Birds *of* ISLAY

Richard E. Elliott

CHRISTOPHER HELM
London

© 1989 R. E. Elliott
Line illustrations by John Davies, John Govett, Brian Southern, Brett Westwood
Christopher Helm (Publishers) Ltd, Imperial House, 21–25 North Street, Bromley,
Kent BR1 1SD

ISBN 0-7470-0803-5

A CIP catalogue record for this book is available from the British Library

Typeset by Cotswold Typesetting Ltd, Gloucester
Printed and bound by Biddles Ltd, Guildford, Surrey

Contents

Scene and Sound

Embrace awhile the scene and sound
   On moor and cliff, on farm and shore;
As loch is still, or gale intense,
   How much we gain from Islay's store
Of natural inheritance.

A fleeting glimpse of Peregrine,
   A Curlew cry, a startled cock,
A duck on windswept water rides,
   A diver out on darkened loch,
Perchance a grebe is there but hides.

In swamp not drained the Heron creeps,
   In pools the gull its feathers preens,
A Teal secludes and Peewit wades,
   The 'chic-ka' call of Snipe unseen;
An air of secrecy pervades.

The Eagle flights across the moor,
   A Raven grunts, a Hoodie calls,
The 'Hawk' with wings in vee appears,
   It hesitates, it angled falls,
And voles around renew their fears.

By Shags and Auks and Kittiwakes,
   A Solan Goose to Ailsa flights;
It skims each wave with stately craft,
   While straight of wing the Fulmar kites
And Chough play-out a strong updraft.

Where coast is low, yet safe for some,
   On rocks just short of Neptune's fling,
The travelled Tern defends its own
   From Herring Gulls that search on wing.
No peace until the brood has flown.

When broods are gone and autumn dawns,
  The mood is change, the isle is host;
All Terns depart, Redwings fly in,
  A flux of waders works the coast,
And Ruff may strut on wet grazing.

A bark is heard, invaders come;
  Just by Ardnave they glide in sight,
At first a few, then groups compound,
  For several hours at lowish height
They pass up-loch to feeding grounds.

When sun is set but sky's still lit,
  The waxing skeins fly overall,
A mass of geese that yelp and bark,
  By whiffle, glide and powered stall
Alight in creeks to roost by dark.

Then, when day is done, think back
  A hundred years, a hundred more;
No gamekeeper, no sporting man,
  What then was heard on ben and moor?
The crackling croak of Ptarmigan?

Were Ring Ouzels frequently seen?
  Did Eagles with white tails prey,
And Puffins watch a busy scene
  Whilst Skuas sat on nests in May?
Were Barnacles confined to flats?

The pace was slow, no oil spill then,
  Did man respect nature's bequest,
Replacing loss with gain elsewhere?
  Do woods that stand here now attest,
Enriched in songs of claims on air?

What will be heard next century
  On more and cliff, on farm and shore?
Let's now inquire and contemplate,
  If change accelerates yet more
Will scene and sound still exaltate?

REE 1987

Preface and Acknowledgements

In this book I present accounts of the occurrence of both regular and vagrant birds seen on the Hebridean island of Islay: a place with many and varied habitats well known to a growing number of people interested in birds, and a place offering scope for the pursuit of interests in many other branches of natural history, geology and archaeology. Migration, the history of habitats, and the problems of conservation in association with the island community are subjects given some emphasis in the preliminary chapters.

From 1968, patient accumulation of ornithological records by C. Gordon Booth led to the publication of his book *Birds of Islay* in 1975 and its updating in 1981; they also provided the foundation upon which the main part of the present book depends. Gordon left his records with the then newly formed Islay Natural History Trust when he left the island in 1985; since then, birdwatchers and students of Islay's birds have continued to contribute valuable data to the Trust's files, thereby improving the basis of my compilation. My own information dates back to 1976.

Keith Verrall, who lived on Islay from 1973 to 1977, ringed a total of 2,054 birds; a small number were later seen during their travels, providing valuable information. Some indication of the relative abundance of species can be judged from his data and this has been taken into account when assessing numbers of breeding passerines.

Malcolm A. Ogilvie, director of the INHT since the spring of 1986, has made detailed comments on drafts of all sections of the book; for this and for his full support throughout its preparation, I am very grateful. He also allowed me to use some of his own observations, introduced me to data collected on behalf of the Wildfowl Trust, to some important references, and to articles and reports written by students who have worked on the island in recent years. John French, a biologist living on the island, kindly agreed to read the final draft and made some useful suggestions.

David B. Boyd, the Islay Estates Factor, generously allowed me free access to the estate records; these provided a basis for parts of Chapters 2 and 3. Pete Moore, warden of the Gruinart Reserve, made available to me reports prepared for the Royal Society for the Protection of Birds and the 'Birds of Estuaries Enquiry'; he also discussed the development of the reserve and helpfully commented on relevant sections of the book.

Ivor Rees of the Department of Marine Biology at the University College of North Wales contributed a note on abundant flightless auks on the seas off Islay, and Gordon Yates of Rochdale provided data on the recovery of ringed Hen Harriers. Ron Hickling commented on an early draft of Chapter 3.

Jane Dawson, who founded the INHT in memory of Rodney, her late husband, took on the painstaking task of typing from my manuscript. Laurie B. Smith, a retired veterinary surgeon, and J. Malcolm, a public health officer, gave helpful advice on the section entitled 'Herring Gulls and food poisoning'.

To each of these and to other friends who have helped in various ways, however small, and to the many birdwatchers who have submitted information, but who are too numerous to be mentioned individually, I wish to express my sincere thanks. I am also indebted to many islanders for freedom of access to various parts of the island, and most especially I am thankful for the indulgence shown by my wife Cherry during the last three years.

R. E. Elliott, 1988

1
An Introduction to Islay and its Birds

Perspective

This book is about Hebridean birds, many of which are migratory, and an island called Islay (pronounced eye-la) that is much loved but subject to change, now as in the past. Many of the resident people have moved to Islay at some stage of their lives, and many truly Islay families are now overseas. Within this changing scene the birds and the people have a varied relationship that in many ways enters into the economics of the island and is periodically given space and time by the media. A collation of facts about the birds and some ways in which they interact with human aspirations is attempted in the pages that follow.

Islay is the most southerly island of the Hebrides (Figure 1), lying 24 km (15 miles) from Kintyre on mainland Britain, across the approaches to the Sound of Jura, and 32 km (20 miles) across the North Channel from Rathlin Island in Northern Ireland. It has an area of 615 sq. km (237 sq. miles), 220 km (137 miles) of coast and about 250 km (155 miles) of road.

Islay's maritime climate has lower summer and higher winter temperatures than the mainland (Boyd and Bowes 1983). Frosts and snowfalls are infrequent, and an icy ground cover rarely lasts all day. The mild winters attract birds moving southwest away from more severe conditions in the highlands, encouraging them either to use Islay as a staging post en route for Ireland or to stay rather than cross the North Channel. High salt-laden winds are common and restrict the growth of trees (Bibby and Heslop 1986), particularly on west- and north-facing slopes, thereby limiting the avifauna.

In the Hebrides, cloud amounts are less than on the mainland and the power of the sun is consequently greater, especially on the Rhinns, the western limb of Islay, where the clarity of the air is greatest. There are

1

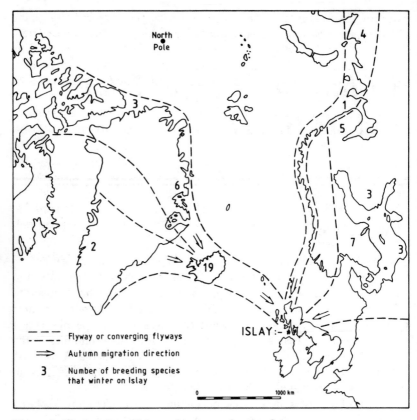

Figure 1: The location of Islay and autumn migration flyways

occasions when anticyclonic conditions persist for a few weeks and soils dry out to such an extent that walking conditions over normally boggy moorland are excellent. A warming sun and calm clean air can produce superb conditions for watching wildfowl on Loch Indaal (Figure 2). At other times gales from the south or west throw much seaweed and marine animals on to the loch shores, providing food for gulls and crows. Special feeding and flying techniques are adopted and large birds gather where the pickings are rich, while small passerines seek shelter on farms and in woods. Flight and wind are the subjects of the section on pages 8–11.

About 100 species of birds are usually present on Islay, and this number is exceeded at times, especially during the change-over of species from mid-March to the end of May and again from mid-August to the end of October. The winter months are enlivened by abundant waterfowl, including Whooper Swans, over 20,000 geese and large rafts of Wigeon and Scaup. Barnacle and White-fronted Geese come from Greenland, and they select Islay from among the Hebrides because of its extensive pastures and the saltings at the heads of the two sea-lochs which they use as roosting areas. Along the shores of these lochs up to 3,000 waders gather and there are constant changes in the species present. Nine or ten raptors can be found on the island; there are good chances of seeing eagles, harriers and Peregrines. The Chough is a speciality and Glaucous Gulls are present in most winters.

Western Islay ranks among the most important seawatching stations in Britain (Verrall and Bourne 1982) and both migrants and vagrants, seabirds and landbirds, contribute to the Islay list of over 270 species, subdivided in Table 1. The migrants follow two major flyways (Figure 1), roughly along two great circle routes. One, along which Islay's geese and many other birds are channelled, extends from arctic Canada via Greenland and Iceland to fringe the Hebrides and pass south to Ireland and beyond. The second, from the northern coast of Siberia, crosses the Barents Sea to follow the Norwegian coast to Scotland. Many birds on

Table 1: Subdivision of Islay's species by origin

		Percentages (no. of species)
Residents:		
Including at least 6% irregular partial migrants		27 (74)
Migrants:		
Breeding on Islay and wintering south, mainly in Africa	12 (33)	
Breeding mainly in Iceland, Greenland or arctic Canada	14 (38)	
Breeding mainly in Fennoscandia, arctic Russia or Siberia	13 (36)	
Breeding on Islay and living out over the Atlantic	03 (08)	
Breeding in Eurasia and wintering on Islay	03 (08)	
Total migrants		45 (123)
Dispersive migrants:		
From British Isles outwith Islay		07 (19)
Vagrants:		
From Eurasia south of the sub-Arctic	11 (30)	
From the Arctic or sub-Arctic	05 (14)	
From North America	04 (11)	
Atlantic wanderers	01 (03)	
Total vagrants		21 (58)
Total species		100 (274)

this latter route continue down the east coast of Britain, but some join west coast migrants or cut across northern Scotland, perhaps down the Great Glen and on southwest, following the Firth of Lorne to Jura and Islay. Additional hard-weather movements from northern Scotland appear to be channelled down the latter route and occasional influxes of raptors may arrive this way. Similarly, Islay's Lapwings and Skylarks often visit Ireland for a few weeks in January and February.

Vagrant species have been identified in all months, but 70 per cent are found in May, June and July, or in September, October and November. Many come from the Arctic and Eurasia; a few are driven off the open Atlantic by storms, or even across from North America on favourable winds. Movements account for three-quarters of Islay's birds, only one-quarter being residents.

Islay's 'Top Ten' birdwatching localities

These localities (see Figure 2) are selected from a wide choice; their order is largely a matter of personal preference.

Upper Loch Indaal

One or more days' birdwatching are feasible at various points from Gartbreck to Port Charlotte, including visits to the mud and shingle from Saltpan Point to Ronnachmore, the saltings and Traigh Cill an Rubha at Bridgend, Blackrock Bay, the spit at Traigh an Luig, the shingle and rock shores of Bruichladdich and several burn mouths where birds congregate. There are convenient elevated observation points at the Bowmore Power Station, Blackrock headland and the Bruichladdich Monument (Figure 2). On calm days, all the birds on the upper loch can be identified and counted from these three localities with the aid of a telescope. Divers, grebes, cormorants, swans, geese, ducks, waders, gulls and terns frequent the loch. Whooper Swans, Barnacle Geese, Wigeon, Mallard, Teal, Oystercatchers, Dunlins, Curlews and gulls each have their particular roosting sites in Bridgend Bay during the winter. In the same season, Slavonian Grebe, Long-tailed Duck and more rarely Smew are specialities more likely to be seen between Bowmore Pier and the Power Station. Common Scoter and divers can be found from Bruichladdich monument most readily in the winter months, but it is still worth a search in good conditions during the summer. A Peregrine sometimes hunts over the shores, particularly over the Bridgend saltings. Fifty-seven species were recorded on monthly counts around the loch during 1986.

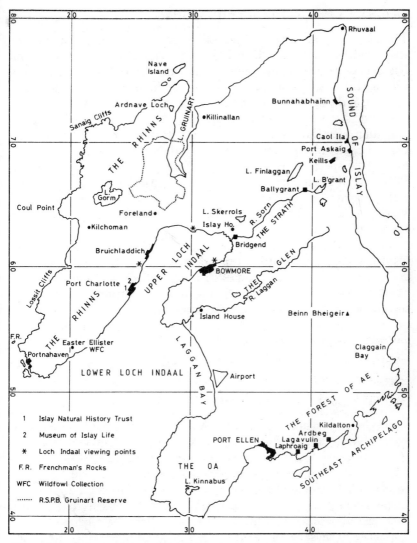

Figure 2: Some key localities on Islay. Other places referred to in the text are listed in the index with British National Grid references; most of them may be found on the Ordnance Survey Landranger map, sheet 60, 1:50,000 scale, or located approximately using the grid on this map

Gruinart Flats, saltings and mudflats

This area forms an important part of the Gruinart Reserve. The reserve was acquired by the RSPB in 1983 and holds large concentrations of Barnacle Geese during the winter. Greenland White-fronted Geese and occasionally other goose species also feed in the area. A few fields on the east side of the flats are outside the reserve; these include one adjacent to the saltings at which most geese arrive as they complete their autumn migration. Hen Harriers and other raptors cross from moor to moor; even Golden Eagles may penetrate down from the wild north of the island. A total of 86 species was recorded in this area during 1986, including Shelduck, Wigeon, Sparrowhawk, Kestrel, Merlin, Peregrine, Corncrake, Golden Plover, Greenshank, Short-eared Owl, Grasshopper Warbler, Twite and more rarely Shoveler, Goshawk, Little Stint, Jack Snipe and Barn Owl.

The RSPB plans to attract visitors interested in birds and natural history in general; a visitor information centre is planned in a location giving good views of geese and other birds. School parties are welcome and it is hoped to give them the opportunity to study wildlife at all seasons. Pools will be created for resident and migrant waders and the moorland and woodland parts of the reserve will be managed with wildlife in mind. The archaeological site at An Sithean will be given due consideration in the plans and has been appropriately signposted.

Ardnave Loch and Peninsula

Little Grebe, Mallard, Teal and Tufted Duck are usually on the loch and a pair of Mute Swans breeds in some years. Many migratory and casual waterfowl give a total of some 22 swimming species (Table 4, page 29). Lapwing, Redshank and Common Sandpiper breed around the shore and Grey Herons and Oystercatchers visit. A walk around the peninsula shores north of the loch is worthwhile; a few waders feed at Traigh Nostaig and others might be on the rocks at Sgeir na Nighinn. Arctic Terns nest at these localities, and divers, Shags, Eiders, gulls and Black Guillemots are usually to be found in Nave Island sound. Choughs frequent areas where cattle graze.

Sanaig Cliffs

These cliffs are best approached from Sanaigmore; they hold colonies of Fulmars, Shags, Herring and Lesser Black-backed Gulls, Kittiwakes, Guillemots and Razorbills. Access to some parts is difficult and dangerous, but all species can be readily seen from viewpoints reached by walking down the main gully sides.

Kilchoman

Fulmars nest up to 1.25 km (over $\frac{3}{4}$ mile) inland on the old cliffs east of the church. Jackdaws and Choughs roost on ledges and in crevaces on the cliffs of Creag Mhor. The dune area between these cliffs and Traigh Mhachir is the most convenient place on the island to watch the flight and feeding of Choughs in any month. Birds of prey sometimes fly over or along the cliffs.

Claggain Bay

Great Northern Divers, Gannets, Eiders and Red-breasted Mergansers are often present offshore. Calm weather and a telescope are desirable. During the breeding season, visitors should avoid disturbing the few terns and Ringed Plovers by not traversing the length of the pebble-bar. Betweeen the pebbles and the grass leading down from the road is a quagmire that is best avoided!

Southern Rhinns Moorland

Hen Harriers, Merlins and Short-eared Owls divide up the moors into hunting ranges, and Golden Eagle and Peregrine are occasionally seen. This area is difficult of access and birdwatchers are advised to search from vantage points on the peripheral roads. Cars are not advised on the Octofad-Ballimony track, but a walk here can be very rewarding. In addition to the raptors, Black Grouse may be sighted.

Bridgend Woods and the River Sorn

These are mixed woods with a variety of deciduous and coniferous trees planted during the last 160 years. There is a wide range of trees and undergrowth densities providing habitats for about 30 avian species (Table 3, page 23). The woods are interspersed with open fields, which together extend over some 6 sq. km (2.3 sq. miles). All the common woodland species are present; Wood Warblers sing in groups of beech trees; Spotted Flycatchers feed on wood edges by field or river; and Sparrowhawks hunt over and around the trees. A Peregrine sometimes hunts overhead, scaring Woodpigeons in the tree tops, and a Buzzard may scan over pasture from a prominent perch. Garden Warbler, Blackcap and Bullfinch are rarely recorded. Tawny Owl and Woodcock are most readily found at dusk from March to July. Grey Wagtail and

7

Dipper establish territories along the Sorn, but they have been irregular in recent years. Grey Heron and Mallard visit the river regularly, but Kingfishers are very rare.

Loch Skerrols

This fishing loch may be viewed from the lane west of Skerrols farm or by following a track near Knockanbearach, taking special care not to disturb wildlife or fishermen. Twenty-two species have been recorded (Table 4, page 29), including most of the island's freshwater wildfowl. Wigeon, Teal, Mallard, Pochard and Tufted Duck sometimes build up to impressive numbers, and one or two Red-throated Divers may visit the loch to fish. Greenland White-fronted Geese and Common Gulls often use this loch as a comfort station and the geese may roost there.

Frenchman's Rocks

As a result of seawatching over a period of nearly five years, 46 seabird species were recorded from the vicinity of these rocks by Verrall and Bourne (1982). Here, many seabirds swing from a southerly to a southeasterly heading or from a northwesterly to a northerly one. These include divers, shearwaters, petrels, Gannets, cormorants, ducks, skuas, gulls, terns and auks; in addition, many land migrants pass by. Seabird movements are on a large scale during the period May to November and reach a peak in October; they start one or two hours after sunrise and most activity takes place during the following three hours. A south to west wind produces most birds, and counts of the order of 10,000 per hour have been noted following the clearance of depressions to the east. Coul Point, 11 km (6.8 miles) to the north, is also a useful seawatching station.

Flight and wind

The major aspect of Islay's climate that affects the daily life of its birds is wind. The island faces the Atlantic and the prevailing winds are from the western sector. The Hebrides are ranked as the fifth most exposed inhabited region of the world (Bibby and Heslop 1986); strengths on the Beaufort Scale range from calm up to storm force 10 (25 to 28 m/s) and occasional hurricanes are known (force 12: 32–37 m/s). The flying performance of many bird species under these varying and sometimes testing conditions is fascinating. Most birds fly at between 7 and 20 m/s, the larger species being faster than the smaller ones. Geese, ducks, falcons and pigeons usually rely on sheer strength and speed to face strong winds, whereas passerines and gamebirds tend to escape high winds by remaining on the ground, often in cover or even seeking shelter in crevices in dry-stone dykes. There is, however, a third group of birds that are capable of flying at between 10 and 14 m/s and use special techniques of flight on windy days; this includes Fulmars, shearwaters, Gannets, gulls and some members of the crow family.

Birds fly in order to travel, to scan the countryside or sea, and to find food. Aerial insect-eaters are limited by high winds; under these circumstances Swallows fly back and forth in the lee of woods. A good area to look for this behaviour is Gruinart, where there are several small woods and shelter belts. Aerial divers such as terns and Black-headed Gulls are hampered by rough water, particularly when white horses and spray are produced at over force 6 (14 m/s). Even Gannets do not fish in winds stronger than force 8 (17–21 m/s) (Nelson 1978).

Flight in calm air requires the expenditure of much energy, and up to force 2/3 (3.4 m/s)—or when the Airport windsock flies steeper than 45 degrees—little energy can be extracted from the wind by birds. However, in these light breezes, Buzzards, gulls and Choughs may be seen spiralling on the rising air of thermals and, after reaching a sufficient height, gliding to their destination or to another thermal. On Islay, thermals develop readily over bare rock or bare soil, and expecially over fields being ploughed and then drying out on a breezy day. Owing to the high value of solar radiation transmitted through the clear Hebridean air, thermals occur in almost every month. They cannot develop in winds stronger than force 6, but they may be present, dragging markedly downwind, in forces 4 and 5. Under these conditions gulls and some raptors often glide along a trochoidal path, following a flight pattern known as 'lee-looping'. Watching gulls reacting to thermals developing over a field being ploughed is most rewarding; the author has had most success studying this reaction in the Mulindry, Skerrols and Sunderland areas.

Updraughts also occur on the windward side of topographic features such as raised beaches (Kilchoman), present-day sea cliffs (Port Charlotte), eskers (Cnoc Fada, Sunderland) and many other prominent hills (Cnoc Don Mor, Bridgend). Perhaps the most efficient and precise flight of any bird around Islay is that of Fulmars taking advantage of updraughts adjacent to the higher sea cliffs. Raptors, gulls and crows, including Choughs and Ravens, all soar on these updraughts in wind forces 3 to 8. Soaring sites are numerous and widespread on Islay, the larger birds use them as lookout posts and as a means of travel along their lengths or from one to another. Large gulls are also adept at utilising

9

updraughts along quite small topographic features. For example, it is interesting to watch large gulls flying along the 8-km (5-mile) coast of Laggan Bay into or obliquely across a strong breeze or gale (forces 6 to 8). Sometimes these birds are able to glide along wave troughs, taking advantage of a small updraught in the lee of a wave just before it breaks. At other times skilled birds glide over the low bluff at the top of the beach near the Airport. Out of 100 gulls flying along this bluff, 92 per cent of those with adult plumage kept to a steady glide within a height of 2 m (6$\frac{1}{2}$ ft), whereas only 46 per cent of the immatures succeeded, the rest using much energy in corrective flaps and manoeuvres. This is a skill that has to be acquired through experience.

At a still lower flight level, some help is gained from a cushion of air trapped between wings and ground or water; cormorants, Eiders and gulls are adept at flying with wings virtually touching the water. Ideally, this technique requires smooth water under calm or near calm air; it is often seen around Upper Loch Indaal.

In fresh to strong breezes and near gales, forces 5 to 7, when the Airport windsock approaches the horizontal, some raptors, gulls and crows are seen flying obliquely upwind and riding eddies in a kind of 'billowing flight'. Those birds best in control of such apparently erratic flight flap only occasionally to maintain a sound flight path. Energy is extracted from the wind by constantly adjusting wings and tail to give maximum lift from and maximum time in short-lived updraughts, and then by gliding swiftly to minimise time spent in the associated downdraughts. Forces 5 to 7 are the wind strengths typified by swaying branches and whole trees in motion; this adds to the complexity of the eddies in the airstream where it passes over woods. Gulls are capable of gaining considerable height over a coppice such as that at Cluanach.

It is possible for a bird, using the 'billowing flight' technique, to make headway against winds that are blowing faster than the bird's maximum airspeed; many gulls and crows are adept at this, and their performance is often to be seen in the vicinity of Bridgend Woods. Another way of making headway is to fly low into the wind; conventionally wind speed is measured at a height of 10 m (33 ft) and that speed reduces logarithmically towards the ground. A large gull flying at an airspeed of 13 m/s could make some headway against a force 7/8 (17 m/s) gale by keeping within 3 m (10 ft) of the ground. Portnahaven is an excellent place to watch gulls in a gale.

Over the sea or open ground, where eddies are less well developed, a technique similar to 'billowing flight', composed of alternate steep soaring rises against the wind and swift downward glides to leeward, produces an average flight path orientated at a high angle to the wind.

Large gulls sometimes fly in this way over Loch Indaal; their flight paths approach that of the spectacular dynamic soaring of albatrosses and have been called straight-line soaring.

The next chapter is concerned with changes in climate and landscape that have taken place on Islay since man first arrived. These changes, including variations in the wind regime, have determined and still are determining the success or otherwise of species within the avian assemblage, both visiting and breeding on the island.

2
History and Habitats on Islay

From the Ice Age to the present

As the last phase of the Ice Age waned about 10,000 years ago, the sea was rising towards its present level and the harsh climate began to ameliorate. At first birds were scarce, but as grasses and low herbs colonised the coastal areas some geese were probably attracted; Barnacle Geese may have bred on the sea cliffs and White-fronted Geese probably occupied marshy hollows. Seabirds, including the Great Auk and various gulls, are likely to have found the cliffs and shores to their liking.

Sea level continued to rise, gradually spreading over low-lying land until it reached about 8–10 m (26–33 ft) above its present level about 7,000 years ago. The shoreline can still be traced following old pebbly beaches and cliffs now partially vegetated. Some cliffs, such as those some distance back from the present shore between Bholsa and Killinallan and also those around Laggan Farm, were cut in solid rock, while others were eroded in various glacial and fluvial deposits, including gravels such as those on which the wood behind Blackrock stands. At this time the Rhinns became separated from eastern Islay, but remained almost linked by gravel ridges west of Erasaid and Uiskentuie (Figure 5, pages 20–1). Extensive shallow-water areas, flanked by saltings and marsh, were present between Lochs Gruinart and Indaal and these habitats were probably attractive to considerable numbers of swans, geese, ducks and waders. The White-tailed Eagle and a large falcon such as the Gyrfalcon are likely to have bred; at the present day both are capable of taking ducks and the Gyrfalcon is known to take Barnacle Geese.

Seven thousand years ago the climate had reached an optimum, perhaps somewhat warmer than at the present day. Mesolithic Man camped on Islay's shores next to the now raised beaches referred to above. His middens have been excavated near Ardnave Point, on

Oronsay 15 km (9 miles) to the northeast, and on Risga, an island in Loch Sunart north of Mull. The bones of Gannet, Cormorant, Red-breasted Merganser, Water Rail, gulls, terns, Guillemot, Razorbill, Great Auk and a possible crane have been identified (Morrison 1980).

Inland, the temperate climate encouraged the growth of a variety of trees, including alder, hazel, birch, willow, oak and probably elm. A rich assemblage of insect life and woodland birds would follow; thrushes, warblers, flycatchers, tits, finches, buntings and others would spread into Islay as their food resources developed, but the farmland species present today are likely to have been rare or absent.

Around 5,500 years ago, at the beginning of the Neolithic period, farming practices were introduced and land clearance became necessary to provide areas for crops and grazing; trees on the lower and flatter ground were burnt. These early farmers gradually penetrated up some of the more promising glens and straths. With increased resources the population grew; their tombs and standing stones help define the areas cleared (Figure 3). The accumulation of peat started in abandoned low-lying areas (Simmons and Tooley 1981).

From about 4,000 to 2,500 years ago, during the Bronze Age, the climate deteriorated and became much wetter with strengthening winds. This created landscape changes: sand dunes accumulated around the heads of bays and many soils developed iron-rich layers or otherwise became impervious. Poor drainage, stronger winds, a greater need for fuel, and continued clearance for farming combined to accelerate the elimination of forests. Impeded drainage also encouraged the accumulation of peat, and bogs replaced some low-lying forest. Many inland lochs became acid and much less productive, greatly reducing the numbers of wildfowl that they could support.

During this period sea level was falling towards its present position, and the shallow waters between the Rhinns and eastern Islay became extensive marsh with a freshwater loch of about 1.5 km^2 (370 acres) where Loch Raoin and Foreland Marsh are now (Figure 5). Another broad irregular area of lochs and marshes probably extended from Island House to Ballivicar.

Throughout the Bronze Age and succeeding periods, many treeless raised bogs gradually replaced marshes and some lochs while the clearance of forested areas for agriculture continued. Barnacle Geese probably found more and more suitable grassland on which to graze and White-fronted Geese began to utilise the raised bogs for feeding and roosting. Throughout the millenia since the Ice Age the highest ground with thin soils on quartzite had been barren (Figure 3), and now the encroachment of blanket peat on to areas where trees were windthrown,

13

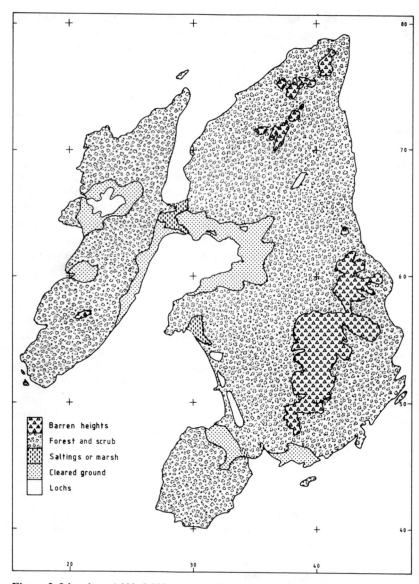

Figure 3: Islay about 4,000–5,000 years ago. The coast approximated to the present 8-m (26-ft) or 10-m (33-ft) contour; sand dunes and most areas of peat had not started to accumulate; Loch Gorm extended over areas now covered with thick peat; Neolithic Man had cleared small areas of forest for agriculture and the higher hills stood bare above extensive forests

and then cleared by man, extended these unproductive areas. Reduction of the forested area and wind sculpturing, producing low and thinly scattered trees or scrub, reduced the number of woodland birds. Moorland birds now found a developing habitat.

From 400 AD and particularly from 1100 AD, the names now appearing on topographic maps were first applied to the landscape; some indicate treeless tracts, but others refer to native trees now absent. Northeast of Craigens, Gruinart, names such as Maol na Coille refer to woods that once covered what is now heather-clad moorland. On the shores of the Sound of Islay, references to alder and willow suggest that the wooded cliffs from Ardnahoe to Caol Ila were once much more extensive. As ground between the barren hilltops and the farmland and peatlands of the lower ground was gradually cleared, summer grazing prevented the regeneration of trees, leaving forest remnants confined to steep-sided glens. Between these glens, some Gaelic names refer to summer pastures (Airigh) whereas others indicate the bare nature of the ground. Destruction continued up some valleys whose names refer to the presence of trees, although scrub is still found in a few sheltered glens up to heights of almost 300 m (985 ft). Two large areas were slow to lose the tree cover: the 'Forest of Nae' in the southeast, which is still represented by woods scattered on the many steep slopes and ridges of the district; and 'Kilchoman Forest', which appears to have extended south from Kilchoman inland of Kilchiaran to Beinn Tart a'Mhill. This latter forest is now represented only by small clumps of trees or scrub hidden in the many small glens of that area.

In 1772, the Islay landscape was described by Pennant as heathland 'absolutely in a state of nature' with a few stunted woods of birch and hazel giving cover to Black Grouse. Even Islay House was surrounded by open land with a few gorse bushes. The population of the island reached a peak of 14,992 in 1831 and there was said to be a great scarcity of wood. The Reverend Dr John Walker also reported on a visit to Islay in the same decade as Pennant. He stated (McKay 1980) that the island was formerly well stocked with timber but that the trees had largely been destroyed by cattle and the people. He wrote of many coppices of 2 to 12 ha (5–30 acres) and one wood of 40 ha (100 acres); the coppices consisted of osier, 'grey willow', 'laurel-leaved willow', birch, hazel, oak, hawthorn, blackthorn and rowan. Most trees were not as high as a man but some ash grew to 7 m (23 ft). He suggested that the remnants should be enclosed and that planting be undertaken.

In some places these recommendations appear to have been carried out: there are many wood remnants on steep east- or southeast-facing slopes that were probably more extensive some time prior to the first

Table 2: Statistics of Islay's habitats and protected areas (Dec. 1987)

Habitats	km²	(%)	km²	(%)	% in Britain
Arable land, including leys:	20	(3)			
Permanent pastures:	70	(11)			
Total Farmland:			90	(14)	
Natural woods and scrub (approx.):	25	(4)			
Estate woodlands	10	(2)			
Planted copses and shelter belts:	2	(0)			
Forestry plantations:	36	(6)			
Total Woods:			73	(12)	10
Lochs and reservoirs:			11	(2)	
Peatlands, uncut, including some rough grazings:			95	(15)	
Peatlands, cut (approx.):			65	(11)	
Moorlands, including some rough grazings:			240	(39)	
Hilltops and high slopes with thin or no soil:			28	(5)	
Sand dunes:			7	(1)	
Saltings:			1	(0)	
Villages, Airport, other buildings and roads:			5	(1)	
Total land surface:			615	(100)	

Protected areas			km²	(%)	% in Britain
Gruinart Reserve (RSPB):			12	(2)	4
SSSIs:			157	(25)	9
Total protected area:			169	(27)	13

Coastline			km	(%)	
Cliffs and seabird colonies:			10	(5)	
Other cliffs:			155	(70)	
Beaches:			55	(25)	
Total coastline:			220	(100)	

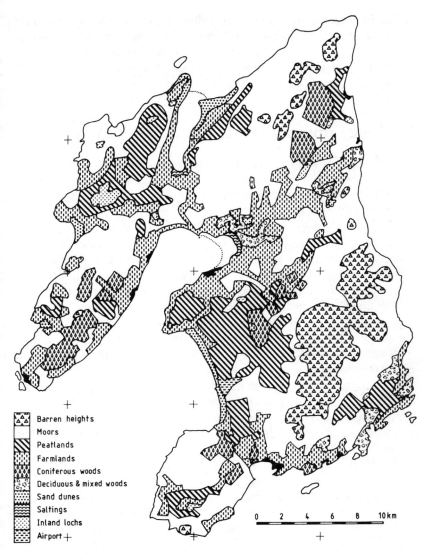

Barren heights
Moors
Peatlands
Farmlands
Coniferous woods
Deciduous & mixed woods
Sand dunes
Saltings
Inland lochs
Airport +

0   2   4   6   8   10 km

Figure 4: Generalised areas of present-day habitats on Islay

Ordnance Survey maps of 1880. Small wooded areas on the northwest side of the strath between Emeraconart and Ballygrant, between Ballinaby and Leek, and at Cnoc Mor by Cragabus on the Oa are all associated with larger areas where shade-loving bluebells survive. There are also many native woods today that are larger than Walker described.

17

In recent decades, the fences around these woods have been allowed to lapse into a state of disrepair and livestock are again being allowed to trample and graze within them, reducing their chances of regeneration.

The present extents of broad categories of habitats (Figure 4) and conservation areas (Figure 9, page 55) are given in Table 2.

Drainage improvements in the 19th century

During the 1800s, many drainage schemes modified the wetlands and waters of Islay. In 1812 a sea bank (Figure 5) was constructed across the saltings at the head of Loch Gruinart; this was breached near the Craigens end. Further work was carried out from about 1830 and completed with government aid in 1847; this involved rebuilding the eastern part of the bank on a less ambitious line. The Gleann Mor river that then meandered across Gruinart Flats from Eresaid to Loch Gruinart was diverted past Loch an Raoin to join the Allt na Coite (Coracle or Punt Burn). It was directed along a new channel with the minimum of bends to debouch into Loch Indaal at Uiskentuie. Together these works enabled 400 ha (990 acres) of land to be reclaimed. Much of the area had been salt- and freshwater marsh. A 40-ha (100-acre) inland loch was partially drained; this is now replaced by a large area of reeds and a number of small pools totalling only 2 ha (5 acres). As the name 'Allt na Coite' suggests, a large number of wildfowl and waders may have visited the loch in the past, but now only a few Teal and Mallard are normally present. Other waterbirds were probably on the Gruinart Flats for much of the year, the range of species being greater than that commonly seen now.

A second scheme in the Carrabus and Islay House areas (Figure 6) was probably executed during the same period. Loch Skerrols appears to have been very shallow and marshy in the 1700s, with a local catchment in the Scarrabus and Octovullin areas. It drained to the northwest via the Carrabus Burn, which meandered through ill-drained pastures. An earth and rock dam was constructed across the place at which this stream issued from the loch, causing the water level to be raised and overflow southwest into the Eallabus Burn, which then, as now, debouched into Bridgend Bay near Bluehouses. A second dam with two sluices was added at the southern outlet to enable the water flow to be controlled and the water level raised still further, so that the loch became 3 m (10 ft) deep and the first dam was nearly breached, sending any seepage or overflow down the Carrabus Burn. The water from one sluice was led into a millpond and used to power a mill at Eallabus, as shown on a plan dated 1825; that from the second sluice fed a small distillery at Newton in the 1830s. About 1900, the Meal Mill near Bluehouses replaced the Eallabus Mill.

The Carrabus Burn had always flowed down to Loch Carrabus, a shallow elongated loch held back by a gravel ridge that was deposited when the sea level was about 9 m (29 ft) higher than at the present day. This loch extended from the southwest edge of land now planted and called Winter Covert, to the bend in the road below West Carrabus. Its waters drained through the gravel ridge into marshes between the Coullabus Road and the site of Glenburn House (British National Grid reference 308630), and also down a tortuous channel issuing from near the west end of the loch and draining into Blackrock Bay immediately west of the Glenburn House site. This channel can still be traced south of the minor road. Loch Carrabus was drained by digging a deep trench east of Tayandoch directly towards Blackrock Bay east of Glenburn House. This is now an extension of the Carrabus Burn, which itself was straightened and deepened as shown on a plan dated 1865. At a latter date a tree belt around Loch Skerrols and much of Winter Covert were planted: the last trees, in the west corner of Winter Covert, in the 1880s.

These various works have modified the landscape in many ways, by:

(a) eliminating shallow, probably well-vegetated habitats at both Loch Carrabus and Loch Skerrols;
(b) enlarging and deepening Loch Skerrols so that divers and diving ducks now feed there;
(c) creating shelter at Skerrols so that many waterfowl now roost or shelter from storms;
(d) reducing the seepage into the marshes southwest of the Coullabus Road and probably lowering their ornithological value;
(e) creating the mixed wood known as Winter Covert, which is now rich in bird life; and
(f) adding an area of fertile land to the Carrabus Farm with only minor ornithological value.

Many other lesser works dammed burns to provide enlarged lochs for fishermen, drained smaller areas, or provided water for villages and distilleries or for flax and meal mills. Early in the 1800s, Loch Cam was deepened by constructing a small dam at the outflow to the south; depth may be an important factor contributing to the lack of waterbirds there. A sluice was installed to control the outfall from Loch Ballygrant. The normal water level was slightly raised, but extensive shallows and reeds remain in several sheltered bays, allowing a moderate range of bird species to find suitable habitats. The Lily Loch southwest of Dunlossit

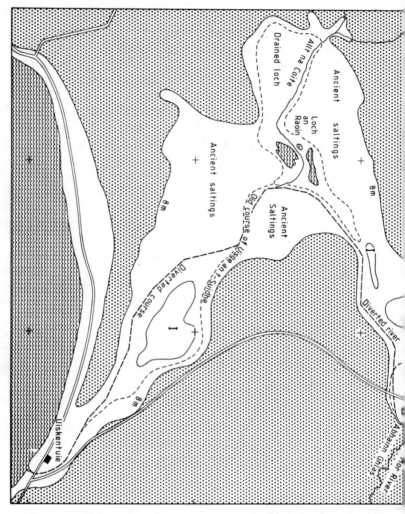

Figure 5: The area between Loch Gruinart in the north and Loch Indaal in the south, which was once a shallow arm of the sea separating the Rhinns from eastern Islay. The Neolithic shoreline approximated to the present day 8-m (26-ft) contour as shown; ancient saltings are backed by this line, and are recognised by traces of sinuous creeks revealed by subtle variations in vegetation seen on aerial photographs. A few creeks are

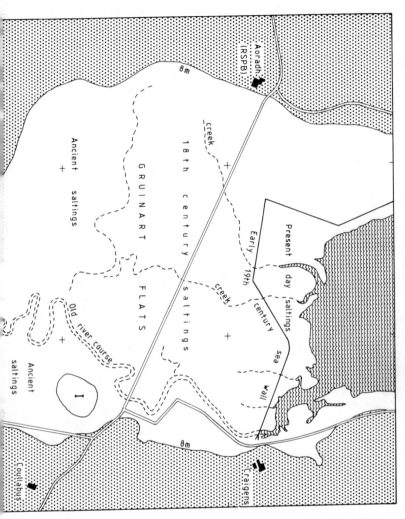

shown crossing 18th-century saltings in the north. Drainage works carried out in the early 19th century are indicated by the sea wall and the diverted course of the Gleann Mor river. The previous tortuous course is shown by finely pecked lines, and several areas slightly raised above the 18th-century floodplain are indicated by the symbol 'I'

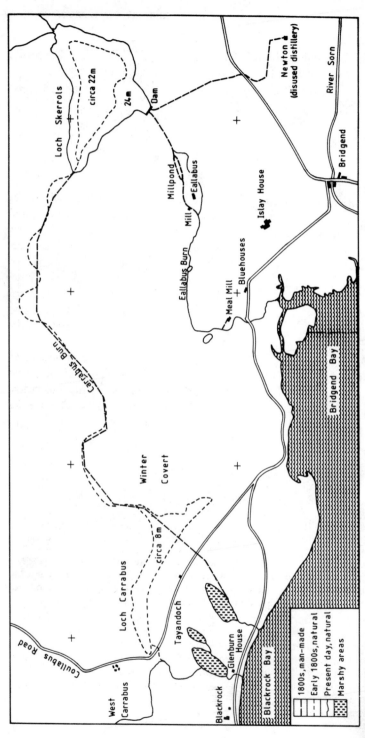

Figure 6: The canalisation of the Carrabus Burn, drainage of Loch Carrabus, enlargement of Loch Skerrols and associated works carried out in the early 19th century. Approximate water levels at the lochs are shown in metres above ordnance datum

House is natural, but about 1900 it was enlarged by the construction of a dam 0.6 km (650 yds) downstream, creating Loch Allan with a comparable water level. This loch now has a species list very similar to that of Loch Ballygrant (Table 4, page 29).

Woodlands and afforestation

From about 1820 a wide variety of trees, mainly deciduous, was planted on estate policies around Foreland House, Islay House and Ardimersay Cottage, the predecessor of Kildalton House. Paintings by Heath about 1830 show young trees in the vicinity of Islay House and Ardimersay Cottage. Dunlossit House and Kildalton House were built later that century and much of the planting around the former was accomplished between 1868 and 1890. Some of the older trees throughout the estate woodlands have now been felled and ring counts on their stumps commonly give 100 to 160 years. Shelter belts in open flat areas and copses of sycamore adjacent to some of the farms were also planted in the 19th century.

The estate woodlands now hold about 30 species of birds, including the Blackcap, Wood Warbler, Lesser Redpoll and Bullfinch, whereas the natural woodlands have an overall total of 15 species. Most individual natural woodlands hold fewer than ten species (Table 3); twelve species

Table 3: Woodland birds

Sparrowhawk	Bp	Song Thrush	Bo	Long-tailed Tit	Ps
Buzzard	Bp	Mistle Thrush	Bs	Coal Tit	Bp
Woodcock	Bo	Garden Warbler	(N)o	Blue Tit	Bp
Woodpigeon	Bs	Blackcap	Po	Great Tit	Bp
Tawny Owl	Bo	Wood Warbler	Po	Treecreeper	B(n)
Tree Pipit	Bn	Chiffchaff	B(n)	Rook	BYo
Wren	Bb	Willow Warbler	Bb	Starling	BXo
Dunnock	Bo	Goldcrest	B(n)	Chaffinch	Bb
Robin	Bb	Spotted Fly-		Lesser Redpoll	PZ(p)
Blackbird	Bb	catcher	BZn	Bullfinch	BX(s)

Key: In estate woodlands or Gruinart shelter belts: B = breeding proved; P = probably breeding; N = species recorded; X = breeding recorded in the Bridgend district; Y = breeding recorded in the Ballygrant district; Z = breeding recorded in the Kildalton district. In native woods: b = breeding proved; p = probably breeding; s = possibly breeding; n = noted; o = not recorded.
Parentheses indicate scarcity.

23

have been recorded in the woods overlooking Loch Tallant, southwest of Bowmore. The greater variety of tree species and the low level of grazing in the estate woodlands have led to the development of a richer habitat, encouraging more birds. These woods are of interest to a wide public.

Early in the 1950s conifers had been planted only in small areas, the largest being that around the distillery at Laphroaig. In the 1960s, more extensive areas were planted in the Laggan Strath from Cluanach to Avenvogie Cottage (Figure 4). Then, in the mid-1980s, there was another more extensive phase of planting in the southern Rhinns, in the areas northwest of Lochs Staoisha and Finlaggan and in the northeastern parts of the Oa. Each of these woods is composed largely of one conifer species, but some small areas are devoted to larch or deciduous trees. Plantations of conifers outwith the estate woodlands now cover some 6 per cent of Islay's land surface (Table 2).

There are severe limitations on the suitability of the island for afforestation. The main factor is that of exposure to gales causing restriction of growth and windthrow. The latter is all the more likely on gley soils, where shallow rooting is likely, and on wet peat, where roots do not find firm attachment. Other factors are the low organic content of soils above about 250 m (820 ft), which in association with strong winds is prohibitive, and the steep or rocky ground which occurs in many small areas. Some Sitka spruce trees on the moors of the Rhinns are, after only two or three years, showing signs of failure to get established, supporting the contention that strong winds are the key limiting factor. This suggests that the area currently planted is near the economic limit, and it seems probable that there will never be a desire to increase the area to above, say, 10 per cent of the land surface.

The successful plantations are likely to reduce the number of bird species within their boundaries from a maximum of 18 to a maximum of ten (Figure 7). This decline includes a reduction in raptors from seven to one and in quarry species from four to one. Typically in coniferous plantations, the moorland community is eliminated as the first trees grow to a height of about 3 m (10 ft). Meanwhile a maximum of eight scrub species becomes established, but eventually declines as the canopy closes. Then, as the trees mature and these woods lose their uniformity by the supression of weak trees and successive windthrows, a true but impoverished woodland community of four to ten species (Figure 7) is established, particularly around the peripheries of the blocks of trees, in the developing gaps and in the tree tops. Raptor losses in the surrounding country, caused by reduction in the size of their hunting ranges, may be serious on the Rhinns, where the Hen Harrier, Merlin and Short-eared Owl have until now been well established. Many species likely to be

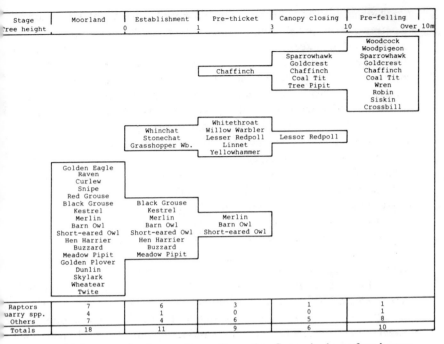

Figure 7: Bird-community changes due to afforestation. Successive boxes from bottom left to top right enclose moorland, scrub, and coniferous-plantation bird communities

represented in the pre-thicket and canopy stages are found elsewhere on the island and will not in any way compensate for the loss of raptors. On the other hand, any encouragement given to Whitethroat, Grasshopper Warbler, Lesser Redpoll, Siskin or Crossbill would be welcome, for the last species especially, since it currently visits Islay only in some winters.

Farming on sporting estates

In the mid-1800s the island became subdivided into several estates; most were then managed as sporting and farming concerns with some degree of conservation in support of field sports. They attracted those who wished to fish for trout and salmon, or shoot deer, grouse, Pheasant, Snipe, Woodcock or wildfowl. These activities continue today on a reduced scale. Gamekeepers, who are now employed in much reduced numbers, are concerned with the conservation of fish and game stocks and therefore with the minimisation of river pollution, the maintenance of heather moors and the preservation of many small areas of scrub and woodland giving cover to game. Pheasants feed on the enclosed farmland and deer sometimes stray there, doing damage to crops; close co-operation is required between keeper and farmer.

For over a century to the Second World War there was a gradual improvement in farming practices, involving better drainage, the introduction of crop rotations and the use of horse-drawn or horse-driven mechanical aids. Increased fodder production enabled larger numbers of livestock to be exported. This required full use of all enclosed fields in an efficient manner, limiting the possibilities of providing cover for game and, incidentally, wild birds.

Since the Second World War, changes in farming practices have been more rapid and directed towards the improvement of crops and even greater efficiency. These changes have been fuelled by increasing support from government coffers. In 1946 there were 670 working horses on Islay's farms; these were gradually replaced by tractors until very few were left in 1950, and in 1986 only four remained on the island. Leys of selected grasses replaced hayfields between the mid-1950s and the mid-1960s. The area of grasses sown and mown in the same year increased from 1406 ha (3474 acres) in 1956 to 2053 ha (5073 acres) in 1966. Grasses have been improved to give faster growth, more powerful tractors now pull larger ploughs, and silage-cutting machinery was introduced in the early 1960s. Chemicals for the control of weeds and insect pests have never been extensively used in Islay.

These post-war changes allowed a major increase in the number of cattle without recourse to importing winter fodder, except after a bad summer. Some 8,707 cattle were on the island in 1946, and this figure had risen to 17,097 by 1976.

Hayfields are now largely confined to the Portnahaven district, while elsewhere rich green leys are harvested for silage two or three times during the course of a good growing season. The early cutting that this requires is detrimental to the breeding efforts of the Corncrake and other birds that require undisturbed ground nest sites and adequate concealment. There has been a considerable loss of food for seed-eating birds; hayfields with their great abundance of wild flowers were not harvested until late July or August.

Many fields have been much improved with better drainage, fertilisers and new, more productive strains of grass; these grow early in spring and, under the influence of the mild climate, even for a short period during some winters. Both Barnacle and White-fronted Geese feed on these rich leys throughout the winter. Today's farmland is shown on Figure 4 (page 17).

The area sown with oats steadily decreased from 1346 ha (3326 acres) in 1946 to only 113 ha (279 acres) in 1986, and over this same period it became possible to grow new strains of barley. About 200 ha (494 acres) are now sown on the better soils and combine harvesters were first used in the 1970s to process this crop. These machines eliminate lengthy cutting, gathering, binding, stacking and thrashing, allowing time for autumn ploughing. The period over which stubbles are available to a wide variety of grain-eating birds is reduced, and food is scattered in a more limited area than it was in the extensive oat fields. For a few weeks these stubbles provide a feeding bonanza to members of the goose, gull, pigeon, crow and starling families, as well as to some sparrows, finches and buntings. In the past, small passerines were probably favoured by more thinly scattered seeds after the harvesting of oats and pigeons fed on stooked oats, whereas other large birds found a visit to the fields less profitable than now.

Over the four decades since the war, the agricultural labour force on Islay decreased from 521 to 109, while the number of holdings fell from 475 to 115; this trend has left many farm buildings abandoned and in a state of disrepair. Barn Owls, Choughs, Jackdaws and Starlings are currently benefiting from nest sites available in these and other abandoned places, although the present phase of cottage restoration and the replacement of old steadings by structures of concrete and metal threatens to reduce the opportunities for these species. Swallows and House Martins, may, however, be encouraged by an increase in the number of accessible roofed buildings.

Inland lochs

The inland lochs of Islay (Table 4) vary in area from 1 ha (2.47 acres) up to the 268 ha (662 acres) of Loch Gorm; many are shallow and a few become dry in rainless periods. Their attraction for waterbirds is based on many factors: food resources around the shores and at depths within up-ending or diving capabilities, nest sites among reeds, in long grasses around the shores or on small islands; suitability for bathing, loafing and roosting; shelter from storms or rest from migration; and the extra safety found at remote hill lochs. Geese, gulls, Lapwings, Curlews or Oystercatchers may use any small shingle beach by an inland loch as a comfort station. The number of feeding birds frequenting each loch gives some indication of the biological productivity of its waters: most birds and most species are found on the better fishing lochs and the least number are recorded at acid hill lochs (Table 4).

Food resources at shallow depths are best provided by the slightly alkaline fishing lochs receiving drainage from limestone country or old dunes: Lochs Allan, Ballygrant, Skerrols, Ardnave, Lossit, Finlaggan and Cadhan. Twenty-two species have been sighted at Loch Skerrols (page 8); this loch is well sheltered and is convenient for birds escaping severe conditions in Bridgend Bay. Several hundred White-fronted Geese and similar numbers of Teal, Mallard, Pochard, Tufted Duck and Wigeon have been recorded there. Particularly significant are records of the normally marine Scaup: exceptionally, 1,100 were present on 2nd January 1972, sheltering from a storm. Ardnave Loch (page 6) sometimes receives tired migrants by virtue of its northern position among conspicuous dunes: there are instances of 98 Whooper Swans, 164 Teal, 100 Pochard and 170 Wigeon being present; 24 species have been recorded there. The other alkaline lochs have lists of 13 to 15 species, except Cadhan which has produced only five, probably because of its small size and the infrequency of visits by birdwatchers.

Although Loch Gorm is in an acid environment, 25 species have been found there and it is regarded as an important fishing loch. It has several favourable features: it is nowhere greater than about 2 m ($6\frac{1}{2}$ ft) deep; it is large and has many bays offering shelter, some having reeds; it is near the west coast and receives spray from heavy seas, reducing its acidity; it receives visitations from passing migrants; and it contains several small islands on which birds can nest in relative safety, although rats, stoats and ferrets can reach the easternmost island when the water is low. In spite of these features Loch Gorm rarely holds large numbers of birds, and it is difficult to watch owing to its size, waves generated in the open situation, and low or distant viewing points. A good telescope is essential to facilitate a satisfactory search for waterfowl.

Small numbers of up to eleven species have been found at many less popular fishing lochs with neutral waters. These include Lochs Kinnabus and Glenastle on the Oa, Loch Nigheadaireachd by Laggan Farm, Loch Eighinn near the Airport, and Loch Fada southeast of Ballygrant. Eighty Wigeon have been reported on Loch Kinnabus and 100 on Loch Eighinn. Some small reservoirs also have neutral waters and many carry small groups of waterbirds; eleven species are known from Claddach Reservoir, near Portnahaven. Whooper Swans sometimes call there as they migrate in short hops down the west coast towards Ireland; Red-throated Divers have bred there and Shoveler have been recorded. This is also the only inland locality at which Eiders have been seen. The Gearach Reservoir, inland from Port Charlotte, can boast nine species; 19 Teal have been recorded and a small group of feral Canada and Greylag Geese have nested there. Small ponds at Port Charlotte, Lagavulin and Port Ellen Distillery, and the Laphroaig Reservoir are in

Table 4: Species of birds recorded at inland lochs

The maximum number of birds recorded is shown, except for 'Other species' where the number of species is given (other species are Great Northern Diver, Great Crested Grebe, Slavonian Grebe, Bewick's Swan, Shelduck, Gadwall, Garganey, Ferruginous Duck, Eider and Long-tailed Duck). Geese, Lapwing and gulls are not listed but may use any convenient loch or burn mouth as a comfort station. r=recorded.

Inland lochs	Alkaline fishing lochs							Neutral fishing lochs						Neutral ponds and res.						Peaty lochs					Acid hill lochs							Unclassified			
Classification	Ardnave	Skerrols	Allan	Ballygrant	Lossit	Finlaggan	Cadhan	Kinnabus	Nighealaireachd	Eighinn	Glenastle	Diol	Fada, Ballygrant	Claddach	Gearach	Laphroaig	Lagavulin	Port Ellen Dist.	Port Charlotte	Gorm	Loch Gorm Pools	Corr	Staoisha	Murchairt	Sholum	Uraraidh	Allalaidh	Airigh nan Caisteal	Beinne Brice	Giur Bheinn	Leorin	Tallant, Bowmore	Siphinn	Ardnahoe	Craigens
pH value of water	7.8	7.8	8.3	7.9	7.6	7.6	7.5	—	—	—	—	—	7.0	—	—	—	—	—	—	—	—	—	—	—	—	—	—	4.2	4.2	—	4.2	—	—	—	—
Red-throated Diver	7	3	—	2	2	4	—	2	—	—	—	—	—	2	—	—	—	—	—	3	—	1	—	—	2	2	2	4	2	—	1	—	2	3	—
Black-throated Diver	—	2	—	2	—	—	—	—	—	—	—	—	—	—	—	—	—	—	—	—	—	—	—	—	—	—	—	—	—	—	—	—	2	2	—
Little Grebe	4	3	2	7	1	1	r	1	2	—	—	—	r	—	—	—	—	—	—	1	r	—	1	—	—	—	—	—	—	—	—	2	—	—	—
Cormorant	6	1	2	1	—	—	—	—	—	—	—	—	—	—	2	1	—	—	1	3	2	4	—	—	—	—	—	—	—	—	—	—	—	1	—
Grey Heron	4	18	20	2	2	8	4	4	—	4	—	—	4	—	2	1	—	8	—	3	1	1	—	11	—	—	—	—	—	—	—	9	—	—	—
Mute Swan	2	9	8	10	2	—	—	8	—	—	—	—	2	—	—	—	—	—	—	6	—	—	—	—	—	—	—	—	—	—	—	—	—	—	—
Whooper Swan	98	9	—	9	—	7	—	—	—	—	7	—	—	—	—	—	—	—	—	40	57	—	—	—	1	22	—	—	—	—	—	6	—	—	—
Wigeon	170	300	—	20	20	20	—	80	2	100	—	—	—	20	19	—	8	5	—	40	26	—	—	—	7	2	—	—	—	—	—	—	—	—	—
Teal	164	204	2	50	20	21	26	1	2	65	30	—	—	4	—	4	14	1	—	800	63	3	2	—	1	—	—	—	—	—	—	110	4	—	450
Mallard	24	463	13	7	20	7	—	64	12	50	40	4	3	32	12	4	2	—	—	55	18	12	13	6	—	—	2	2	—	—	—	75	5	—	5
Pintail	20	4	—	—	—	—	—	—	—	2	2	—	—	—	—	—	—	—	—	—	—	—	—	—	—	—	—	—	—	—	—	—	—	—	—
Shoveler	4	—	—	2	2	—	—	—	—	—	—	—	—	3	—	—	—	—	—	3	—	—	—	—	—	—	—	—	—	—	—	—	—	—	—
Pochard	100	320	45	128	50	50	30	30	—	—	40	1	—	—	3	3	—	—	1	54	—	64	64	30	—	—	—	—	—	—	—	—	—	—	r
Tufted Duck	55	200	200	27	21	21	4	20	4	—	16	5	—	—	6	3	8	—	2	41	—	4	37	4	—	—	—	—	—	—	—	—	—	—	1
Scaup	8	1100	—	3	—	—	—	—	—	—	—	—	—	—	—	—	—	—	—	20	—	—	—	—	—	—	—	—	—	—	—	—	—	—	—
Common Scoter	1	6	—	—	—	—	—	—	—	—	—	—	—	—	—	—	—	—	—	17	—	—	—	—	—	—	—	—	—	—	—	—	—	—	—
Goldeneye	4	8	1	1	2	—	—	4	3	20	8	1	—	—	1	1	1	—	2	15	2	6	5	1	4	—	—	—	—	—	—	—	—	—	—
Red-breasted Merganser	20	—	2	2	2	2	—	—	5	—	—	—	—	1	—	—	—	—	—	2	—	1	1	—	—	2	—	—	—	—	—	—	—	—	—
Goosander	2	1	1	—	—	—	—	—	—	—	—	—	—	—	r	—	—	—	—	—	—	—	—	—	—	—	—	—	—	—	—	—	—	—	—
Moorhen	—	—	1	—	1	—	—	—	—	—	—	—	—	—	r	—	1	6	—	r	r	—	—	—	—	—	—	—	—	—	—	—	—	—	—
Coot	4	120	2	30	2	1	—	1	—	—	r	r	r	—	2	—	1	—	2	—	1	—	—	—	—	—	—	—	—	—	—	—	—	—	18
Redshank	6	6	1	—	2	2	—	2	—	—	—	—	—	—	—	1	1	—	—	—	—	—	—	—	—	—	—	—	—	—	—	—	—	1	4
Common Sandpiper	2	—	—	—	—	—	—	—	—	—	1	—	—	1	—	—	—	—	—	2	—	—	—	—	—	—	—	—	—	—	—	—	r	2	—
Other species	3	2	0	0	0	0	0	0	1	0	0	0	0	2	0	0	0	0	0	6	1	0	0	0	0	0	0	0	0	0	0	1	0	0	1
TOTAL SPECIES	24	22	15	14	14	13	5	11	8	8	7	6	5	11	7	6	5	5	4	25	11	8	7	5	6	4	3	1	1	0	1	6	5	5	7

this category and have each held between four and seven species (Table 4).

Small, remote, weakly acid hill lochs are the breeding haunts of Red-throated and, rarely, Black-throated Divers. Often a pair of divers are the only birds present unless some reedy shallows attract a pair of Teal or Mallard, or a flock of gulls is using a corner as a comfort station. Lochan Sholum, the source of Lagavulin's water, is perhaps an exception: as well as Red-throated Diver, Little Grebe, Wigeon, Teal, Mallard and Goldeneye have been spotted there.

There are also some small lochs set among peat on the low ground with species lists of up to eleven, dependent on loch size and frequency of visits by birdwatchers; Teal and Mallard are most commonly present. Lochs Clach a' Bhuaile and na Cachle, alongside Loch Gorm near Rockside Lane end, are often searched; they have sometimes appeared in records as the 'Loch Gorm Pools'. Some of Loch Gorm's birds may roost there; 57 Whooper Swans and 63 Teal have been counted on their 5 ha (12 acres). Loch Corr near Sanaig holds very few birds, but eight species have been noted. Loch Staoisha near Bunnahabhainn and Loch Murchairt on the northeast side of the Oa are also in this category (Table.4).

Loch Ardnahoe, north of Port Askaig, receives drainage off peaty areas and is probably the deepest loch on Islay. It has recently been surveyed and the maximum depth found was about 35 m (115 ft). Less than 10 per cent of its area is of suitable depth and slope for diving ducks, and indeed grebes, ducks and Coots are not recorded. Divers are sometimes present and have been seen commuting to the Sound of Islay to obtain fish. Common Sandpipers and Redshanks feed along the shores and Grey Herons pay visits.

Coastal habitats

Islay has a wide variety of coastal habitats. The saltings and sandflats found particularly at the head of Lochs Gruinart (page 6) and Indaal (page 4) are of special importance to bird life. In winter these localities are roosts for large numbers of Barnacle Geese, often of the order of 10,000 at each, as well as for many Whooper Swans and ducks such as Shelduck, Wigeon, Teal, Mallard, Eider and Red-breasted Merganser. Oyster-catchers, Lapwings, Curlews, Redshanks and hundreds of gulls also roost, each on their preferred sections of the flats. A flock of Scaup roosts and feeds offshore on Loch Indaal, usually within Bridgend Bay, and builds up to between 600 and 1,500 birds each winter. Down loch, often

often in the narrow section west of the Laggan Peninsula, there is usually a flock of Common Scoter, occasionally with Velvet Scoter.

Pebble and boulder beaches are plentiful all around the island. Those around Loch Indaal are feeding areas for Dunlin, Turnstone and Purple Sandpiper; some are roosting places for Eider and there are breeding sites for terns. Where boulders predominate and accessibility is difficult, Black Guillemots breed. Birds are sparsely distributed along the sand and shingle beaches of Laggan Bay, Machir Bay, northern Loch Indaal, northern Loch Gruinart and east to Gortantaoid Point, except where they are adjacent to rocky areas or crossed by a river or burn; here gulls, Oystercatchers, Lapwings and Curlews have comfort stations. Gulls, Oystercatchers, and a few Dunlins and Sanderlings search and probe the swash areas and strand lines, whereas Pied Wagtails visit the higher storm beaches. Large gulls, Hooded Crows and occasional Ravens take carrion from both beaches and dunes. Where seaweed is piled up by wild seas, the food it contains is sought by waders, gulls and crows when it is fresh and by wagtails, Starlings and Jackdaws when it is dry and teeming with insects and other small arthropods.

Many kilometres of low cliffs with geos and caves are occupied by ledges serving as nest sites, rich in bird life in the breeding season, are located at Sanaig (page 6) in the northern Rhinns and between Lossit and Tormisdale in the southern Rhinns. These cliffs hold Fulmars, Shags, Herring and Lesser Black-backed Gulls, Kittiwakes, Guillemots and Razorbills. High cliffs on the Oa also hold a similar range of seabirds but in smaller numbers. Peregrines nest at intervals along the coast except where beaches are backed by grassy slopes.

Waters southeast of Islay

North of mixed waters flowing through the North Channel out of the Irish Sea, in the approaches to the Sound of Jura, there is an area of organically rich stratified waters crossed by the ferry routes to Port Ellen and Port Askaig. During August and into September this area is a nursery for flightless auks; the numbers of Razorbills and Guillemots are so great that they must come to moult from colonies on the north and northwest coasts of Ireland as well as from Islay (Dr E. I. S. Rees, Univ. Coll. of North Wales, private communication).

3
Birds and Man on Islay

Introduction

The pleasant scenes and tranquillity of Islay are valued by most of its inhabitants and many of its visitors. Most of the latter have at least a mild interest in wild flowers, birds or some other natural history or cultural aspect of the island. From time to time, however, conflicts arise between the conservation of some part of the island and proposals to introduce a new enterprise, perhaps on a larger scale than usual, or involving brash innovations. So far Islay has remained relatively unspoilt.

Since at least the early 1800s, wildlife has been conserved to some degree by estate management. Under the present low level of keepering the persecution of birds of prey is much reduced, and this favourable situation is likely to improve further as the researched knowledge of selective predation becomes fully accepted. It is now well established that birds of prey take unfit, ill-adapted or weak individuals and that some species suspected of killing are essentially carrion-eaters. Hen Harriers, once heavily persecuted by egg-collectors and gamekeepers, have returned in good numbers to the island. Like Sparrowhawks, Golden Eagles and Peregrines, they are now successful members of the Islay fauna. The re-introduction of White-tailed Eagles from Norwegian stocks to the island of Rhum may one day lead to that magnificent species breeding again on Islay's cliffs. The exceptional range of birds of prey seen on Islay is one of the main attractions bringing birdwatchers to the island.

The main purpose of this chapter is to review some past and ongoing interactions between birds and man. The first pages are probably the most sensitive: they involve wintering geese, which help prolong the island's tourist season but are not welcome by many farmers because they take a share of the food grown for livestock.

32

The Barnacle Goose (*Branta leucopsis*) and farming

Barnacle Geese occur in three discrete breeding populations; one of these winters in west Scotland and Ireland and breeds in east and northeast Greenland. Some 8,000 wintered in Islay in 1961/2, when there were only 40,000 in the world (Ogilvie 1978), compared with about 19,000 in 1985/6, when there was a world population of 110,000.

Variations in arctic weather between different breeding seasons cause major fluctuations in breeding success and therefore in numbers, but in the case of all three populations improvements of pasture and increased protection on the wintering grounds have benefited the geese. Improved pasture produces birds in a better condition, which is vital prior to the spring migration and subsequent breeding. Increased protection reduces the numbers killed and allows the geese to feed relatively unmolested, thereby both saving energy that would otherwise be used in flight and gaining energy reserves from uninterrupted feeding.

Greenland Barnacle Geese in Scotland and Ireland outwith Islay feed largely on small uninhabited islands where inaccessibility severely limits shooting. A steady increase in the area of improved pasture on Islay, and in the degree of improvement, have been major factors contributing to the rise in the goose numbers. The numbers of geese on uninhabited islands increased one-and-a-half times from March 1961 to March 1978, whereas those on Islay increased fourfold over the same period.

Since 1961/2, consistent counting on Islay together with estimates of the proportion of young in flocks has enabled the percentage of young birds entering the population to be compared with the number of birds dying (Ogilvie, in Boyd and Bowes 1983). This has revealed a healthy situation, sufficient to account for the increase in Islay over two decades without a contribution from geese transferring to the island from other wintering areas, although transfers cannot be discounted. This situation was temporarily reversed in the late 1970s by increased shooting after numbers had reached a peak of 24,000 in November 1976. Only 15,000 were present in November 1981, but since then more protection has been followed by an increase to 22,000 in late November 1986. The Protection of Birds Act 1954 gave the Barnacle Goose on Islay full protection, but an Order made in January 1955 allowed some shooting in December and January. For the next 20 years about 400 to 600 geese were shot each season under the close control of the few large estates. During the early part of this period, pastures on Gruinart Flats were in a reasonably good condition; about two-thirds of the geese were held in that area during November, but by spring this had dropped to a half.

33

In November 1976, when goose numbers reached their peak, farmers lobbied strongly for increased action, and in 1978 the shooting season was lengthened by starting on 1st September and continuing until 20th February in areas below high-water mark, in keeping with other wildfowl seasons. The estates began letting shooting to paying visitors and one or two hotels acquired shooting rights. The combined effect was an increase in the annual kill to around 1,500 by 1980. The population growth was reversed, autumn concentrations were broken up, and the geese dispersed earlier and moved on to a larger number of farms; as a result, more farmers felt that they had cause for complaint, although smaller goose flocks were involved.

The natural foods of Barnacle Geese include clover stolons and grasses found on sea-washed islands and saltings. Over recent centuries the geese have been tempted inland on to improved pastures and now especially on to young leys and modern well-fertilised rye-grass fields (Figure 8). The birds select the best fields by sight from the air, and, after landing, choose those grass blades which have a high energy content, presumably by pecking at those having a rich green colour. They spend a high proportion of the winter daylight hours feeding. Geese damage young leys mainly by over-grazing them before they are properly established; any fertiliser spread on damaged fields has limited value. Occasionally they uproot young grass plants and puddle bare soil, which cakes and then restricts the growth needed for livestock in the spring. Attempts have been made to assess goose damage: small areas are fenced off to prevent access by geese, and differences in growth within and without measured. Recent improved trials, particularly on reseeded fields, have revealed up to 30 per cent losses of silage from heavily grazed fields and around 70 per cent losses of grass available to livestock at the end of April (S. Percival, Glasgow University, private communication).

The Wildlife and Countryside Act 1981 again gave full protection to the Barnacle Goose, but a derogation allows shooting, to prevent serious agricultural damage. Licences for shooting are issued by the Department of Agriculture and Fisheries for Scotland. At first these were issued freely; now they are restricted and are granted only after a joint on-site inspection by DAFS and Nature Conservancy Council officials. They run to the end of April, extending the season into the period of maximum damage. In the first winter of licences about 1,000 geese were shot, but numbers decreased as the procedure was tightened up.

Areas in which shooting is prohibited have been established in two ways. Firstly, Sites of Special Scientific Interest have been notified by the NCC, the first in 1963. They now cover Loch Gruinart and its surrounds, Gruinart Flats, Bridgend saltings, the Laggan Peninsula and other areas less frequented by Barnacle Geese. These areas contain all the regular roosting sites of the species (Figure 8; Figure 9, page 55). The 1981 Act enabled the NCC to object to developments on SSSIs, including important changes in farming practice which they consider to be adverse to the special interest, in this case geese. The Council is also enabled to offer compensation payments for goose damage. In return, the farmer undertakes not to scare geese, becomes ineligible for a shooting licence, and has to abide by a management agreement regarding the reseeding of grassland.

Secondly, in 1983 some 12 sq. km (4.6 sq. miles) around Loch Gruinart were purchased by the Royal Society for the Protection of Birds. The main aim of the Society is to provide a sanctuary for geese and to attract maximum numbers for as long as possible through the winter. Some drainage improvements have been made and a programme of reseeding with grass and clover mixtures is underway. Beef livestock, outwintered on the rougher pastures of the reserve, are put to graze on the goose fields during the summer. The Society's cattle, supplemented by some from other farms, are controlled to provide the optimum degree of grazing, leaving a growth suitable for the geese on their arrival in October. Some harvesting for silage feeds calves that are wintered under cover and sold the following year. It will take some years to establish a satisfactory rotation over the whole reserve.

During the 1983/4, 1984/5 and 1985/6 winter seasons, the percentages of Islay's Barnacle Geese feeding on the reserve were 31, 33 and 28 respectively, giving an average of 31 per cent. In 1986/7 the proportion feeding there fell to 18 per cent: larger numbers than usual fed in the Bridgend-Ballygrant strath and in the Mulindry area; large flocks from the strath were seen commuting over the hills to the Gruinart roost. In 1987/8 the proportion on the reserve returned to about 30 per cent, probably as a result of increased goose-scaring (see below).

The present position concerning Barnacle Geese

Large numbers of Barnacle Geese visiting Islay in winter compete with livestock for food on the same rich grasslands. Somehow it must be arranged that geese and livestock feed in separate areas, at least during the lambing season and when winter fodder is running short. The ways in which this problem can be tackled are limited.

Many of Islay's farmers in winter calves and feed cattle and sheep daily close to the farm steadings. This is especially necessary in the case of the 15 dairy farmers. Extensive leys of selected and fertilised grasses are

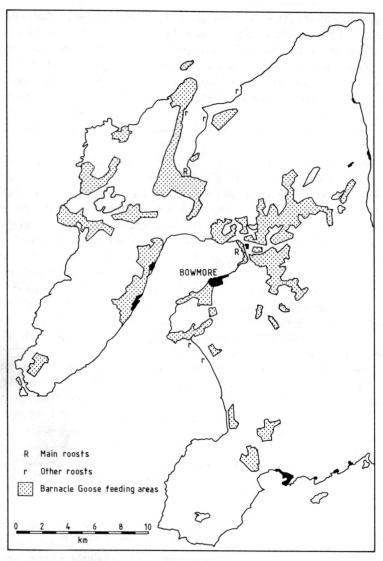

Figure 8: Barnacle Goose feeding areas and roosts

required to yield rich grass for silage; and these fields cannot contribute to the general cause of conservation, except that they do attract geese and they have been the principal cause of the expansion in their numbers in the two decades prior to 1978. The farmers' need for silage is accepted, and compensation for food taken by geese but intended for livestock is

36

now paid by the NCC to those who farm on SSSIs. Many would agree that it is reasonable for the public to contribute to the easement of the conflict between goose and farmer through the medium of taxation.

There are two conservation side-effects of feeding stations and inwintering. Lifestock are concentrated on pastures for artificial feeding, and so well-trodden ground, numerous cowpats as well as the leftovers are an attraction to gulls, Starlings, Jackdaws, Choughs and other farmland passerines. On the negative side, however, waste products from steadings and silos are often difficult to dispose of without polluting drainage systems and other watercourses.

The outwintering of hardy breeds takes advantage of Islay's mild climate. Pastures and grassy moorland, not used by Barnacle Geese, are used to a maximum, and supplements to natural feeding are kept to a minimum, except during critical periods. Top-quality beef is produced. Conservation interests are well favoured by minimising the area of leys and producing a minimum quantity of silage liquor and byre waste. Starlings and Pied Wagtails take advantage of the insects disturbed by animals feeding their way through long grasses and on pastures not treated with any chemicals. Cowpats produced by outwintered cattle are important feeding sites for the Chough.

The Gruinart Reserve has the advantage of including one of the major Barnacle Goose roosts and, therefore, birds feeding in the fields on the reserve save energy on 'commuting'. Also, geese arriving in October concentrate their feeding in the Gruinart area before many disperse to other parts of the island. Pastures on the Gruinart Flats were reclaimed in the early 1800s, but special drainage problems remain. An attempt to improve the drainage in the southeast part of the flats has recently met with some success, although some restriction to the passage of water downstream, out of the reserve and past Craigens, requires attention. In the poorly draining fields it is difficult to grow grass that is as attractive to geese as are rich leys elsewhere on the island, and, moreover, to maintain its quality throughout the winter.

A road divides Gruinart Flats into two and the geese are easily scared by passing vehicles. Feeding flocks are usually well back from the road, except when there is no traffic for an hour or so. On the north side, a low-voltage electricity power line cuts across the fields and appears to be an additional deterrent; it coincides with the boundary between well-grazed grass and a greener strip 50 m (160 ft) wide next to the road. These features appear to reduce locally the attraction that the flats have for geese, and mitigate against the contribution that the reserve gives towards resolving the island's goose problem. Another subject for debate is the provision of supplementary food for the geese in the form of grain;

the RSPB is contemplating an experiment on these lines, growing their own barley for this purpose.

Goose-scaring has been tried by many farmers. It takes various forms, such as firing flares or bangers from a Véry pistol; mounting a gas gun set to fire at intervals; flying kites tethered to stakes in sub-gale-force winds, but removing them in gales; setting up an arrangement of posts and cords or string carrying brightly coloured twisting or flapping plastic strips; deploying models of geese with their heads and necks raised in the alarm attitude; and erecting scarecrows with arms that flap in the wind. Geese are capable of getting used to any of these devices within periods varying from a few hours to a few weeks. Farmers sometimes shoot over the heads of the geese, and it has been shown that shooting to kill a single bird in a flock and leaving the carcase lying in the field has the most permanent effect; also, gas guns are more effective when shooting to kill has recently occurred in the vicinity. During the winter of 1987/8, the Farming, Forestry and Wildlife Advisory Group planned to coordinate a goose-scaring programme with estate-organised shooting under licence in non-protection areas (Figure 9). It is hoped that a significant proportion of the birds can be driven on to the reserve or SSSIs. Even this is unlikely to have a permanent effect, but the method may be viable for the critical grass-growing period late in the winter.

A basis for the easement of the conflict of interests centred on Barnacle Geese should involve action on all fronts:

(a) by making the reserve more attractive to geese, minimising disturbance, preparing rich grasslands and providing extra food;

(b) by compensating farmers on SSSIs for losses due to geese and perhaps extending this to include all dairy farmers, while allowing only accidental disturbance of geese where this applies;

(c) by shooting limited numbers of geese spread widely over farms not covered by (a) or (b) and supplementing this by manual scaring where necessary, the number shot being in accordance with annually reviewed plans that take account of goose population trends and the needs of farmers and estate management; and

(d) by maximising the outwintering of beef cattle on rough pastures and minimising the production of silage.

The Greenland White-fronted Goose (*Anser albifrons flavirostris*) and peatlands

The world population of the Greenland White-fronted Goose was 17,000 to 23,000 in the late 1950s; it declined to around 15,000 in the 1970s and has increased to over 20,000 since 1984 (Ruttledge and Ogilvie 1979; Ogilvie, personal communication). It breeds in west Greenland and winters in Ireland and Scotland. From 2,250 to 4,700 visited Islay in the late 1960s (Ogilvie 1978) and from 4,200 to 6,000 in the years 1981 to 1986. Flocks have been observed flying to or from Ireland or Kintyre, probably accounting for much of the variation in counts on Islay. The rate of loss of geese exceeded the rate of recruitment of young in the late 1970s, probably as a result of increased shooting.

Most of these geese arrive during a period of a few days some time in October and quickly become spread over the island, but their small numbers and small flocks have generally not brought them into serious conflict with farming interests. In the last few years, however, some flock sizes have increased and farmers are beginning to call for action.

The traditional feeding and roosting habitat of the species seems to have been the extensive peatlands in Ireland and Scotland, where dark brown birds with black belly markings are well camouflaged. In many areas there has been habitat loss due to drainage and reclamation; this has encouraged these geese to move on to farmland for daytime feeding. Most of Islay's Whitefronts spend a large part of the day feeding on farms, sometimes on pastures or on stubbles in the early autumn, and often in more poorly drained areas than those used by the Barnacle Geese; some feeding is known to occur at night near the peatland roosts. On farmland they sever grasses and sedges and dig for underground storage organs; in the peatlands their food plants are the white beak-sedge (*Rhynchospora alba*), cotton grass (*Eriophorum angustifolium*), bulbous rush (*Juncus bulbosus*), bogbean (*Menyanthes trifoliata*), white water-lily (*Nymphaea alba*) and deergrass (*Trichophorum cespitosum*).

White-fronted Geese have a complex roosting pattern. On Islay the majority attend three main roosts on peatland sites that have scattered lochans. These are on Eilean na Muice Duibhe, 4 km ($2\frac{1}{2}$ miles) south of Bowmore; in the vicinity of Feur Lochain between Loch Gorm and Ardnave; and in the Loch Leathan area, 6 km ($3\frac{3}{4}$ miles) north of Bridgend. Several flocks usually fly into these roosts, but watching them on a succession of nights soon reveals considerable variation in the numbers attending any one site. Sometimes over 500 and occasionally over 1,000 birds enter, although there are nights when fewer than 500 assemble. A few sites are irregularly occupied and appear to function as alternatives to the large roosts, dependent on weather conditions. A roost of 300 or more geese is also known at Kinnabus on the Oa, and there are at least 20 others housing single flocks of fewer than 100 birds, or even single families. A small flock feeding at Callumkill, for instance, has been seen to fly over Kildalton towards Ardmore at dusk. Altogether there are about 30 known roosts which have the capacity to house all the island's White-fronted Geese. Since these geese now form about a quarter of the world population, the larger roosts are regarded as important to their well-being, especially since habitat loss has reached serious proportions in western Ireland.

Because they are more palatable than the Barnacle Goose, Whitefronts have in the past been shot in small numbers while flighting into a roost. The 1954–67 Protection of Birds Acts allowed shooting during September to January, but the 1981 Wildlife and Countryside Act now protects them at all times. Subsequent to this latter Act both numbers of geese on Islay and their productivity on the breeding grounds have increased, reflecting a reduction in shooting throughout the subspecies' range.

The continued well-being of the Greenland White-fronted Geese on Islay has recently been threatened from three directions:

(1) Despite objections by the NCC, the Secretary of State for Scotland gave planning permission in July 1984 for peat to be cut by a firm of distillers from the vicinity of the major roost on Eilean na Muice Duibhe. Cutting the peat required preparatory drainage ditches to be dug and one was commenced, contravening the programme set out in the planning permission documents. Complaints were raised that the plans breached the European Directive on the Conservation of Wild Birds, and it was feared that the ditch would destroy boglands in the roost area, based on case histories of similar damage in Ireland.

Representations were made to the European Commission, and in October 1985 their representative, together with officials of the NCC, inspected the site and alternative peatlands. All work on site was stopped and the Commission instigated proceedings in the European Court against the British Government. In 1987 an agreement was finally reached to transfer the proposed peat extraction to a site near Castlehill, 6 km (3¾ miles) north of Port Ellen. The distillers agreed that the characteristics of the Castlehill peat were suitable for their purposes. Unfortunately drainage continued from the ditch at Eilean na Muice Duibhe for over two years before it was dammed, and an area of peat has been drained; it is hoped that the effects of this will not extend too far towards the area containing the roost.

(2) A 1986 proposal to construct a holiday complex in northwest Islay gained planning permission, but was referred to a public inquiry in 1987. This was to encroach on to the Loch Corr area which is the site of a White-fronted Goose roost, a 'satellite' to the main roost in the Feur

Lochain area. The proposals also had impacts on birds of prey and the Chough, all of which are 'specially protected' by the 1981 Act (Appendix 1). In the face of strong objections from the NCC and most inhabitants of the Rhinns, the proposal was withdrawn.

(3) Afforestation started in a small way on Islay in 1949, and larger plantations were developed in the Glen area (Figure 2) in the 1960s; furthermore, extensive planting has recently been carried out in the southern Rhinns, on the northeast side of the Oa and in northern Islay. Now about 35 sq. km (13.5 sq. miles), 6 per cent of Islay, are planted. In the Glen area some White-fronted Goose feeding areas were planted, and on the Rhinns planting has been taken right up to the edge of a roost site by a small lochan in Gleannagaoidh near Easter Ellister. These are minor factors acting against the well-being of the geese and further major additions to these plantations are unlikely, especially following the designation of most of the Rhinns as an SSSI in the spring of 1987.

The Chough (*Pyrrhocorax pyrrhocorax*) and livestock farming

Two recent studies of the Chough on Islay (Monaghan and Thompson 1984; Warnes 1982) have provided most of the information on which the following account is based.

During the period 1820 to 1950, there was a gradual reduction in the number of Britain's counties occupied by the Chough from about 24 to seven, but the distribution hardly changed from 1963 to 1982 and on Islay there has been an increase in recent years. The island held about 170 to 180 birds in April 1981 prior to the breeding season, that is about 6 per cent of all Choughs resident in the British Isles and 85 per cent of those in Scotland. About 300 birds were present in 1986.

After the decline, the 1954–67 Protection of Birds Acts and more recently the 1981 Wildlife and Countryside Act provided this member of the crow family with special protection at all times. This is particularly necessary for the British Chough because it is a species at the northern limit of its European range and it has been shown to produce only two breeding adults from 26 clutches averaging four eggs each. Nesting traditionally takes place on ledges in caves and in crevices around cliffed coasts, but since the 1960s some pairs have occupied old buildings and barns with roofs intact, even though inland nest sites are not so well situated with respect to feeding grounds. This change suggests that the population is near the island's maximum carrying capacity.

Choughs feed mainly within 1.5 km (nearly 1 mile) of the coast, using their curved bills to scrape, dig and probe for invertebrates. They find prey under rocks and by turning over cowpats, root-mats, stones and seaweed; breaking up the dung of domestic stock provides a major food source. Their diet is supplemented by grain found in stubbles, at stock-feeding stations and at other places where spillage occurs. They commonly hunt on bare soil or well-grazed pastures and heath along the coasts of the western Rhinns and the Oa; sheep, cattle, feral goats and rabbits all feed in these maritime areas. On the Irish Sea islands of Ramsey, Bardsey and the Calf of Man, the numbers of breeding Choughs have varied directly with the density of grazing animals. If arable farming is carried right up to the cliff tops, the population declines; historical events such as the repeal of the Corn Laws and the world wars have also been cited as probable causes of the major decline from 1820 to 1950.

The Chough is therefore greatly dependent on livestock farming and it may be significant that the east-central coast of Islay, with no farms, has no Choughs. There is little, if any, persecution of the Chough on the island and inwintering of cattle is probably the main threat to its continued presence. Two small areas have been ploughed up to the cliff tops in recent years, but this is unlikely to become common practice because of the strong prevailing southwest winds. These same winds will also prohibit afforestation on the species' main feeding grounds.

The Corncrake (*Crex crex*) and silage

In the late 1800s, a decline in Corncrake numbers was noticed in the southeast of England; through the succeeding decades this spread north and west into most of Britain. By 1939 the grating call of this rail was heard only locally, but the species was still numerous on the Scottish islands. In June 1978 the Hebrides held 70 per cent of all calling birds in Britain; 22–24 were calling on Islay, and in June 1986 23 were located. Both surveys were carried out between dusk (22.30 hrs) and dawn (03.00 hrs) and 80 calling sites, recorded over the previous 25 years, were visited and checked (Moore 1987).

The Corncrake pecks food from the ground and off plants, taking chiefly small invertebrates, seeds, buds and some green plant parts. It requires lush vegetation of sufficient height and density to give good cover; tall grass, sedges, rushes, iris clumps and nettles are chosen. Its traditional habitat is one of damp pastures that support abundant life. In recent decades there has been a tendency for these birds to select improved leys intended for silage or hay. Islay's Corncrakes can be found in or near both the traditional habitats and the modern leys. Most leys are harvested, using machinery, in June, before these birds have had time to breed. Hay is not gathered before late July.

At Coul, strips a few metres wide on either side of drainage ditches are fenced off and prevent grazing; consequently, the ditch margins have become well vegetated. Four males were regularly heard calling from these strips each season from 1981 to 1985, and five were heard in 1986. Failing provision of this sort and retention of other sites in their present state, the future of the Corncrake looks bleak.

Other threats on Islay include the predation of eggs or young by small mammals such as feral ferrets and feral or domestic cats. In Sutherland the latter are on record as bringing in adult as well as young Corncrakes. It is also known that these low-flying migrants are sometimes killed by colliding with overhead cables. The main reason for the decline of the species in Britain, however, is the change from the July gathering of hay to rapid and early harvesting of grass by machinery for silage.

The Corn Bunting was abundant last century; it remained resident until perhaps the 1940s and has been an occasional visitor since, with the last record in 1981. Its decline preceded that of the Corncrake and was probably due to changes in agricultural practices involving the introduction of horse-drawn machinery. It probably nested close to the field boundaries, and the tilling of these margins has been suggested as a factor in its decline.

The Hen Harrier (*Circus cyaneus*) and afforestation

In mediaeval Britain, the forest cover probably limited the open habitat suitable for Hen Harriers, but by the 1700s they had become widespread. Then, during the 1800s, this species was persecuted by gamekeepers and egg-collectors, and it became extinct on Islay in the latter part of that century. By 1900, it was confined to Orkney, the Outer Hebrides and Kintyre. It was not until keepering was reduced in the Second World War that this raptor began to recolonise parts of mainland Scotland from the north southwards. By about 1960 it had reached Islay, but it probably did not breed there until the late 1960s.

Gamekeepers have been concerned that these predators took grouse chicks and frightened quarry during drives. A study of a grouse moor in Kincardine showed that the grouse available for shooting were reduced by not more than 7.4 per cent by August. Grouse are now rare on Islay

43

and are not recorded as taken by this harrier, but Pheasants are among a range of smaller birds and animals listed as prey.

Since this species returned to Islay there has been some afforestation which in the 1980s has reached significant proportions on moorlands, especially in the Rhinns. During the establishment stage of plantations the vole population increases, and Hen Harriers may continue to hunt the area until the trees are about 1 m ($3\frac{1}{4}$ ft) high. They require tall rank vegetation for nesting and may continue to breed at the traditional sites in plantations up to the thicket stage if there is good access to hunting ground. They leave well before the canopy closes and this may not be until the trees are at least 15 years old. When a forest is felled and restocked it is unlikely that they will return.

The Protection of Birds Acts of 1954 and 1967 and the Wildlife and Countryside Act 1981 protected all species of harriers at all times; in addition, pairs that do occupy plantations are usually free of persecution at the nest. It seems unlikely that Islay's Hen Harriers are at serious risk, because grouse are rare, an SSSI covers the Rhinns moorlands, and the planting of conifers is not likely to cover much more ground. A few nest sites are, however, likely to be lost as the trees begin to close canopy.

Moorland birds and muirburn practice

True moorland birds nest and usually feed at ground level; this makes them vulnerable to the practice of muirburning. On Islay these birds include the Hen Harrier, Merlin, Red Grouse, Black Grouse, Golden Plover, Dunlin, Curlew, Short-eared Owl, Skylark, Meadow Pipit and Twite; and also the Cuckoo, which lays eggs in the nests of Meadow Pipits. The adverse effects of muirburns on a moorland bird community are minimised by the Hill Farming Act 1946, which limits the practice to the period from 1st October to 15th April. Burning during the first half of April is likely to affect only early-nesting Golden Plovers and Curlews. If the period is extended to 30th April, however, as the landowner may do under the 1946 Act, all the species listed above could be affected except the Merlin and Twite, which do not nest until early May.

Controlled muirburning was introduced in the face of much opposition in the second half of the 18th century. The objective is to manage moorland vegetation in favour of the nutritious growth of heather or grasses suitable for grouse and livestock, and also to provide small areas of cover for grouse. Correct burning preserves a *status quo* in plant succession, suppressing shrub or tree saplings, but does not destroy the existing plant regime. However, it is often not possible to avoid disturbing the balance between the species present.

The experienced man is able to burn back heather that is seven to 15 years old or eliminate accumulations of dead grass and leaves, without damaging buds around the base of heather plants or seeds within tussocks of grass, thus allowing new growth to flourish afterwards. Restoration of heather from root stocks takes three or four years. It is recommended that strips be burnt in rotation, each strip of heather every eight to 15 years and each strip of rough grass every three to five years, the latter being in larger strips (DAFS and NCC 1977). Carefully controlled fires should be planned to burn downwind in a gentle breeze towards a firebreak. Fires that are too fierce owing to too much woody material or too strong a wind kill plants and seeds or may burn off surface layers of peaty humus which may smoulder for days. In extreme cases, mineral soils are exposed and there is little hope of the original plant cover being regenerated.

Smoke from all muirburns contains minerals such as potassium, magnesium, calcium and phosphorus; these and others are also present in ashes left after fires, a proportion of which may be lost to the area in drainage waters or high winds. Losses of minerals from well-controlled burns every ten years, and from the sale of ewes and lambs, are likely to be replaced from rainfall and sea mists (DAFS and NCC 1977). Phosphorus, however, is the exception and is probably being depleted. Red Grouse depend heavily on heather for food and sometimes select young shoots with relatively high nitrogen and phosphorus contents (Watson 1971). Depletion of phosphorus on heather moors may eventually result in phosphorus deficiencies in Red Grouse.

There is a serious risk of overburn if muirburning is carried out in unsuitable conditions or with an inadequate number of helpers. This must have happened frequently in the past, well before the days of agricultural science, when fires were started to clear scrub and forest. Some place names such as Maol Dubh (black bare hill, British National Grid reference 3851) and Pliadan Dubh (black plots of ground, grid reference 4259) probably refer to areas badly burnt in the past. MacAlpine's Gaelic dictionary records that in Islay the word *dubh* also means disastrous.

Several stages of vegetation and soil degradation, initiated by past muirburning or clearance, can be recognised (McVean 1959) by:
(a) bracken colonising areas burnt in previous years; its rhizomes are unaffected by burning and it has spread widely in western Scotland over the last one or two centuries (Darling 1947);
(b) bare lichen-encrusted patches among heather and a tough leathery skin to peat;

(c) bare soft peat with isolated tussock plants;

(d) moss and thin peat burnt from around stones, boulders and rock outcrops;

(e) sheet erosion of thin peat with downhill washing of underlying bleached sand and gravel; and

(f) gullies developed on steep slopes where thin peat overlies sand and gravel.

The latter stages are created by the natural forces of erosion taking over from old, probably successive, overburnings. Even where some grass or heather remains but encrusting lichens are developed, it is difficult for the natural succession of plants to restore the habitat under Islay's maritime climate. It is generally accepted that muirburning is least beneficial in the west of Scotland and that the amount of heather on the hills appears to be steadily decreasing. Furthermore, muirburns reduce the diversity of vegetation and therefore also the richness of insect and other animal life that forms the prey of moorland birds (DAFS and NCC 1977). The early stages of insects have no means of escape from a severe burning, but some in the winter resting stages are protected from well-controlled fires that generate lower temperatures. Wildlife is, however, best conserved where muirburning is not practised.

Islay has its share of accidental fires: one in February 1985 raged for two days and swept across 5 or 6 sq. km (1.9–2.3 sq. miles) of moorland on the Rhinns, requiring firefighting reinforcements to be brought from the mainland. The productivity of the land can be seriously reduced by such events, and a similar accident during the breeding season would eliminate all nests and their contents. In 1987, the land burnt in 1985 was slowly recovering and was at least supporting Meadow Pipits.

Marine pollution and the Loch Indaal incident

The pollutant affecting birds at sea is oil; heavy oil clings to feathers and light oil penetrates them, destroying insulation and waterproofing properties. Birds that have many oiled feathers die either from ingesting oil during attempts to preen, by exposure, or through an inability to hunt for prey leading to starvation. Detergents used for dispersing oil slicks are also toxic to wildlife. Those species that feed by dipping their heads in search of prey or by surface-diving and then swimming to hunt for prey often dive to escape oil, but usually resurface still within the oil. These are the worst-affected birds and it has been confirmed by ringing recoveries that auks are most at risk, with Eiders second; others that may be killed are Scaup, scoters, mergansers, Cormorants, Shags, grebes and divers.

Substantial numbers of oiled birds are sometimes found on beaches and other coastal areas. Cleaning and rehabilitation has been tried but with very limited success, and in general this is not now thought to be worthwhile. The worst incidents occur where and when numbers are swelled by winter visitors.

There have been instances of oiled birds in Islay's shores. Fortunately the numbers of carcases have been small, except in 1969, when there was an oil spillage at Bruichladdich. On 19th–20th October, a leak of 114,000 litres (25,000 gallons) of heavy fuel oil developed overnight and flowed down a burn into Loch Indaal (Ogilvie and Booth 1970). A prompt attempt was made to contain the oil behind a boom, but the combination of a very high spring tide and a southwesterly wind caused the boom to be breached. The oil was then driven towards and deposited on to the 18 km (11 miles) of shore from the Bruichladdich Monument around the head of the loch to just beyond Saltpan Point. It was pushed well up the beaches and rocks into a narrow belt, except at Bridgend saltings where it occurred in patches of several square metres. By March 1970, the remains of the oil had become partially buried in stranded seaweed and sand.

Over the days and weeks following the spillage, a minimum of 450 birds was found dead or dying. Of these, 338 were Eiders, 31 Red-breasted Mergansers, 27 Guillemots and Black Guillemots, 18 Scaup and seven Common Scoters. Eiders were found walking up to 0.8 km ($\frac{1}{2}$ mile) inland, and some were picked up in the main street of Bowmore. During the following spring farming activity, several carcases were found. In November 1969 there were only 100 to 150 Eiders on Loch Indaal, whereas 600 were estimated before the incident. With this as a basis, the full casualty list of all species may have totalled between 600 and 700 birds.

The spillage occurred while the Scaup flock was building up. On 21st October 1969 between 600 and 650 had arrived, and no affected birds were noted until 16th and 17th November, when 18 were found. The main rafts must have fed at oil-free parts of Loch Indaal.

The pollution of watercourses

The rivers and burns of Islay provide habitat for Grey Heron, Mallard, Moorhen, Common Sandpiper, Grey and Pied Wagtails, Dipper, and rare visiting Kingfishers. The distribution of these birds along watercourses is dependent on the speed, quantity and quality of the

47

water, and especially on its acidity and oxygen content. These factors affect the abundance of insects and fish upon which the birds prey. The Dipper is particularly sensitive to changes in the riverine habitat: from 1975 to 1987 there were from zero to possible three pairs along the River Sorn, normally one near Bridgend and another near the Wool Mill; there may have been three in 1977, but none was recorded in either 1985 or 1986.

The catchment areas of Islay's rivers contain farmland to varying degrees; some have none, but the River Sorn catchment has a particularly high percentage. A technical report, prepared for Islay Estates by the Clyde River Purification Board in 1974, was based on both chemical and biological examinations of water samples from eleven localities on the Sorn between Ballygrant and the river's mouth. This report referred to two places at which the biotic index, based on a range of small invertebrates, was depressed; in each case, however, the condition of the river recovered within 1 km (0.6 miles) downstream.

It is recognised that pollution by silage liquor is most serious. Other potential sources associated with farming are fertiliser nitrates in run-off, sheep dip, byre wastes, milking-parlour waste and sewage; garbage tipped into watercourses can also be detrimental. Some of these pollutants enhance biological growth in waters to such an extent that the oxygen content is depleted and fish are seriously affected. Although a few farms on Islay are equipped to deal with pollutants and others do not significantly pollute any watercourse, there are clear cases where periodic pollution should be better controlled to enhance the prospects of fishermen and wildlife.

The 1974 Sorn report suggested that the increasing use of fertilisers over the decade or two prior to 1974 might have disturbed the balance of the river's productivity in favour of trout rather than salmon. It also indicated that pollution of the River Sorn could be kept to a reasonable minimum if the small sewage works at Ballygrant were adequately maintained and provision were made for intercepting byre and silage drainage at farms. In both cases the effluent would have to be removed from storage periodically and spread over land away from the river and confluent burns or drainage ditches.

Ferrets and ground-nesting birds

The Rabbit (*Oryctolagus cuniculus*) arrived on Islay about 1780 and was apparently common in 1880. Now there are warrens wherever there are suitable sandy soils. Early in 1979, around ten to 15 Ferrets (*Mustela furo*) were set free in northwestern Islay, with the object of reducing the Rabbit population. By 1985, these predators had become established as feral members of the Islay fauna and their numbers were reported as presenting a problem.

Among the prey of the Ferret are ground-nesting birds, their eggs and their young, as well as the young of Rabbits, Brown Hares (*Lepus capensis*) and other small vertebrates. Present in numbers, this animal threatens domestic, game and wild birds, including domestic ducks, Mallard, Teal, Red Grouse, Black Grouse, domestic fowl, Pheasants, Guineafowl, Corncrakes, Oystercatchers, Lapwings, Ringed Plovers, Snipe, Woodcock, Curlew, Skylarks and Meadow Pipits. As farmers, gamekeepers and conservationists became united against this introduced species, discussions took place that resulted in a programme of intensive trapping in baited wire cages starting in December 1985 under the auspices of the Islay Forestry, Farming and Wildlife Group. This advisory body has a committee of representatives drawn from many organisations in the fields of conservation, farming, forestry, field sports and distilling, and also from local authorities.

The trapping programme was funded by the Manpower Services Commission, with additional grants from the Highlands and Islands Development Board. Traps were set along the boundaries of enclosed fields, covering areas of about 2 to 5 sq. km (0.8–1.9 sq. miles) per week. An average of about 140 cage traps were baited with Rabbit and other carcases. Much of the island was covered in each of the two years of the scheme, except two estates where the matter was tackled independently. Some high-catch areas were visited twice within one year, but unenclosed rough pastures, moorlands and peatlands were not covered for practical reasons. Tables 5 and 6 summarise the results.

The Ferret is likely to be in competition with feral cats and the indigenous Stoats, with which it has a large overlap in choice of prey size and species, and to a lesser degree with feral Hedgehogs and Brown Rats. In general the last two species specialise in smaller prey, but all these carnivores including the Ferret take birds, especially young birds and eggs. The ecological relationship between these species is surely complex, but it has not been researched and the true effect of the introduction of the Ferret on bird life—domestic, game or wild—is unknown. The three largest weekly catches of 1987 were 23 at Saligo, 14 at Kilchoman and 14 at Lossit, Rhinns; each of these was in the vicinity of large Rabbit warrens.

Islay's feral Ferrets have not been exterminated by this programme; these animals are likely to be present in the unfenced areas (as they are on the island of Mull), though in lesser numbers than they are in the fenced

Table 5: A summary of Ferret-trapping results

	Dec. 1985 to Dec. 1986	Feb. 1987 to Dec. 1987
Number of weeks worked	45	40
Number of Ferrets trapped	290	177
Weekly average in NW	9.5 over 24 weeks	9.0 over 9 weeks
Weekly average elsewhere	3.0 over 21 weeks	3.1 over 31 weeks
Weekly average overall	6.4 over 45 weeks	5.3 over 40 weeks
Other known catches/ kills	112	35
Total number of Ferrets	402	212
Percentage of females	48	43

Note: The northwest in which the higher catch rates were recorded comprised the Rhinns north of Bruichladdich, including areas around Loch Gruinart. The highest catches were 34 and 23 in the first weeks of November 1986 and 1987 respectively, when traps were set in the Saligo-Sanaigmore district.

Table 6: The number of Ferrets trapped compared with numbers of other animals

Carnivore species	D = domestic F = feral W = wild	1986	1987	1987/ 1986 %
Ferret (*Mustela furo*)	F	290	177	61
Cat (*Felis silvestris lybica*)	D, F	289	132	46
Brown Rat (*Rattus norvegicus*)	W	183	81	44
Hedgehog (*Erinaceus europaeus*)	F	161	71	44
Stoat (*Mustela erminea*)	W	129	79	61
Total carnivores	—	1052	540	51

Note: Cats, Hedgehogs and some Stoats were set free and it is likely that a proportion of these were retrapped. Bearing this in mind, it is clear that significantly more Ferrets were trapped than any one of the other four carnivores.

areas because on average the biological productivity of the former areas is lower. The reservoir of Ferrets outside the trapping areas is almost certainly sufficient to support a rapid recovery in numbers. After the termination of the programme, however, the traps were distributed among the farmers with the aim of keeping the numbers low.

Herring Gulls and food poisoning

On 10th September 1982, a case of salmonella poisoning was reported at the Cottage Hospital, Bowmore. During the following fortnight a total of 45 people were clinically affected by an outbreak, but no new cases were identified after 25th September 1982. The bacterium responsible was identified as *Salmonella typhimurium* phage type 12, and the same strain occurring elsewhere had been identified in milk, red meat, cattle, pigs and poultry. Unpasteurised milk was the only factor common to the infected households and other establishments, and five other facts arising out of detailed investigations pointed to milk being the most probable food vehicle. A government regulation made in November 1982 required that all milk retailed on Islay after August 1983 be pasteurised, and the dairies distributing milk to the affected eastern parts of the island were equipped to do this at an early date.

It is known that gulls can be carriers of the bacteria, and that *Salmonella* strains found in gulls include those found in humans with gastro-intestinal infections. Gulls can be carriers for a few days or years, but they are rarely affected themselves by the infection. Also, gull droppings on pasture are likely to infect cattle only if the latter are rendered susceptible by illness or stress.

Numerous outbreaks of salmonellosis among livestock in Scotland have been attributed to infections brought to farms by gulls that are presumed to have fed at a sewage outfall or on a refuse tip. High incidences have been found in gull droppings collected around outfalls, and 10 per cent of Herring Gulls caught at tips in the Clyde area carried these bacteria (Monaghan *et al.* 1985). Some hundred gull droppings collected at the Gartbreck tip, Bowmore, were examined and just five were found to contain *Salmonella typhimurium* phage type 12; no sampling at sewage outfalls on Islay was reported. A correlation has been found between the occurrence of human and gull infections in the same areas (Monaghan *et al.* 1985).

Over 90 per cent of the gulls feeding at Gartbreck are Herring Gulls; some of these commute from the Port Ellen district, while others stay around Loch Indaal and visit farms in the central part of the island, including dairy farms close to the tip. It seems likely that Herring Gulls were involved in the 1982 outbreak in some way, feeding either at the Gartbreck tip or at a sewage outfall on the island. Gulls are, however, highly mobile and it is possible that they were contaminated beyond Islay's shores.

At one time the refuse from Jura and Islay was tipped along a continuous slope at Gartbreck; now a system of trenches is filled in sequence and quickly covered over with sand and gravel from a nearby quarry. This change has much reduced the area of refuse exposed at any one time, and the attendant gulls can take only food that has been dumped recently. The number of gulls present at the tip also appears to have declined. Thus, the chance of these birds transporting *Salmonellae* incubated on the rubbish tip to pastures grazed by livestock has been minimised. Little can be done to reduce the chance of bacteria being collected by gulls from effluent at sewage outfalls without incurring considerable expense. Meanwhile, healthy dairy cows and pasteurisation remain the main safeguards against outbreaks of the September 1982 type.

Poisoned baits and non-target species

Poisoned baits are illegal except when they are used carefully to kill ground vermin; they may be placed only where they cannot be taken by species other than ground vermin. Such baits placed in the open countryside kill indiscriminately; unfortunately they are still widely used in Britain. They place domestic animals and even children at risk: cases of fatally poisoned sheepdogs and one human death are on record.

Poisoned baits sometimes kill avian predators or scavengers which are not regarded in law as vermin or 'pest species' (K of Appendix 1) and which often are not the objective of the person responsible. Since the late 1970s 15 incidents on Islay have been reported, involving the death of four Buzzards, a Golden Eagle, a Gyrfalcon, a Raven, and some more common birds; there have also been several cases of domestic animals being killed by this means.

Buzzards are widespread and common. They eat a variety of small prey, especially young Rabbits, but have a negligible effect on gamebirds. They may be seen around sheep at lambing time but are not lamb-killers; they scavenge for afterbirths and feed on stillborn lambs, or visit sheep carcases opened by larger scavengers.

Golden Eagles are powerful predators. They take a variety of mammals and birds, usually favouring hares and Rabbits; a full list of prey recorded on Islay is given in the species account. Although grouse are not on this list eagles do take Red Grouse on the mainland, but careful research has shown that they do not affect population or bag sizes. Sheep and Red Deer carrion can be an important source of food, and lambs are occasionally taken alive, probably when mother and lamb are separated.

The Gyrfalcon is rarely seen on Islay; the first record was in 1862 and only eleven birds have been noted in 125 years. Ravens are not listed as a 'pest species' in the 1981 Wildlife and Countryside Act and, like raptors and most other birds, are protected at all times. They are mainly carrion-eaters and as such are beneficial, unlike some members of the crow family. They take carrion of cattle, sheep, Rabbits and hares, as well as some found on the shore. Live food includes voles, mice, rats and beetles. They occasionally attack incapacitated lambs and sheep.

The case against any of these species is weak. By contrast, the case for them is strong: it is arguable in terms of the clearing of carrion, the eating of ground vermin, an interest in their behaviour, heritage and the attraction of visitors to Islay.

The disturbance of birds

The legal status of Islay's wild birds, under the Wildlife and Countryside Act 1981, is summarised in Appendix 1. All birds, their nests and eggs are protected by law. Under the 1981 Act, it is an offence intentionally to disturb any wild bird unless you are authorised to kill or take a 'pest species' or to shoot a 'quarry' species between dates limiting the open season, or have obtained a licence to carry out activities involving specified birds in connection with education, research, conservation, photography, public health and safety, or the prevention of serious damage.

Serious disturbance resulting from leisure activities is often avoidable. Birdwatching and other natural history activities are generally pursued by persons who wish to conserve the heritage of nature, but there are unfortunate exceptions and the Royal Society for the Protection of Birds has produced a leaflet explaining a recommended code of conduct; ten points abstracted from this leaflet are listed in Appendix 2.

Unwitting disturbance of birds is not an offence under the Act, but morally should be minimised. Disturbance interrupts feeding or resting, causing birds to use extra energy on swimming, running or flying. To compensate they must feed more intensively in the available time left, but if this is impossible some will move to other sites, fail to breed or die prematurely.

The disturbance of shore-nesting birds by visitors, islanders and their dogs is concentrated mainly on a few beaches and is not normally significant. Within the constraints of their habitat requirements, birds tend to choose the least-frequented places for nesting. Occasionally, however, there is an unfortunate use of a part of a beach that needs careful conservation in the breeding season. Colonies of Little Terns provide a good example; only 200 to 300 pairs breed in Scotland and up to 26 pairs have attempted to breed in recent years on Islay. These birds, like several other species, nest among shingle or pebbles in specific places above the high spring-tide level. Horse-riders, dog-walkers and others, even Land Rover and motorbike 'joy riders', may unwittingly cross these places during May or June and endanger well-camouflaged eggs or chicks. Alternative routes should be taken during the breeding season, and walkers, who have to pass by, cause less disturbance if they keep to the firmer wave-washed lower part of the beach. Any frantic calling or dive-bombing birds, or birds performing distraction displays, should be heeded and a small detour made to obviate further, more serious disturbance.

Another, potentially serious threat to waterbirds comes from water sports such as sailing, windsurfing and power-boating. Since the 1950s there has been a rapid growth in these activities in mainland Britain, particularly on inland waters. On Islay, fishing interests prohibit this development inland, but all three sports are practised on sheltered coastal waters, albeit on a very small scale. Also, the majority of wildfowl on Loch Indaal and other waters are winter visitors and no serious conflict of interests arises. The use of wet-suits, however, is capable of extending water sports into colder places and seasons, and the future situation may need careful consideration. Apart from birds, seals and Otters such as those that frequent Loch an t-Sailein (Loch of the Seals), near Ardbeg, and the nearby archipelago, are easily disturbed by water sports.

An overview

Histories of some habitat modifications by climate, changes in farming practice, keepering and incidents detrimental to wildlife have been briefly described in Chapters 2 and 3. The reader has been given an indication of how Islay has been constantly changing since it became hospitable to man after the Ice Age, and of how the rate of change has increased during the last 200 years at the hands of man.

The accounts of Chapter 4 contain a summary of the occurrences of over 270 bird species seen on Islay. The data record or suggest changes in the status of some species, and these are summarised in Table 7. These events are largely linked to habitat changes and to the activities of man, and on general grounds it is likely that others are unrecorded. The concern of conservationists is that unilateral actions by individuals or organisations based within and outwith the island may further accelerate these environmental modifications, resulting in serious declines in

numbers or even losses of species. Birds, other animals and plants are
invaluable for reasons given below. Conservation areas are shown in
Figure 9.

Wildlife is part of the original beneficial environment of man, within
which he evolved and with which he was in tune. This contrasts with the

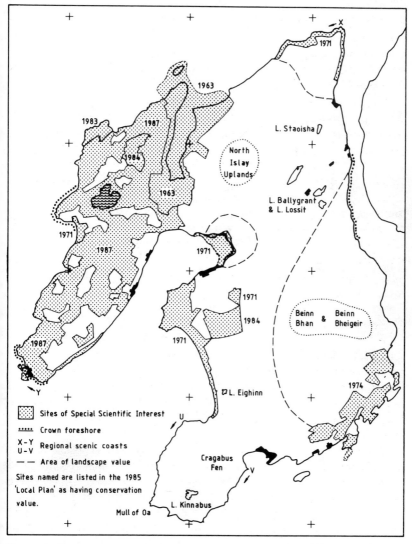

Figure 9: Conservation on Islay; showing areas and coasts designated for conservation
purposes by the Nature Conservancy Council or the local authority

Table 7: Changes in the status of some bird species on Islay

GAINS

Species	Year/Period
Natural colonisation:	
Fulmar	First pairs found 1924
Mute Swan	Arrived about 1900
Tufted Duck	First bred about 1950
Curlew	First bred in late 1800s
Little Tern	First reported in 1925
Collared Dove	Arrived in 1961
Sand Martin	First reported in 1913
Willow Warbler	Arrived in late 1800s
Jackdaw	Arrived in mid-1800s
Starling	Arrived in 1843
Lesser Redpoll	First bred in 1953
House Sparrow	Appears to have arrived between 1800 and 1850
Benefited from estate woodlands planted from 1820 onwards:	
Woodcock	Probably arrived between 1800 and 1850
Tawny Owl	Arrived in mid-1800s
Tree Pipit	Probably arrived in late 1800s
Mistle Thrush	Arrived in 1822
Wood Warbler	Probably arrived in late 1800s
Benefited from reduced persecution:	
Hen Harrier	Recolonised Islay in 1960s
Sparrowhawk	Increased in recent years
Golden Eagle	Improvement in numbers during 1980s
Peregrine	Increased mid-1960s to mid-1970s
Hooded Crow	Increased 1980 to 1987
Introductions:	
White-tailed Eagle	A few sightings of Rhum birds from 1978
Partridge	Periodic introductions of both species
Pheasant	First introduced about 1840
Woodpigeon	Introduced as estate woodlands matured
Others:	
Wigeon	Became numerous from mid-1800s
Arctic Tern	Expanded this century as Common Tern has decreased
Goldfinch	Increased after caging of species was prohibited

Species	LOSSES/DECLINES Year/Period
Losses of breeding species:	
Storm Petrel	Bred prior to 1871; Rabbits may have taken over nest holes
Gannet	Last bred in 1703
White-tailed Eagle	Last bred in mid-1800s
Hen Harrier	Was exterminated in late 1800s
Arctic Skua	Said to have bred in 1700s
Great Auk	Probably bred prior to 1800; now extinct
Puffin	Bred in some numbers prior to mid-1900s
Nightjar	Probably lost to Islay in 1970s
Ring Ouzel	Year of last breeding pair not recorded
Corn Bunting	Bred until 1940; abundant in 1892
Marked reduction in number of breeding pairs:	
Golden Eagle	Persecuted from early 1700s to about 1980
Kestrel	Declined since 1900
Corncrake	Abundant in 1849; only 23 calling in 1986
Moorhen	Reduced by drainage improvements since mid-1800s
Common Tern	Colony of 1,000 pairs in 1907; only 23 in 1986
Rock Dove	Abundant in 1800s; declined into 1900s, but now recovered
Barn Owl	Far fewer sightings since mid-1970s
Whitethroat	Marked reduction since 1950s
Hooded Crow	Almost exterminated in 1939
Reduction in winter visitors:	
Bewick's Swan	Common in 1800s; now rare
Bean Goose	Visitor prior to 1871
Greylag Goose	Over 1,000 in 1825; fewer than 100 in 1980s
Brent Goose	1,500 wintered in mid-1800s; now seen only on passage
Reduction in summer visitors:	
Sand Martin	120 nest holes in Laggan River cliffs in 1972; only 20 in 1986

alien and crowded cities that generate crime and moral degradation. City-dwellers have a need to 'get away from it all': wildlife programmes on television have a very large audience, and the therapeutic value of contact with pets and other animals, or of gardening, is well known.

In the case of Islay, it is clear that wildlife is an asset to the economy. The island has an attraction to many who have an interest in flowers, birds and other branches of natural history; also, the clear atmosphere and subtly changing light are valued by artists. With careful planning it would be possible to improve these attractions and increase the benefits to the island economy accruing from an appreciative section of the British and overseas public.

Wildlife is a resource. Plant-breeders obtain genetic material from wild species to improve the resistance of existing crops to pests and diseases and to create new crops. Numerous organic substances in plants, insects and other animals await investigation; many are likely to be useful to man.

Wildlife has educational value at levels from primary school to university and beyond. Islay is visited by students of the natural sciences who wish to carry out research into a wide variety of topics, including some associated with birds.

4

Species Accounts

The following accounts are headed and arranged according to the *List of Recent Holarctic Bird Species* (Voous 1977). They give brief information concerning the status, migration, distribution, feeding and roosting of all species regularly seen on Islay; and also statements of the origin and occurrence of all rarities seen on the island. Inevitably there are some species for which the available information is inadequate, imprecise or vague, and readers who birdwatch on Islay are likely to collect data that will help improve these accounts; it would be helpful if they reported their findings at the Natural History Trust in Port Charlotte.

Throughout this section of the book, the terms 'fishing loch' and 'peaty lochan' or 'peaty loch' are used in conformity with the general classification of Table 4; 'estate woodlands' is used to indicate the well-established mixed plantations started in the early 1800s by estate-owners and now forming Islay's richest habitats for woodland birds (pages 23–5; Figure 4; and Table 3).

Nearly all place names are taken from the 1987 edition of sheet 60 in the Landranger Series of Ordnance Survey maps on a scale of 1:50,000. These, and the exceptions, are listed in the index with National Grid references for easy location.

The accounts are based on information received up to 31st December 1987. Statements in the present tense, such as population estimates, are as at that date.

Red-throated Diver *Gavia stellata*

A summer visitor and regular breeder, occurring in small numbers; also a winter visitor and passage migrant. It is likely, but not proven, that many passage migrants come from Greenland and Iceland. In winter some Scottish birds remain in Scottish waters, but two recoveries of British-ringed birds on the

59

Red-throated Diver, summer plumage (John Davies)

French coast suggest that others migrate south. Small numbers are recorded flying south past Frenchman's Rocks in late August and September, a similar period to that of the well-known movements along the east coast of Scotland. The Islay birds return in March and displaying has been recorded on 22nd of that month. Fifty-four birds were noted on Loch Indaal on 14th February 1987, and 20 were in the Sound of Islay in March 1981.

This diver ranges from small shallow peaty lochans, where it breeds, to the larger fishing lochs or sheltered coasts, especially bays and sea-lochs, where it feeds. It is one of the very few species found on the soft-edged peaty lochans; the largest area of water for which evidence of breeding is recorded is 5 ha (12.4 acres). Most wintering birds are seen on Loch Indaal or in Port Ellen Bay. It flies high and direct to and from the sea on feeding trips and, in spite of its large size, has an ability to take off from very small areas of water. It normally fishes in the sea, but will take food from fresh water if it is readily available. These birds dive without a forward spring, slipping gently beneath the water's surface and pursuing prey to depths of 2–9 m (6–30 ft). They take a variety of fish species, which they seize rather than spear; also fish spawn, frogs, crustaceans, molluscs, water insects and annelid worms. Birds sleep on water in their small breeding territories, and on the sea, singly or in small flocks, at other seasons. The breeding success of this species can be seriously affected by frequent human disturbance.

Black-throated Diver   *Gavia arctica*

A passage migrant and occasional summer visitor. Pairs were seen on 12th July 1962 and in late April 1963 and it was recorded as breeding in two squares during the *Atlas* survey of 1968-72; a nest was recorded in 1982. Birds on spring passage are seen from mid-February to late May. Summer visitors are present from the second half of April to the first half of August, and are likely to winter in British waters.

On autumn passage this species is usually observed from early September to the end of November. Passage birds are seen either on Upper Loch Indaal, in bays on the outer coasts such as those at Claggain and Sanaigmore, in the Sound of Islay or at Frenchman's Rocks. The rare summer visitors have been seen on both fishing lochs and peaty lochs. They are most likely to breed beside deep lochs greater than 10 ha (25 acres) in area and which have islets and a clear view of the surrounding terrain not obscured by forestry plantations. These are very restrictive requirements and few lochs on Islay satisfy them. This species surface-dives down 3–6 m (10–20 ft) and takes mainly fish, but sometimes also crustaceans, molluscs and aquatic insects. It sleeps on the water of loch or sea.

Great Northern Diver   *Gavia immer*

A winter visitor and passage migrant; in summer, there are only two records of single birds from mid-June to mid-September. Both visitors and migrants come from Iceland or Greenland. The earliest dates are of movement south past Frenchman's Rocks on 16th September 1980 and of the arrival of eleven birds near Killinallan on 18th September 1976. The grouping of records suggests that the passage continues until the end of October. On 27th January 1974, from 14th to 21st April 1979 and on 28th December 1979, counts indicated an island total of over 30, probably 35 to 40 birds. Temporary small parties of up to 20 birds are recorded throughout May during spring migration, and over 200 passed northwards by Frenchman's Rocks on 4th May 1975. Nearly half of the 170 records are from around Upper Loch Indaal; others are from most readily accessible coastal sections, with notably high frequencies in the Claggain and Port Ellen Bays. Fourteen birds were between Bruichladdich and Port Charlotte on 14th March 1973 and on 14th February 1987. There is only one inland record, perhaps of a storm-driven bird, at Loch Skerrols on 27th March 1968.

This species searches for prey by dipping its bill and forehead under water. It then dives for up to one minute, using feet and sometimes wings for propulsion. It takes principally fish up to 28 cm (11 in) long, crabs, shrimps and prawns; also some shellfish, worms and aquatic insects. Outside the breeding season this diver roosts mainly on the sea, both singly and in small flocks. After nightfall on 29th February 1976, 19 were found off Port Charlotte.

White-billed Diver *Gavia adamsii*

A vagrant that breeds in arctic Russia, Siberia, Alaska and Canada. Some winter southwest down the Norwegian coast and a very few reach Scotland each year. They have been recorded from October to June, but most Hebridean records are of isolated birds, usually in breeding plumage, sighted in April, May or June. One was found oiled at Bowmore on 27th March, 1986, and another was said to have been at Kildalton on 7th April 1986.

Little Grebe *Tachybaptus ruficollis*

Resident in small numbers; there has been little change in status since Gray (1871). From August onwards, some disperse to larger lochs or to sheltered coasts, especially from waters likely to freeze. Six records off the southeast coast, five on the sea-lochs and five on Loch Gorm are all dated August to January; February records are under-documented. Evidence of the immigration of Continental birds has been noted in eastern Scotland in some years. The largest count on Islay, seven on Loch Ballygrant on 25th October 1978, may have included immigrants or have been an assembly of locally bred families.

The Little Grebe requires shallow fresh water with a good supply of submerged vegetation and cover for nesting. It is most regularly seen on the fishing lochs sheltered by woods and on a few open but small productive lochs near the west coast. Loch Ballygrant has sheltered reedy embayments to which these small birds retreat in stormy weather; Loch Gorm is six times larger with very little shelter, and only single birds have been seen there, principally in October. This grebe dives to a depth of only 1 m (3 ft) or so, often with a distinct jump and splash. It also seeks food by swimming with head and neck immersed; takes items from the water's surface; and snatches insects from the air, reaching them from a floating position. Its food consists of small fish, insects and their larvae, small molluscs, crustaceans, amphibian spawn and some vegetable matter. It roosts on or near the nest when breeding, but at other times in small groups on water, within reeds or under overhanging bushes.

Great Crested Grebe *Podiceps cristatus*

An occasional winter and rare summer visitor that bred in 1969. It is resident nearby in Donegal, Antrim and Ayrshire, dispersing in late July and August.

These birds probably move short distances with a bias southwards, but occasionally they explore the Hebrides, usually leaving in March or April. In autumn or winter there have been four records from Upper Loch Indaal and one from Loch an t-Sailein; one bird stayed on Indaal from 27th January to 3rd April 1974. In the breeding season these grebes occur on open inland waters with emergent vegetation, on lochs of at least 1 ha ($2\frac{1}{2}$ acres), or in sheltered bays of much larger areas of fresh water. A pair bred on the 8-ha (20-acre) Ardnave Loch in 1969 and in June young were seen. Two were on the sea at Kilchoman on 15th November 1985.

This species searches for, and chooses prey from, a smooth surface-dive, foot-propelled to depths of 2–6 m (6–20 ft). It also dips its head and neck to search and up-ends to feed, occasionally pecking from the water's surface and snatching insects from the air. It takes chiefly fish; also aquatic insects, spiders, frogs and tadpoles. It loafs and roosts singly or in family groups in the shelter of a lee shore or among aquatic vegetation. Great Crested Grebes form loose parties when not breeding.

Red-necked Grebe *Podiceps grisegena*

A rare winter visitor, with singles recorded in March 1975, December 1979, January 1981 and February 1981. Another in Kilnaughton Bay on 3rd July 1976 may have summered in the Hebrides. Migrants from the Continent, where the nearest breeding sites are in Denmark, usually arrive in winter plumage and are in Scotland from October to March, although a very few have arrived earlier, from the end of July. The main Scottish wintering area is in the Firth of Forth and numbers are greatest in years when Continental weather is most severe. A few penetrate to the west of Scotland, but in some years nearly all remain on the Forth.

This species winters on salt water; four records are from around Upper Loch Indaal and one from Loch an t-Sailein. It locates food by swimming with its head submerged and dives to a few metres, taking insects and their larvae; also some fish, especially in winter. Red-necked Grebes roost on water by night and day.

Slavonian Grebe *Podiceps auritus*

A winter visitor in small numbers, recorded in 1892, 1939, 1962 and each year from 1970 onwards, with no overall change in numbers. Some birds may be passage visitors. Islay's birds are probably from Iceland; they arrive in mid-September and depart in late March or early April. Over 80 per cent of the records refer to localities around Upper Loch Indaal. These grebes are often seen with a raft of Scaup in autumn, or occasionally taking shelter in Bowmore Harbour; often they are revealed by a careful search from the Blackrock headland or the vantage point outside the Bowmore Power Station. Numbers

Slavonian Grebe, winter plumage (John Davies)

have varied from a single bird up to twelve seen on 21st March 1981, 13 on 24th September 1986 and 49 on 18th February 1987. Other sightings of single birds have been in outer coast bays at Sanaigmore, Kilchoman, Port Ellen, Claggain and near Kildalton; only four have been inland, at Lochs Gorm, Skerrols, and Tallant by Bowmore.

The Slavonian Grebe takes small fish and aquatic insects and their larvae; mainly by dives, which usually start stealthily, gliding down without a splash, and also by picking prey off the water's surface or snatching insects from the air. It roosts on water by day or night, depending on feeding opportunities. Marine grebes are at risk from oiling, although none was found to be affected by the October 1969 spillage in Loch Indaal.

Black-necked Grebe   *Podiceps nigricollis*

A very rare winter visitor to the Hebrides that breeds in small numbers in the Central Scottish Lowlands. It is in its winter quarters from November to March, and one in winter plumage, found on Loch Indaal on 18th March 1976, provides the only Islay record. It feeds chiefly on insects and their larvae, but also on small molluscs, crustaceans, shellfish and fish. It roosts on water by night and day.

Fulmar *Fulmarus glacialis*

A visitor to Islay, breeding in large numbers; also periodically at the nesting ledges outside the breeding season. However, there are very few records of birds in the vicinity of cliffs from 27th November to 24th January. Fulmars have gradually expanded their British range over the last 110 years; they prospected Sanaig Cliffs in 1918, this leading to the first few pairs breeding on Islay in 1924.

There are three records from Frenchman's Rocks of single dark-phase birds, a form that breeds in the high Arctic. Up to 500 light-phase birds per hour have been counted passing south by these rocks in late August, September, and October, whereas fewer than 50 per hour pass at other times. These movements are thought to be dispersive rather than migratory. Ringing has shown that juveniles disperse throughout the whole of the North Atlantic, but Scottish adults appear to feed in the eastern part of this ocean. When they are breeding, at over six to twelve years old, they probably have a range extending up to only 320 km (200 miles) from their cliffs.

The Fulmar breeds on all the cliffed coasts of Islay except those in the east remote from the ocean. Ledges are occupied up to 1.2 km ($\frac{3}{4}$ mile) inland, east of Kilchoman House. Most were counted in 1986, suggesting a population of about 1,700 birds; on 22nd June 1987, about 525 nest sites were counted around the Oa from a boat. The species' natural food is zooplankton such as crustaceans and cephalopods; it also takes fish, fish offal and marine carrion, attending trawlers at sea and taking other opportunities offered by man. It has been suggested that its sense of smell aids detection of offal and carrion. Food is normally obtained by surface seizing while floating or swimming, and occasionally by pursuit-plunging to depths of over 4 m (13 ft). Feeding is curtailed in very rough seas. On-duty birds roost at or near the nest, while off-duty birds sometimes sleep in rafts. Outside the breeding season all roost at sea.

Cory's Shearwater *Calonectris diomedea*

A vagrant in Scottish waters, mainly in August and September. It breeds on Mediterranean and East Atlantic islands off North Africa and Spain, and migrates around tropical and warm-temperate Atlantic seas. Single birds were recorded on 19th August 1973 off Frenchman's Rocks and on 30th August 1981 off Coul Point; two flew north past the latter locality on 30th May 1981.

Great Shearwater *Puffinus gravis*

A vagrant in Scottish waters, mainly in August and September. It breeds on South Atlantic islands, and has a probable loop migration route around a major part of the Atlantic Ocean. One was recorded off Laggan Strand in August 1963, but these birds are normally well offshore over the ocean.

Sooty Shearwater *Puffinus griseus*

A passage migrant which is regular and is usually among Manx Shearwaters. It breeds on sub-antarctic islands; non-breeders virtually circumnavigate the Atlantic Ocean clockwise, almost all passing Islay southwards. The earliest sightings have been in the second half of July, but the main passage is from mid-August to the end of September, with a peak in the first half of September; the last few seen are in mid-October. These seabirds are occasionally sighted in other months; one was north of Colonsay on 29th April 1983. Nearly all records are from Frenchman's Rocks, where a maximum of 115 was counted passing on 4th September 1977. They can also be seen off Coul Point and crossing the path of the ferry between Islay and Gigha. They obtain their food from the surface of the sea or by making short shallow dives, using their wings for propulsion underwater, and take squid, crustaceans and fish.

Manx Shearwater *Puffinus puffinus*

A passage migrant commonly seen off Islay. Adults visit their colonies from February to September; a very large one is on Rhum, 130 km (81 miles) to the north of Islay, and another is on Rathlin Island, just 30 km (19 miles) to the south. Several small colonies have been discovered in recent years and, although there is no evidence, it is not impossible that a few pairs have nesting burrows on Islay. Movement off Islay's shores begins in April and continues to the end of September, reaching 300–600 per hour under favourable conditions during June, July or August; one seen on 4th December 1982 and 20 off Frenchman's Rocks on 3rd Febuary 1984 were exceptional.

The great majority fly south down the west coast, although many are also seen to the east of Islay. A raft of about 1,000 was in the Sound of Islay on 29th August 1975. Most are likely to come from Rhum and in autumn many travel to the east coast of Brazil, where they stay until the end of the year. They appear to return via Newfoundland waters, approaching Scotland from the west, which probably explains the lack of a northward movement off Islay early in the year. In stormy conditions a few have been seen in Lower Loch Indaal and in western bays such as Saligo Bay, but most records come from seawatching at Rubha na Faing, where parties pass west of Frenchman's Rocks. Two ringed immature birds have been found on Islay beaches: one was ringed on Copeland Island, near Belfast,

Manx Shearwater (Brian Southern)

on 14th July 1975 and found at Machir on 21st May 1976; the second was ringed on Bardsey Island, North Wales, on 11th July 1980 and found freshly dead at Kilnaughton on 4th June 1981.

Manx Shearwaters generally feed on the open ocean, but some feed inshore; 20 were seen feeding in Saligo Bay on 11th May 1977. Their principal prey is small fish, such as pilchards, herrings and sprats, taken by pursuit-plunging, pursuit-diving and surface-seizing, and sometimes from hovering flight with foot-paddling on the surface. Underwater, both wings and feet are used for propulsion. They presumably roost on water, except when on duty in burrows during the breeding season.

Little Shearwater *Puffinus assimilis*

A vagrant in Scottish waters, breeding on islands in three oceans including the East Atlantic, where the Azores are the nearest haunt; it disperses rather than migrates long distances. Irish records are mainly in August and September. One off Frenchman's Rocks on 30th June 1974 with 100 Manx Shearwaters provided the first record of this species for Scotland.

Storm Petrel *Hydrobates pelagicus*

A passage migrant; Gray (1871) stated that it bred on Islay. A small colony was found on Colonsay in about 1975 and one may even exist on Islay. The Storm

Petrel winters at sea off the west and south coasts of Africa, and breeds in western Europe between April and November. Most of Islay's records are dated mid-August to mid-October.

These tiny birds are seldom close to land, but are sometimes found there in stormy conditions, when they may be off Frenchman's Rocks or Coul Point; 26 were seen off the former on 28th August 1977 and seven off the latter on 24th August 1981. Many have sheltered in Loch Indaal and one was in Port Charlotte Harbour on 26th May 1972 during a force 9 gale; also, four were at Loch Gruinart on 12th September 1980, and one was at Bowmore on 17th October 1983. They feed from the surface of the sea, pattering, hovering and pecking without alighting, and taking crustaceans, small fish and squid brought up to the surface by turbulence, as well as floating jellyfish and offal fragments.

Leach's Petrel   *Oceanodroma leucorhoa*

A passage migrant; there have been only eight records since the 'wrecks' of 1891 and 1952. Most birds winter between West Africa and Brazil; they breed on remote islands, the nearest being St Kilda. The few records are dated September to January. This species is normally seen in September or October, as a single individual travelling south off Frenchman's Rocks in stormy conditions. Some may be driven into Loch Indaal or even inland during severe gales; they are then found dead or in a weak condition. Leach's Petrel feeds mainly from the surface, hovering, skimming and snatching, and takes planktonic crustaceans, squid, small fish, or fish spawn and offal.

Gannet   *Sula bassana*

The Gannet is said to have bred on Islay in 1703; the nearest colonies now are on Ailsa Craig, 90 km (56 miles) to the southeast, and on St Kilda, 250 km (155 miles) to the northwest. Birds seen off Islay either are on feeding trips or are passage migrants.

From late July to mid-October, movement off the west coast is predominantly southwards, reaching a peak of around 250 per hour in August or September. Many young birds migrate to northwest African waters or into the Mediterranean, but with increasing age the distance south at which Scottish-ringed birds are recovered decreases. Breeding birds confine their feeding trips to within a range of 480 km (300 miles) from the colony. Usually there is a minority of birds travelling north past Islay; these and a small percentage of those travelling south may be on feeding trips, dispersing in July and August before migration proper, backtracking on autumn migration, or returning to colonies in the spring.

From mid-November to late February, when well over half of Scottish Gannets are in winter quarters to the south, they are scarce off Islay. At other times they are readily seen from seawatching stations, especially from Rubha na

Faing, Coul Point or the Mull of Oa. In spring and summer tens and twenties may be seen feeding in Loch Indaal; they are often seen also in Port Ellen Bay or passing through Nave Island Sound. They are much less frequent off the eastern and northern coasts. Dead, but not oiled, Gannets are sometimes found on the beaches.

Gannets generally feed within the continental shelf, sometimes well inshore and where strong currents bring fish near the surface, as around Frenchman's Rocks. Groups rapidly converge on shoals, indicated by the first individual to dive. Plunge-dives start from just above the surface or from heights of up to a maximum of 27 m (89 ft), but usually from 9 to 15 m (30–50 ft). They penetrate up to 3.5 m (11 ft), but if powered by legs and wings a maximum of 15 m (50 ft) is attainable. The species also feeds by diving from the surface and pursuing fish, swimming among fry and scooping them up, or by robbing other birds, especially gulls, at a shoal. Fishing by any method is curtailed by a force 8 gale. A Gannet takes fish 25–45 cm (10–18 in) long and also offal from fishing boats. Herring and mackerel are its preferred foods. The birds roost at their breeding site or in the nearby 'club'. Outside the breeding season, or when temporarily absent from a colony, they roost on the sea.

Cormorant   *Phalacrocorax carbo*

A resident, occurring in small numbers. Most Scottish Cormorants disperse southwards from mid-September onwards, but very few leave British waters. Some are known to cross from west to east; unfortunately, no Islay birds have been ringed. A nestling ringed in Orkney in June 1969 was shot on Eilean a' Chuirn off the southeast coast in November 1969. A few sometimes fly inland to fish at freshwater lochs.

The Cormorant occurs on shallow coastal waters and on inland fishing lochs. It breeds on rocky islets and shelved cliffs, and spends much time in comfort behaviour on low islets and boulders, both around the coast and within inland lochs (for example, on Ceann a' Chlachain southwest of Bowmore and Carraig Dubh west of Bridgend); many occur among the islands of the southeast archipelago, and on rocks off the tip of peninsulas such as those extending into Loch Gorm. Nearly half of the records relate to Loch Indaal, particularly around the Laggan Peninsula and the directly opposed coast. Cormorants are probably under-recorded along the Sound of Islay.

Birds of this species prefer relatively sheltered shallow water, where their main prey is bottom-living fish, especially the small flat-fish known as dabs (*Limanda limanda*). They are solitary daytime feeders, diving from the surface with or without an initial leap, to depths of up to 9 m (30 ft), average 2 m ($6\frac{1}{2}$ ft), for periods of up to one minute. They also take prawns and shrimps from salt water and trout and salmon from fresh water. It has been demonstrated that predation by Cormorants is unlikely to have any significant effect on fish stocks inland, or on commercial interests in coastal waters.

Nocturnal roosts assemble at sites similar to those occupied by breeding colonies. A few birds were oiled after the October 1969 incident at Bruichladdich.

Shag *Phalacrocorax aristotelis*

Perhaps half of the resident Shags disperse in the winter, and up to 30 per hour fly past Frenchman's Rocks in August and September, but most Scottish adults remain within 100 km (60 miles) of their colonies. First-year birds disperse further, but nearly all remain in British waters. Those returning to Islay do so in March. A bird ringed as a nestling on 9th July 1981 at Loch Sween was found on 7th January 1982 in a lobster pot off Rubha Bhachlaig in the Sound of Islay, only 50 km (31 miles) from its natal area.

The Shag can be seen off most of Islay's shores, but rarely in Bridgend Bay. Large fishing flocks are seen in most years between mid-July and November, and exceptionally in winter: in Nave Island Sound they peaked at 350 birds on 12th September 1973 and in August 1975; in Port Ellen Bay there were over 180 in December 1979; 200 were off the southeast archipelago on 3rd November 1979; and 330 were in Claggain Bay in February 1983. Some 127 nest sites were counted around the Oa on 22nd June 1987, and there are probably over 250 pairs nesting on Islay. In accord with its generally marine habitat elsewhere in Britain, the Shag does not visit inland lochs as the Cormorant does, and only 15 per cent of the records relate to Loch Indaal. It breeds chiefly in caves and on ledges in gullies; colonies are regular on the Oa, on western and northern coasts and on the cliffs around Laggan Farm, while on other cliffed coasts nesting is more solitary. It spends much time resting, drying, oiling and preening on rocky waterside vantage points, typically at the extremity of a promontory.

This species usually takes free-swimming fish by surface-diving to about 4 m (13 ft), with or without an initial leap, often staying under for less than one minute but sometimes for up to three minutes. Birds frequently fish alone but also gather at fish shoals. Roosting, like nesting, is mainly communal, with a few solitary birds, on cliffs or stacks.

White Pelican *Pelecanus onocrotalus*

Four possible escapes were seen from 1st to 10th May 1973, first near Ardmore, then at Ardilistry, Port Ellen, Blackrock and finally at Loch Clach a' Bhuaile by Gorm. Wild birds breed in southeast Europe and migrate to Africa; they are beginning their return migration in May. There was a report in a Yorkshire newspaper early in May 1973 that some pelicans were missing from Flamingo Park Zoo.

Bittern *Botaurus stellaris*

A rare visitor that bred in 'a good many parts' of Scotland up to about the end of the 18th century. Currently, visitors to Scotland are usually found dead or weak and are thought to have dispersed from their breeding haunts, which are thinly scattered in England and well distributed on the Continent. One was shot on Islay on 2nd February 1864.

American Bittern *Botaurus lentiginosus*

A vagrant to Scotland; most records are dated October or November. One was shot on Islay's shore at the end of October 1875. It is thought that autumn migrants in the Gulf of St Lawrence, caught up in westerly storm tracks are those most likely to end up in Britain.

Little Egret *Egretta garzetta*

A vagrant to Scotland, occurring mostly in spring. One was at Loch Gorm and Loch Gruinart from 25th May to 4th July 1970; during this period, Little Egrets are normally breeding in southern Europe.

Great White Egret *Egretta alba*

A vagrant or escape that breeds locally in the Netherlands, Hungary and many other places worldwide. European birds winter in Mediterranean countries. Three were found in Scotland during the 1970s, in the months of March, April and June. One was on Gruinart Flats on 14th June 1986.

Grey Heron *Ardea cinerea*

A resident and partial migrant; breeding was recorded in 1772, 1849 and at various times in the present century. Three herons flew at about 150 m (500 ft) over Port Ellen Bay towards Ireland on 19th August 1973. There is a general dispersal from the end of August to October, and at the same time an influx of birds from further northeast; this explains the maintenance of numbers until November. In late December, January and the first half of February records are few and chiefly of single birds, but, by March, numbers are often back to normal. Twenty were already at Loch Allan on 18th February 1987. Few Scottish birds disperse more than 100 km (60 miles) from their natal area, although one found

71

dead by Loch Indaal on 23rd May 1981 had been ringed near Dunning, southwest of Perth, on 25th May 1979.

The Grey Heron is found feeding on sheltered marine shores, at the edge of inland fishing lochs, by many rivers, streams and ditches, and also in poorly drained fields with rushes. It occasionally uses a peaty lochan as a comfort station. Islay normally has four heronries, perhaps five in some decades. They are sited in scrub surrounded by bog or in dense coniferous woods with much undergrowth and next to sea, loch or bog. The home ranges fulfilling feeding and breeding requirements are centred on: the southeast coastal strip; Ballygrant and Port Askaig; the Laggan Strath, Bowmore and Bridgend; and Loch Gorm, Foreland House and Gruinart (Figure 10 opposite). Observations of herons in the southern Rhinns are rare and there is no record of a heronry in that district. There are Islay counts of eight nests in 1928, six in 1954 and 13 in 1972; since then, numbers appear to have been within the same range.

Feeding is usually solitary, but up to about ten birds may gather in loose groups. The heron stands still or stalks slowly with neck tensed for grabbing or spearing; it often forages in early morning or late evening, and has been seen stalking up a burn by moonlight. It is an opportunistic feeder, taking a wide variety of prey: fish, amphibians, shrimps, crabs, small mammals, insects, earthworms and young birds. Roosting can be communal or solitary, nocturnal or diurnal, at the colony or near feeding grounds, often in trees or among reeds. Heronries are abandoned if damaged by gales or disturbed by frequent human visits. Those on Islay are particularly difficult to approach, and it is recommended that they be viewed from a distance.

White Stork   *Ciconia ciconia*

A vagrant to Scotland, recorded mostly from April to mid-June after the normal northward migration through western Europe is completed. Singles were at Gruinart in May 1975, on the roof of Aoradh Farm, Gruinart, in early June 1976, and again at Craigens, Gruinart, on 25th April 1978. This last bird accompanied gulls following a plough at Farkin Cottage, Port Ellen, on 27th and 28th April, but was back at Craigens in the evening of 28th; on 30th it was seen down the Rhinns at Octofad and Easter Ellister, was back at Craigens on 3rd May and again at Ellister on 8th. In 1979 a bird was in the Daill area in late May; then, in 1981, reports of a single bird came from the Sanaig area on 16th May, Kindrochid on 17th and West Carrabus on 18th. The only British breeding record is of a pair that nested on St Giles' Cathedral, Edinburgh, in 1416. The nearest pairs currently nesting are in Denmark and the Netherlands.

Glossy Ibis   *Plegadis falcinellus*

A vagrant to Scotland, usually arriving in the autumn. An immature female was

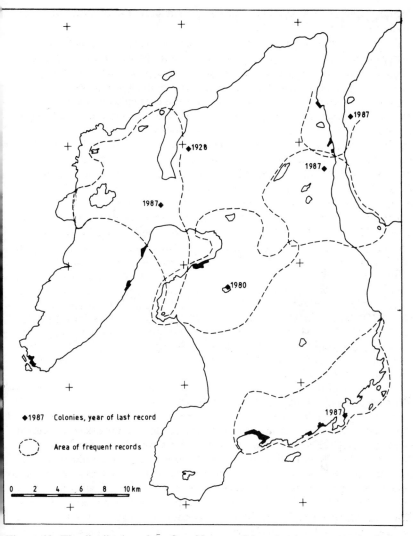

Figure 10: The distribution of the Grey Heron on Islay, showing ranges and colonies

shot near Kildalton on 30th October 1902; two were in an old reedbed on Gruinart Flats on 6th September 1920 and three were there on 13th; and two were again on the island in 1926. The species breeds in southern Europe, but its distribution has receded eastwards so that the nearest regular haunts are in Yugoslavia; it now rarely reaches Scotland and, when it does, it is as single individuals.

73

Spoonbill *Platalea leucorodia*

A vagrant to Scotland that arrives in May to July, or in September to October. One was caught at Bowmore in 1936, probably in May; another flew inland over Portnahaven on 17th September 1978 and was seen to be moulting. This species bred in Britain until the 17th century; now the nearest colonies are in the Netherlands. Scottish recoveries have been of individuals from that country and Yugoslavia. The Spoonbill is endangered in most of its European haunts.

Mute Swan *Cygnus olor*

A resident in small numbers that arrived on Islay around the turn of the century. There is no direct evidence of movement to or from Islay, but, while British adults are generally sedentary, some immatures disperse. One South Uist bird reached Kintyre in its first summer and County Derry in the following year. However, 98 per cent of all British-ringed Mutes move less than 80 km (50 miles). Movements between Islay, Mull, the mainland and Ireland are quite likely.

The Mute Swan is found by the shores of Upper Loch Indaal, in two or three sheltered bays along the southeast coast, and on some fishing lochs, but less often on Loch Gorm. There are up to about ten pairs in total, but in most years cygnets are seen only with two or three pairs. There is a tendency for these swans to concentrate on Loch Indaal and Loch Ballygrant in winter, when the island total is usually around 25 individuals.

This large bird needs extensive shallow water with much submerged, floating or emergent vegetation. It takes aquatic food by dipping head and neck to 45 cm ($1\frac{1}{2}$ ft) or by up-ending to reach down 100 cm (3 ft). It can also graze and dabble at the water's edge and occasionally on land. Mute Swans supplement this vegetarian diet with a few small animals. A family often sleeps on the water together, small cygnets climbing on to the back of the parents; alternatively, they may all return to the nest if it is close by. Mute Swans are particularly liable to oiling, colliding with power lines, or poisoning caused by ingesting lead shot or fishing weights. In October 1969, following the oil spillage at Bruichladdich, six were found on Islay with oil-stained patches of plumage.

Bewick's Swan *Cygnus columbianus bewickii*

A scarce passage visitor, with one or two in only half of the recent years of recording; exceptionally, there were 26 in October 1975, including a flock of 16. In the 19th and early 20th centuries this was a common visitor to the Hebrides, but it has wintered mainly in England since the 1930s.

This swan breeds in the sub-arctic fringe of the USSR and in recent years a few have been found in Iceland in summer. They arrive on Islay in mid-October, but in some years not until November. Most stay less than four weeks and sometimes only a day or two, but two were still present on 12th December 1975 and three in January 1980. One at Loch Gorm on 25th February 1977 may have been beginning its return migration; otherwise these swans are not seen passing north and probably follow a more direct route from wintering grounds in Ireland. They are usually seen with Whooper Swans in the Gorm, Gruinart or Bridgend districts feeding on stubbles, loafing in shallows, or roosting on the loch of the area. Bewick's Swans have also been seen passing Frenchman's Rocks on route for Ireland or calling at Claddach Reservoir, and more rarely at floodwater on pastures elsewhere. They up-end or dip their head and neck in water less than 1 m (3 ft) deep to obtain aquatic plants, and also graze or dig for roots and runners, especially of clover, on flooded pastures. They roost with Whooper Swans.

Whooper Swan *Cygnus cygnus*

A passage migrant and also a winter visitor in small numbers, breeding in Iceland and northern Europe. On 9th December 1967, a flock at 8200 m (27,000 ft) over Tiree was flying south when spotted on radar descending to Ireland; a specially diverted plane identified them. They were taking advantage of a northerly 180 km/h (110 mph) airstream, and meteorological calculations backtracked the birds' path to Iceland. These birds passed high to the west of Islay; many others are recorded at a low level travelling down the coast, either calling in at or leaving the Ardnave, Gorm or Cladville areas, leaving Portnahaven or passing Frenchman's Rocks. Similar southward movement has been noted down Lochs Gruinart and Indaal, some flocks continuing towards Ireland or Kintyre through the gap from Kintra to Port Ellen.

The first birds arrive in late September or early October. There is a passage with stop-over groups in October and a maximum number of short-term visitors is normally reached in November; this has fluctuated from around 20 to over 100 (1878: 70; 1905: 98; 1968: 67; 1972: 21; 1973: 61; 1974: 54; 1975: 73; 1976: 26; 1977: 98; 1978: 106; 1979: 103; 1981: 116; 1982: 54; 1983: 48; 1985: 86 and 1986: 184). By early December most have gone south, leaving from two to twelve birds overwintering. A few are seen on their northward passage from mid-March to late April, the maximum being 25 going north at Ardnave on 1st April 1979 and 24 flying north past Bruichladdich on 20th March 1982. One or two that are probably unfit to breed or migrate sometimes stay through the summer.

The Whooper spends most time in the Bridgend or Loch Gorm areas, but may call at Ardnave Loch and is occasionally seen in very small numbers on other lochs and ponds. Flocks commute for periods of a few weeks between a selected field and either Loch Gorm or Loch Indaal, or feed in vegetated sections of one of these lochs and roost in a sheltered part. This swan obtains aquatic vegetation, including eelgrass (*Zostera*) from near the Sorn River channel, by dipping or up-ending; it also feeds on stubbles, grass, or occasionally root crops.

Whooper Swan (John Davies)

Any rusty stains on head and neck are acquired by feeding in iron-rich Icelandic waters and are lost as the affected feathers are moulted in winter. The stain on some birds may be renewed in Islay's peaty water.

Roosting occurs on the waters of Bridgend Bay, Loch Gorm or nearby lochans, or on Sunderland Pond, the birds arriving at late dusk and leaving just before sunrise. On Islay, this species is occasionally accompanied by a few Bewick's Swans.

Bean Goose   *Anser fabalis*

A rare vagrant that was a winter visitor in small flocks prior to 1871 (Gray) and was the only goose known to a gamekeeper in 1849. By 1939 its visits were irregular, and there have been only a few records since. A decline has also occurred in mainland Britain.

Bean Geese breed in northern Scandinavia and Russia. Fifteen were on Islay on 31st March 1962 and the last five left on 7th April, during the spring migration. Thirteen Scandinavian birds (*A.f.fabalis*) stayed for about four days from 14th November 1981, during the autumn migration. On 18th October 1985, two were at Loch Skerrols with Greenland White-fronted Geese. Ardimersay, Kindrochid, Bushmill and West Carrabus are recorded localities, indicating that these birds foraged on pastures. They roost on large areas of open water, in flocks and at night.

Pink-footed Goose   *Anser brachyrhynchus*

A winter visitor; individuals are regularly present in goose flocks and in some years flocks of passage migrants stop over briefly. It breeds in Iceland and east Greenland and passes over Islay on migration to winter on mainland Britain. Sometimes a skein touches down briefly or stays for up to a few days. The main passage is between mid-September and early October, but there is only one record of birds on spring passage: 26 flew over Bridgend on 31 March 1977. These geese move around northern Britain mainly in response to weather conditions and food supply; 16 spent 9th February 1978 near Island House on Islay.

Individuals have been seen on most of the feeding grounds (Figure 8) within the wintering flocks of Barnacle and White-fronted Geese; they total one to four each year. The flocks are usually heard flying over, or seen feeding on the Bridgend or Gruinart Flats. Flocks of 30, 70 and 120 passed over the island on 14th to 16th September 1986. Maximum numbers feeding are related to date, diminishing as the autumn progresses: 300 on 19th September 1977, 99 on 23rd September 1985, 75 on 6th October 1977, 27 on 26th October 1980 and six on 26th November 1977. Small groups have also been noticed near Island House and in the Loch Gorm area. The flock of 23rd September 1985 fed on grassland adjacent to the Gruinart saltings. In addition to several kinds of grass, these geese take a variety of other plants and on the mainland half of their feeding is on stubble and potatoes. They have not been noted on arable land on Islay. The vagrants roost with their companion species and most migrants staying overnight probably roost at the head of one of the sea-lochs.

European White-fronted Goose   *Anser albifrons albifrons*

A rare vagrant that breeds east of the White Sea and across the Siberian tundra to the Bering Straits. The most westerly birds migrate to England, Wales and the nearby Continent. One was on Islay in January 1955, and 42 were present from 23rd March to 7th April 1962, first at Bridgend and then at Cornabus. One at Octovullin from 11th to 15th March 1986 was paired with a Lesser White-fronted Goose; the breeding ranges of these two geese overlap near the White Sea but there are differences in habitat, the Lesser preferring wooded tundra to open tundra.

Greenland White-fronted Goose *Anser albifrons flavirostris*

The Greenland White-fronted Goose is a winter visitor and passage migrant. It breeds in west Greenland and migrates to Islay via Iceland or southernmost Greenland. The first birds sometimes arrive in the second half of September, but most of these continue on to Ireland or Kintyre. Some Islay winterers may arrive early in October, but the main influx occurs over a period of a few days between 10th and 25th October. In 20 years from the mid-1960s, there have been

Greenland White-Fronted Goose (John Davies)

3,000–6,000 White-fronted Geese visiting Islay. Counts fluctuate month to month, partly owing to movements across the North Channel which are occasionally witnessed and have been confirmed by ringing. Most flocks leave Islay between 20th April and 5th May; the last skeins are a few days later. A small full-winged flock is present in the collection at Easter Ellister.

After arrival, the geese quickly become widely scattered in small groups of up to a few hundreds, occasionally up to 1,000; these occupy traditional feeding areas within Islay. They feed on all qualities of grassland, but with a tendency to occupy damper areas than those used by Barnacle Geese; they are also found on stubbles and fallows with rain flashes. When feeding, each goose walks slowly forward severing grasses and sedges with the edge of its bill by jerking its head sharply backwards. It also pecks rapidly for grain and probes for underground storage organs. These geese sometimes feed by moonlight, and when in the roosting area take the beak-sedge (*Rhynchospora*) and cottongrass (*Eriophorum*).

Roosts are found in boggy areas with peaty lochans, or by a river. Over 20 such roosts have been identified on Islay. The largest are on the peat bogs near Duich and at Feur Lochain; over 1,500 birds have been counted flying into both sites, coming from several different directions. Counts at all the roosts vary considerably through the winter depending on the availability of good feeding within range.

Late in the day many geese feed close to their roost and gradually walk in among the rushes, tall grasses or reeds as darkness approaches. This can be seen northwest of Loch Gorm, by Loch Tallant (Laggan) and between Leorin and Machrie. Among the damp-loving plants of these roosts, the Whitefront's dark brown and black-barred plumage provides exceptionally good camouflage.

See pages 38–41 for further information.

Lesser White-fronted Goose   *Anser erythropus*

A rare vagrant to the British Isles that breeds across sub-arctic Eurasia in a narrow belt where forest passes into tundra. The nearest birds breed in Lapland and winter in the Balkans and neighbouring parts of southeast Europe. One was at Bridgend on 15th March 1980 with two Dark-bellied Brent Geese from northwest Siberia; a second was by Octovullin from 11th to 15th March 1986, paired with a European White-fronted Goose.

Greylag Goose   *Anser anser*

A winter visitor that last nested on Islay in 1825, when there were well over 1,000 wintering. Around 1960 numbers had reduced to 500 or 600 and in the 1980s to fewer than 100; 65 were at Eallabus on 6th November 1985. These geese may be the remnants of a population that once covered Scotland, Ireland and northern

England. Most Greylags wintering in Scotland, however, including several hundreds in Kintyre, now come from Iceland; 37 which may have been on their way to Iceland flew into Islay from the Kintyre direction on 15th April 1978. The first Greylags of the autumn arrive about the end of September and most are present by mid-October; others may not arrive until mid-November. Departure is poorly documented, but the majority appear to leave between mid-March and the end of April.

The Greylag Geese commute between roost and feeding grounds within 6 km ($3\frac{3}{4}$ miles) of Bridgend; a few sometimes feed in the Gruinart or Gorm districts. More rarely small numbers have been noted in the Ballygrant and Port Ellen areas. Three have accompanied the Rhinns Canada Goose flock, but these appear to be feral and originate from the Easter Ellister collection.

This species usually feeds on farmland, especially pastures, eating mainly grasses, but it may resort to a variety of crops, including root crops. Its thick strong bill enables it to cut pieces from potatoes or turnips. The geese roost in tidal creeks and pools at the heads of the two major sea-lochs. Those by Loch Indaal sometimes frequent an area near Bluehouses.

Lesser Snow Goose   *Anser caerulescens caerulescens*

The Lesser Snow Goose is a vagrant to Islay; individuals have been found in flocks of wintering Barnacle and White-fronted Geese, but they are rare and irregular. A white- and a blue-phase bird were together on Eilean Mhic Coinnich, off Portnahaven, in the first half of August 1975. They flew into Easter Ellister on 10th, well before the Greenland geese arrived. They were probably escapes, like many found on the Scottish mainland. Since at least 1978, a feral flock of both phases has bred on Mull and recently wintered on Coll, rendering status determination on Islay even more difficult. This flock now contains over 50 birds.

The wild birds breed across arctic Canada, but some summer and occasionally breed in west and northwest Greenland; normally they migrate south into the United States. Possibly a few birds in Greenland make contact with Greenland White-fronted Geese and migrate with them to Scotland. Birds ringed in Canada have reached the Netherlands in 1981 and Shetland in 1986. In five winters from 1974 to 1978, a blue-phase goose was closely attached to a flock of Greenland White-fronted Geese feeding mainly in the Island House and Avenvogie areas. There are records in ten winters from 1927 to 1986 of one to four geese of both phases; at least some were with Barnacles in the Bruinart and Bridgend areas.

Both the Greenland geese and the Lesser Snow Geese often feed on grassland, and it is in this habitat that the Snow Geese are found on Islay.

Canada Goose   *Branta canadensis*

Rare vagrant; small and large individuals of various races come to Islay and there is a small group of resident feral large birds. The vagrants probably originate in North America and arrive with wintering geese from Greenland, but some could be escapes. Few records have been kept of the resident flock, but it appears to undertake only short flights within the southern Rhinns. In most years, one to four vagrants are found in wintering flocks of either Barnacle or White-fronted Geese, small individuals in the former and large in the latter. Two were with Greylags in March 1985. Canadas have been seen on most of the goose feeding grounds (Figure 8).

Two pinioned pairs were introduced to Colonsay in 1934; they bred successfully and the flock steadily increased until in 1968 there were 65 birds. In recent years numbers there have decreased, and 40 were counted in 1985. It has been suggested that Otters may have been responsible for this decline, but dispersal leading to the residence of some birds on Islay is also likely. Groups that may have come to Islay from Colonsay include: two at Portnahaven in May and June 1963; five beside Upper Loch Indaal in May 1978; and 13 near Bruichladdich in November 1985. The latter group probably arrived in 1983 and first nested in 1984. They breed close by Loch Gearach, feeding on pastures between there and Loch Indaal.

The Canada Goose often grazes on grasses and sometimes on clover and cereals; more rarely it head-dips and up-ends to reach aquatic plants. The vagrants roost with their companions, and have been seen for example in the Bridgend Barnacle roost. The residents roost communally, sometimes on Loch Gearach.

Barnacle Goose   *Branta leucopsis*

The Barnacle Goose is a winter visitor and passage migrant. It breeds in east Greenland and migrates to Islay via Iceland. The majority arrive on one or two days between 10th October and 5th November, but the first few appear up to 20 days earlier. Numbers build up on Gruinart Flats and later in the Bridgend area. Since 1953, when 3,000 were counted, the numbers of Barnacle Geese on Islay have increased, reaching 10,000 in 1963 and 24,000 in 1976; in 1985 they were about 17,000. John Walker, who visited Islay in 1764, found 4,000–5,000 geese (McKay 1980), which suggests that the number of Barnacle Geese then was as small as in the 1950s. The main departure is between mid-April and early May; the last birds leave betwen 20th April and 10th May. While present, they commute daily between roost sites and feeding areas; the return to roost can be particularly spectacular, especially when birds 'whiffle' down quickly from a large, moderately high flying skein. Those feeding on saltings usually walk up to 1 km ($\frac{3}{5}$ mile) to their roost site.

Feeding on pastures and stubbles in the straths and to the south of Loch Gorm

81

Barnacle Goose (John Davies)

increases as the autumn progresses. It extends to other farms with less rich grasslands such as Ballinaby, or those more distant from the roosts as in the Ballygrant area. Finally, in the new year, small poor pastures and some marginal farmlands are exploited. To some extent this progression is being modified by management of the Gruinart Reserve in favour of geese. A full-winged flock is present in the collection at Easter Ellister.

Flocks commonly of hundreds and sometimes of thousands of individuals feed together but may be split up when disturbed. Families keep together in these flocks, and it is the adults that periodically raise their heads on the look-out for danger. They probe and sever plants as they walk slowly forwards, taking clover, grasses and seeds stripped from sedges. Some feeding may be done by moonlight. Often these geese arrive at and depart from their roost when there is only a glimmer of daylight, but if they are well fed they are likely to roost longer. The main roosting places are on tidal flats at the head of Lochs Indaal and Gruinart; smaller groups assemble in Killinallan Bay and on the beach by the mouth of the Laggan, or southeast towards the Airport (Figure 8). During severe storms, they have been seen on the sheltered Loch Skerrols.

See pages 33–8 for further information.

Brent Goose *Branta bernicla*

The Brent Goose is a passage migrant that stays briefly; it was a winter visitor prior to 1938. Now only single individuals are normally seen between passages.

About 95 per cent of Brent Geese seen on Islay are of the light-bellied race *B.b.hrota* which breeds in northern Greenland and nearby arctic Canada and winters in Ireland. One at Blackrock on 25th May 1979 wore a collar fitted in arctic Canada and was later seen twice in Ireland. The remaining 5 per cent of Islay's recorded migrants are of the dark-bellied race breeding in northern Siberia. At Frenchman's Rocks flocks of 48 and three Brents were seen travelling southwards on 7th November 1976 and 4th November 1982 respectively; all evidence for this passage falls between early September and mid-November. The northward passage appears to be between mid-April and late May, but is poorly documented; one was in Sanaigmore Bay on 15th June 1983.

Exceptionally, 3,000–4,000 Brent Geese called in on Bruichladdich on return migration in April 1971; this was then about half of the Irish population. Normally only a small fraction stop over, 97 per cent of counts being below 50. However, 60 were on Loch Gruinart sandflats on 4th September 1987. They are usually found on or near the saltings of Gruinart or Bridgend Bay, in Blackrock Bay and Port Ellen Bay, or much less frequently at other points en route between the entrance to Loch Gruinart and Port Ellen, where stop-over birds often head towards Ireland. One or two are seen in most years in the Barnacle Goose flocks.

The Brent Goose takes marine algae such as *Enteromorpha*, which forms bright green intertidal spreads near burn mouths in Blackrock Bay, as well as eelgrass (*Zostera*) and some saltmarsh plants. It obtains these plants by grazing, dipping or up-ending. The decline of diseased *Zostera* was probably a principal factor in terminating their wintering on Islay. These geese roost close to their feeding area, the timing depending on the state of the tide.

Red-breasted Goose *Branta ruficollis*

One probable escape was reported to be on Islay on 1st April 1962. Wild birds breed in northern Siberia and migrate to Romania and Bulgaria. An increasing few come to southern England, usually with European White-fronted or Brent Geese.

Shelduck *Tadorna tadorna*

Shelduck pairs occupy about 30 feeding territories and non-breeding birds make up a total of about 130 adult residents. Some stop-over visitors are present in late winter; there were 313 at Loch Gruinart on 9th March 1984. Most depart on moult migration in the second half of July. The great majority of northwest European birds assemble in the Heligoland Bight, but in recent years small moulting flocks have been found in Britain. Returning birds arrive on Islay from mid-November to the end of the year. The very few staying behind for a time on Islay include birds in charge of crèches; one of over 50 juveniles was reported at Gruinart on 23rd August 1979.

The Shelduck winters in the upper half of Loch Gruinart and around Upper Loch Indaal. It breeds by these sea-lochs, taking over Rabbit burrows in raised beaches and dunes. Territories are also found in the southeast archipelago, at Traigh Bhan near Smaull, at Traigh Nostaig by Ardnave, in Proaig Bay and in other storm-sheltered bays that are mostly backed by potential burrow sites in dunes, raised beaches or moraines. It very occasionally visits coastal freshwater lochs such as Nigheadaireachd by Laggan.

The tiny spired shellfish *Hydrobia ulvae*, which is abundant in, for example, Bridgend Bay, is the Shelduck's main food; other small intertidal molluscs, crustaceans, and invertebrates form less than 20 per cent of its diet. It wades slowly forward in very shallow water, scything with its bill through the surface sediment, and also pecks, dabbles, head-dips and up-ends depending on water depth. At non-breeding times, these ducks roost communally near their feeding

Shelduck (John Davies)

territories at any safe location, such as in a saltmarsh or on a sand-spit or open water.

Wigeon   *Anas penelope*

A winter visitor that became more numerous in Scotland from the mid-19th century; fewer than ten birds summer on the island, and probable breeding was recorded in the Port Ellen square for the *Atlas* project of 1968–72. The visitors probably originate in Iceland; recoveries of migrants ringed there have occurred chiefly in Scotland and Ireland. Arrivals begin in late August, but the majority come in September; peak numbers are present in November and departures take place mainly in April. Four were seen travelling south past Frenchman's Rocks on 16th September 1973.

The majority of Wigeon are found on and around Upper Loch Indaal and Loch Gruinart, which together normally carry about 700 individuals. Peak counts were 800 on 14th October 1979 and 535 on 16th November 1981 respectively. Less often smaller flocks are on fishing lochs, especially Skerrols, Ardnave, Kinnabus and Gorm. Up to a few tens occasionally visit other lochans and pools, even if they are peaty and unproductive, such as Loch Eighinn, or Loch Clach a' Bhuaile, where 26 roosted on 10th September 1976.

Wigeon are almost entirely vegetarian and obtain food by grazing on short grass (particularly at Gruinart), by dabbling on the surface of water or less often by dipping head and neck. They associate with Whooper Swans in Bridgend Bay near the Sorn channel, where they pick from the surface thin ribbon-like leaves of the green algae *Zostera*, discarded by the dipping and up-ending swans. They also associate with Brent Geese feeding on eelgrass or *Enteromorpha* in Blackrock Bay. Specialist leaf-eating is aided by serrations at the side of the bill, but seeds are also taken by dabbling and insects are probably acquired accidentally. This duck roosts in large flocks, by day or night, at an undisturbed site. Many assemble on the saltings near Islay House.

Gadwall   *Anas strepera*

The Gadwall has been a winter visitor in very small numbers since at least 1871 (Gray). There are single records in the breeding seasons of 1982 and 1985, and the species first bred in Scotland in 1906. Both Icelandic and Scottish breeders winter in Ireland; the Islay visitors could be wanderers from either country. Islay is on the northern limit of the species' winter range. Gadwall occupy fairly shallow water with some fringing cover. Eleven records from 1962 to 1985 include three from Upper Loch Indaal and three from the Loch Gorm area. The maximum number seen was four near the Bowmore Power Station in September 1963.

This duck specialises in aquatic vegetation supplemented by seeds and cereal grain. It feeds with head dipped or up-ends to reach plants down to 30 cm (1 ft), and occasionally grazes or visits stubbles. Roosting birds are usually out of water on a bank or in a creek in the saltings.

Teal *Anas crecca crecca*

The Teal is a winter visitor in moderate numbers and a resident in much smaller numbers. Breeding was recorded in 1849, 1876, 1952, 1954 and 1981 and has taken place in most parts of the island. An immigration from Iceland starts early in September. Maximum numbers recorded at seven localities have been between mid-September and the end of January and include: 712 around Upper Loch Indaal on 18th September 1973; 500 on Loch Gruinart on 26th October 1979; 800 on Loch Gorm on 19th October 1975; 204 on Loch Skerrols on 15th November 1981; and 155 on Ardnave Loch on 20th January 1983. Most counts are considerably smaller, presumably because these small ducks are usually more dispersed or hidden. Emigration occurs in March and April but is poorly documented. During May, June and July, the few records are each of fewer than 20 birds; the females are nesting and well hidden, while most males may be on moult migration further south.

This duck prefers shallow water with reedbeds or other cover and some marginal vegetation. It is found on saltings, a wide range of inland lochs and boggy areas, and is most readily seen around Bridgend Bay. It is omnivorous, taking spores and seeds up to 2.6 mm ($\frac{1}{10}$ in) in diameter, especially in autumn and winter, and animals up to 11 mm ($\frac{1}{2}$ in) long including midge larvae and *Hydrobia*. It filters, picks and skims food from the water's surface and feeds with its head underwater or less often up-ends. A high proportion of feeding is nocturnal and dependent on water level and moon phases. Outside the breeding season roosting flocks are tightly packed on open water. On 3rd October 1981, 450 on the lochan near Craigens may have been roosting during daylight, since this small pond is unlikely to attract such a large number to feed.

Green-winged Teal *Anas crecca carolinensis*

A rare transatlantic vagrant, most likely to come from the Canadian Maritime Provinces; it winters in the southern United States. The vagrants arrive mainly in the Northern Isles and the Outer Hebrides between October and June, but especially December to February. About 90 males have reached the British Isles in recent years; the females are not distinguishable from European Teal. A male was with European Teal on a lochan southwest of Loch Gorm from 7th to 9th May 1979.

Mallard *Anas platyrhynchos*

The Mallard is a resident and a winter visitor. Some Icelandic birds winter in Britain and Ireland and numbers on Islay increase from early August to mid-September, reaching maxima of: 600 around Upper Loch Indaal on 18th September 1973 and 28th October 1973; 403 on Loch Skerrols on 20th September 1980; and over 200 on Loch Gorm on 3rd October 1976. These visitors appear gradually to decrease through the winter, most having gone by mid-March. Winter counts of up to 100 near Rhuvaal probably represent birds undergoing local movements. Opposite Islay House, 59 males were moulting on the saltings on 6th June 1978; a moult migration of Islay males does not seem likely.

This duck occurs on and in the vicinity of nearly all shallow waters. It is found towards the head of both sea-lochs, within the southeast archipelago and in sheltered marine bays with river retreats, such as Proaig Bay. It also occurs on fishing lochs (64 were on Loch Kinnabus in January 1971) and on peaty lochs with some reedy cover (75 were on Loch Tallant, Bowmore, in September 1976). Single pairs are normally on small ponds and reservoirs, including the distillery reservoirs; however, 32 were on Claddach Reservoir on 20th January 1984. It occurs on slow-flowing rivers and burns, especially the River Laggan, and also frequents ill-drained fields with rushes and partially flooded fields after heavy rains. During periods of ground frost in winter, some flock to the coast; 14 were in Kilnaughton Bay when there was a frost on 30th November 1977.

Mallard take midge and other insect larvae as they emerge in summer, and seeds and green plant parts at other times. They visit cereal and potato fields after harvesting and sift on mudflats for minute molluscs and other invertebrates. They peck, dabble and dip their heads under water or up-end; they graze, grub and nibble; and they shake plants to obtain seeds; but they rarely dive. The may feed at night and, outside the breeding season, roost communally on shores in shelter. Some roost among Bridgend saltings.

Pintail *Anas acuta*

The Pintail is a winter visitor in small numbers. Icelandic birds winter mainly in Britain and Ireland and probably include the Islay visitors. These arrive in September, usually late September, and depart during the first half of April. They have been seen arriving from the north in October at the same time as Barnacle Geese. Average numbers on Islay for each month from October to March are around 20–25 birds.

This duck requires open shallow water with a reasonable water-plant production and accompanying invertebrate animal life. Pintail are found mainly at the heads of the two sea-lochs and at Ardnave Loch. One or two individuals are occasionally found on other coastal lochans or pools such as Loch Eighinn, Carnain Pond and Lagavulin Distillery Pond. Exceptional numbers have

87

occurred at Loch Gruinart: 20 on 19th October 1975; 30 on 7th October 1976; and 30 on 29th November 1981. Fifteen were ar Ardnave Loch in December 1981.

Pintail feed mainly by up-ending, by immersing head and neck or by dabbling while swimming. Their reach, especially that of the drake, is greater than that of other dabbling ducks, enabling them to take food from depths down to 50 cm (20 in) but usually extending to less than 30 cm (12 in). Their diet is varied, including the tiny shellfish *Hydrobia ulvae* from mudflats, seeds from drift lines and other plant material, and also invertebrates and crustaceans. On the mainland Pintail are known to feed on stubbles, and there is a record of a male on stubble by Rockmountain, Sunderland, on 21st March 1981. Most feeding is at dusk or by night. Roosting is largely by day and communally on water or shore with other species of *Anas*, such as the Teal of Ardnave Loch. They are often by vegetated low banks away from the track to Ardnave House.

Garganey   *Anas querquedula*

A rare, irregular summer visitor that breeds annually in parts of England; it nested in East Lothian in 1928 and Ayrshire in 1979. Scottish records are dated mainly between April and October. On Islay one was shot at Machrie on 10th September 1964, there were three on Ardnave Loch on 2nd June 1978 and one on Loch Gorm on 27th June 1982. Remains were found below a Peregrine eyrie in mid-May 1976. The Garganey likes sheltered fresh waters of high biological productivity but will temporarily use small ponds, pools and ditches.

Blue-winged Teal   *Anas discors*

A rare transatlantic vagrant, most likely to come from the Canadian Maritime Provinces; it normally winters in the States bordering the Gulf of Mexico. A few arrive in the Outer Hebrides from September to November. There is a reliable record of a female on the flats opposite Islay House on 19th October 1974.

Shoveler   *Anas clypeata*

A winter visitor in very small numbers and an irregular breeder; no more than one breeding pair was reported in 1918, 1957 and about 1970. Immigration of winter visitors commences in mid-September, continuing into November. Maximum numbers for December (29 in 1983), for January (19 in 1982) and for February (20 in 1979) were each recorded on Upper Loch Indaal. Emigration takes place through March to April. These birds are likely to be from Iceland. The very few summering birds probably winter further south with other British or Irish Shoveler. Two-thirds of all records are from Upper Loch Indaal. A few are from Loch Gruinart saltings and others are from small coastal lochs and pools with fringing vegetation. Shovelers are very rarely seen on fishing lochs, except Ardnave. They have been seen several times at temporary flashes in areas with hummocky grasses or rushes.

The Shoveler swims with head and neck immersed or with bill partly immersed, creating a flow from the tip, through and out of the sides of the bill. This broad spatulate tool is adapted to filter out small food particles. Sometimes a group of feeding birds swims in a ring formation, stirring up food for each other. Shoveler sometimes dabble at the edge of pools, occasionally up-end, but rarely dive; they take small freshwater molluscs and crustaceans, aquatic insects, larvae and the seeds of water plants. Roosting is usually at night, communally and in the same or similar habitat as is used for feeding.

Pochard *Aythya ferina*

Principally a winter visitor, but two or three individuals are often present in summer. Pochard wintering in Scotland come from Baltic countries and Russia. Most of Islay's few hundred birds arrive during August, but a few have been noted in late July and in some years arrival is not until September; 14 were on Loch Skerrols on 21st July 1973. Numbers are maintained until the turn of the year; thereafter they are much reduced and the remaining winterers leave in March, but this is poorly documented.

This duck requires fresh, shallow water with abundant water plants and is found chiefly on the inland fishing lochs. Maxima of 320 on Loch Skerrols, 128 on Loch Ballygrant, 51 on Ardnave Loch and 54 on Loch Gorm are recorded; numbers fluctuate greatly, however, from year to year and in 1977, for example, the largest count was of only 19 on Loch Skerrols. Up to 40 have been seen on the Oa lochs, and there is a record of 45 on Loch Allan on 25th January 1976. There are few records on salt water, but 33 were in a Scaup flock on Loch Indaal on 9th February 1984.

The Pochard obtains food mainly by diving to depths of 1–2.5 m (3–8 ft) and occasionally up-ends or dabbles. It takes midge larvae in the breeding season but at other times concentrates on submerged plants such as pondweeds and stoneworts (*Chara*), as well as various small water animals. The main feeding period starts after dark. It roosts communally on open water during the day and in the middle of the night.

Ring-necked Duck *Aythya collaris*

A rare vagrant that breeds in North America and normally moves south and west to winter, some to Central America. It is now recorded annually in Scotland, chiefly as single individuals from late September to February. On 23rd January 1984, a male was at Easter Ellister; it stayed for some weeks.

Ferruginous Duck *Aythya nyroca*

A rare vagrant, or possibly an escape, that has a scattered discrete breeding range in south and east Europe and western Asia. Northern populations are migratory, wintering in the Mediterranean area and Africa north of the tropics. The nearest migrants breed in East Germany. Single birds have been recorded in Scotland between October and May in most years since 1972. On 6th June 1972, a male was on Islay at the lochan just southwest of Craigens.

Tufted Duck *Aythya fuligula*

A resident, breeding in very small numbers; first bred in about 1950 and was still considered rare in 1962 (*Scot. Birds* 1963). Juveniles were seen on Ardnave Loch on 22nd August 1975 and 14th July 1977, and also on Loch Gorm on 9th July 1977. It is also a winter visitor. In the winter months there appear to be around 100 Tufted Duck on Islay, but on 13th Feburary 1972 Loch Skerrols held 100 and on 15th February 1969 Loch Allan held about 200. These are the only records of more than 65 on any single water; they suggest temporary immigrations of Scottish mainland ducks that had vacated frozen lochs, or of Icelandic ducks. A high proportion of the latter winter in the British Isles, particularly in Ireland. In summer, the total for the island is probably about 40.

This species is recorded on 22 inland waters, ranging from two on the 0.5-ha ($1\frac{1}{4}$-acre) Port Charlotte Pond and on the similar-sized peaty Loch a' Gheoidh (257658) to around 40 on the fishing lochs of Ballygrant, Gorm, Skerrols and sometimes Ardnave. When seen on Loch a' Gheoidh during the 1973 breeding season, the ducks had the advantage of alarm calls from a colony of Black-headed Gulls. This is a well-known species nesting association. There is a small number of records of fewer than ten of these ducks on the sea-lochs during the six winter months, and a few are commonly among the Scaup on Loch Indaal.

The Tufted Duck feeds chiefly by diving to depths of 3–7 m (10–23 ft) and searching the bottom for small molluscs, crustaceans or insect larvae. It occasionally up-ends in shallow water or wades and searches for seeds, and also walks along strand lines or further upshore. It pushes its bill under stones and fallen vegetation, or into water weeds, hunting aquatic invertebrates. It may feed at night, even when the sky is dark, and roosts nocturnally in rafts on still, open water.

Scaup *Aythya marila*

A winter visitor and passage migrant; there are a few records of one to three birds in summer. Scaup arrive from Iceland in the second half of August or early September and numbers gradually build up through September and October. During the immigration period flocks have been noted flying south at Ardnave, passing Frenchman's Rocks, and continuing south, having halted at Loch Indaal. There are 31 counts of 1,000 or more Scaup on Loch Indaal, distributed throughout the wintering months and peaking in December at around 1,400–1,500 birds. Emigration occurs through April and the first half of May. Of 24 records at minor localities, 15 were during the immigration and one during the emigration period; a few tired birds appear to land on any calm water before continuing on to Bridgend Bay.

Three-quarters of all records are from Bridgend Bay; often this gathering is divided into three to five rafts and may be aligned approximately along the River Sorn channel. Small numbers are sometimes off other sections of the Upper Loch Indaal coast; 200 were seen between Bruichladdich and Port Charlotte on 5th October 1986. Scaup have not been recorded on Lower Loch Indaal, and only a very few passage birds are noted on the outer coasts. Sometimes there are gatherings of up to 400 birds on Loch Skerrols and exceptionally there were 1,100 on 2nd January 1972; this may be in response to high winds affecting Loch Indaal.

Scaup dive to obtain food at depths of 6 m (20 ft), and occasionally up-end or dabble in shallows. Molluscs are their chief food, plus crustaceans, invertebrates, worms and occasional small fish. It has been suggested that the large numbers in Bridgend Bay benefit from the distillery effluent, and possibly from the sewage

Scaup (John Davies)

91

outfalls as they do elsewhere. These ducks dive from rafts in various places throughout 5 sq. km (2 sq. miles) of Bridgend Bay. The distillery outfall at Bowmore contains nutrients which are presumably distributed by tidal currents, and these are likely to benefit molluscs and other marine life that are the prey of the Scaup. The outfall has been discharging for 200 years and is due to be diverted into the sewage system in 1988. The communal roosting habitat of these ducks is on the water of Bridgend Bay and perhaps Loch Skerrols, and roosting is both diurnal and nocturnal, probably depending on tides, weather and the consequent feeding conditions. Only 18 were found oiled after the October 1969 spillage at Bruichladdich.

Eider *Somateria mollissima*

A resident that makes only short journeys between feeding areas and roosts, or to form moulting flocks. There are a number of winter records of 500 to 3,000 Eiders flying in parties up or down the Sound of Islay; in about 1890, a gamekeeper recorded 'thousands going and coming with the tide'. There are strong tidal currents in this passage and roosting is likely only in sheltered bays.

Eiders fly close to the water surface where winds are weakened by drag; they are adept at keeping a steady course and making progress against gales or even hurricanes. They are found around all of Islay's coasts, breeding near the more remote shores or on small offshore islands. They are especially abundant in the Sounds of Islay and Nave Island, around Upper Loch Indaal, where from 100 to 350 have often been counted, within the southeast archipelago, and in Laggan Bay, where a flock dominated by drakes builds up to about 200 between late March and mid-July. C. G. Booth recorded a flock in Port Ellen Bay almost monthly between November 1974 and June 1981; it built up to a maximum of 260 and nearly all were drakes from late March to at least the end of September. A third flock peaking at over 200 moulting males roosts on the spit at Traigh an Luig from early June to mid-September. These ducks are rarely found inland, but there were ten on Ardnave Loch on 16th September 1980, and one pair on Claddach Reservoir on 25th May 1985.

Eiders forage chiefly on an ebbing tide and especially near low tide, but they feed morning and evening where the tidal range is small; it is less than 1 m (3 ft) around the southeast coast of Islay. They dive, without a leap, to at least 10 m (33 ft) but usually to 2–6 m (6–20 ft). They also up-end and head-dip in the shallows. Their main prey are mussels (*Mytilus edulis*) and crabs, but they also take whelks, periwinkles, starfish and sea-urchins. They usually swallow shellfish whole, crushing them in their muscular gizzard. While swimming, their feet are occasionally used to excavate hollows in shallow muddy areas, enabling additional food to be obtained by up-ending and probing. These ducks roost communally, often in rafts on the sea but also ashore on sheltered beaches. After an oil spill in Loch Indaal in October 1969, at least 338 Eiders were found dead.

King Eider   *Somateria spectabilis*

A rare vagrant from the Arctic Ocean, with its nearest breeding haunts in
Spitsbergen; some winter off the north and northwest coasts of Norway and
around Iceland. A few males are reported off Scottish coasts annually and in all
months; females are rarely identified. One was seen near Kintra from the cliffs of
the Oa on 25th July 1906; it was presumably a male. Another was reported
southeast of Islay from the Winter Atlas Survey of 1981/2 to 1983/4, but it does
not appear to have been authenticated by the Rarities Committee.

Harlequin Duck   *Histrionicus histrionicus*

A very rare vagrant that breeds on ice-free waters in the Arctic and normally
moves to the nearest coast in the winter; the only European birds are in Iceland.
On 12th November 1954, a male was shot in the old river bed at Laggan during a
period of gales and was identified by an Edinburgh taxidermist; this record has
not been generally accepted. A female or immature was in Claggain Bay and on a
pool near the mouth of the river from 20th to 31st October 1987.

Long-tailed Duck   *Clangula hyemalis*

A winter visitor that comes to Islay in very small numbers. In 1978, a female was
still at Loch Gruinart on 11th July. This highly mobile duck has a circumpolar
arctic breeding distribution and has a complex pattern of migration; the origin of
winter visitors to Scotland is unknown. They usually arrive on Islay during
October and November and leave in April or occasionally May. One was at
Frenchman's Rocks in late October 1977, and three sightings in Claggain Bay in
November 1970 and 1976 may have been of passage birds.

About half of the visitors are drakes. The main wintering locality is Bridgend
Bay and a maximum of nine was there on 16th February 1987; one or two have
occasionally been seen on Loch Gruinart. These birds are rarely found on fresh
water, but one was on Ardnave Loch in March 1968, another was on the main
Easter Ellister pond in November 1974, two were on Loch Gorm in October
1975 and a female was there on 22nd October 1976.

To feed, this duck makes deep dives from the surface, commonly to between 3
and 10 m (10–33 ft), but occasionally to over 30 m (100 ft). It takes mussels and
other bivalves, periwinkles, whelks, crustaceans including small crabs, marine
worms and small fish. The few visiting Islay may roost with the Scaup; normally
this species roosts in large flocks and does not associate with other species of
ducks.

Long-tailed Duck (John Davies)

Common Scoter   *Melanitta nigra*

A winter visitor and passage migrant that is also resident in small numbers. Winter visitors are on Loch Indaal from late August to May. Over 50 have been recorded in some months, but numbers have fluctuated from a few to a maximum of 165 on 14th February 1987. They are probably from Iceland, although there is no evidence from ringing. A few were seen passing south by Frenchman's Rocks from 26th August to 7th October 1973. On return passage, 30 passed by Frenchman's Rocks on 15th May 1976, and 70 flew into Port Ellen Bay and then north to Kintra on Laggan Bay on 27th March 1978. Numbers on Loch Indaal often build up through March; some leave in May or transfer to inland lochs to breed; 87 were off Bruichladdich on 23rd May 1987 and there were still over 50 there in June.

Four or five pairs are on Loch Gorm in most summers and an isolated pair is sometimes found on a peaty lochan. From 3rd July to 17th August, the only records of scoters are of a female with two ducklings; this is approximately the period when males are moulting in rafts at sea. The winter quarters of the Scottish breeding birds are unknown.

Common Scoter (John Davies)

The Common Scoter's principal food is mussels obtained by diving to a few metres depth, exceptionally to 20 m (66 ft). A variety of other prey is taken when necessary, especially on inland lochs. It roosts at night in rafts on the sea, probably on Loch Indaal, and is particularly vulnerable to oil pollution, although no affected birds were recorded after the accident in Loch Indaal in October 1969.

Surf Scoter   *Melanitta perspicillata*

An annual vagrant to Scotland from Canada in very small numbers. It is known in all months, especially in autumn and winter, and normally winters in the United States. Adult males are usually reported, but off Frenchman's Rocks on 15th May 1977 two males and three females were seen travelling south. On 4th October 1982, an adult male was with Common Scoter on Loch Indaal, off Port Charlotte.

95

Velvet Scoter *Melanitta fusca*

A rare visitor in all seasons; eight Islay records have been collected in eight months, none having been seen in February, August, September or December. It breeds in northern Eurasia, many wintering off the west coast of Norway and around Denmark. Four records are from Loch Indaal, and the others are widely scattered around Islay's coasts. Both sexes are seen, often with Common Scoter. Several small flocks were seen on Loch Indaal during November 1867. Seven were in Machir Bay on 20th April 1963, and two were on Loch Gruinart on 2nd April 1982. They obtain food by surface-diving to a few metres, but over 10 m (33 ft) where necessary, taking chiefly shellfish as well as crabs, sea-urchins and starfish. They roost communally on the sea.

Goldeneye *Bucephala clangula*

A winter visitor; there are also eight records of one to four birds in the summer months during the 1970s. The winter visitors to Scotland are mainly of Scandinavian origin. They arrive on Islay about mid-October and numbers build up through November. Their departure appears to be during the first half of April.

The Goldeneye is recorded on the two sea-lochs and in bays around the outer coast; in Machir Bay at the end of December, there were 25 in 1971 and 69 in 1981. It is also recorded inland on fishing lochs, as well as on a few peaty lochs and small reservoirs, and is regular on Upper Loch Indaal, Ardnave Loch and Lochs Gorm and Skerrols. It has a tendency to concentrate near sewage outfalls on the mainland, and the two largest counts on Islay are of groups off Bowmore: over 50 on 1st March 1975 and 100 on about 30th November 1981. Six of the eight summer records were on Loch Gorm.

This duck surface-dives, sometimes synchronously and usually to less than 3 m (10 ft), primarily for molluscs, crustaceans and polychaete worms. It also takes insect larvae in summer and some plant material in autumn, and occasionally catches small fish. It sometimes turns stones in search of prey and head-dips in shallows on the ebb tide. All but large food items are swallowed underwater. The Goldeneye usually roosts at night in a dense raft on open water, away from both the shore and the feeding area.

Smew *Mergus albellus*

A scarce, irregular winter visitor to Islay that occurs annually in the east of Scotland, mostly between November and March, and comes from Lapland or Siberia. Females or first-year males were seen 'on Islay' in 1892, at Bruichladdich in December 1925, and off Bowmore several times each winter since 1984/5.

Red-breasted Merganser *Mergus serrator*

The Red-breasted Merganser is a resident and possibly a passage migrant. Ringed Icelandic birds have been recovered in the Hebrides and Ireland; some migrants may stop briefly on Islay, giving high counts on Loch Indaal such as 142 on 7th October 1972, 108 on 13th October 1974 and 171 on 14th March 1971.

From June to September, male and immature or unsuccessful mergansers move to local moulting sites. There is one in the Sound of Gigha and a probable staging post in Clagain Bay; 92 per cent of the total birds covered by 25 counts off Claggain fall within this period; the average count was 35 and the highest counts were 110 on 4th July 1974 and 109 on 25th August 1977. Other gatherings have occurred in Upper Loch Indaal between late June and late July: 150 were at Blackrock on 21st July 1974. In addition to the flocks already mentioned, from mid-March to the end of June pairs are sometimes seen on fishing lochs, on Ardnave Loch and on Loch Nigheadaireachd near Laggan Farm, on the river downstream of Laggan Bridge and in the more sheltered coastal bays. Crèches of juveniles under the care of one female have been seen on both major sea-lochs in July. Small parties of adults are seen in most months on Upper Loch Indaal and in Kilnaughton and Laggan Bays.

Red-breasted Mergansers immerse their heads just under the water's surface in search of prey, and then dive to depths of up to 4–5 m (13–16 ft); a group may drive prey, forming a semicircle, and then dive together. Their long bills are serrated (giving the species its scientific name), and enable fish up to 10 or 15 cm (4–6 in) long to be caught and held firmly. The species takes a variety of fish, including flat-fish, eels, trout and salmon, and also crustaceans and insect larvae. All but the smaller prey are swallowed at the surface. These birds usually roost communally at night, on land at a gathering place or on the sea. After and oil spill on Loch Indaal in October 1969, some 31 mergansers were found dead.

Goosander *Mergus merganser*

A winter visitor on the edge of its range, with one or two birds recorded in most years. A female on the River Sorn was seen on 12th June 1971, and a pair there on 25th April 1973 may have attempted to breed, but there was no proof. There are twelve other records falling between mid-October and the end of March. Goosanders in Iceland appear to be resident, and it seems likely that Islay's visitors come from mainland Britain.

This species is markedly non-marine, but six records come from the two sea-lochs. Three, however, relate to the Allan, Ardnave and Skerrols fishing lochs and four to the Rivers Sorn and Laggan. Goosanders immerse their heads and search, drive prey, and dive after it to depths of 4–5 m (13–16 ft), just like Red-breasted Mergansers. They have serrated bills and catch similar fish in about the

97

same size range. They roost by night as well as during part of the day, communally on perches surrounded by water or on the water.

Honey Buzzard *Pernis apivorus*

A vagrant to Islay that breeds throughout much of Continental Europe and winters in central Africa. A few pairs nest in England and it is recorded annually in Scotland from late April to September, especially in May and June. Baxter and Rintoul (1953) record one on a gamekeeper's vermin board, probably in the Kildalton area, but no year is given. Another was seen on 1st March 1975; and later in August 1975 one was seen on Colonsay.

Red Kite *Milvus milvus*

The Red Kite is a dispersive migrant or vagrant that bred in Scotland in the 19th century and was occasionally seen over Islay. It was exterminated from most parts of Britain but is now resident in Wales and reported in Scotland in most months. On 17th March 1984 one was over Easter Ellister, and in 1985 one was seen thrice in the Rhinns, over Coultorsay, Eresaid and Loch Gruinart, from 30th November to 1st December.

White-tailed Eagle *Haliaeetus albicilla*

A former resident breeder that last bred 'some years' before 1870 at Bholsa and the Mull of Oa; also possibly some time around 1910. From four to ten Norwegian birds have been released on the island of Rhum annually since 1976 and a few of these have been sighted on Islay, the first in March 1978. The adults are sedentary, but juveniles and immatures wander extensively until they breed at about six years old. It is such wanderers that have so far been seen on Islay.

This eagle is occasionally seen on the north and west sides of the island. Individuals were seen at Loch Finlaggan in March 1978 and rising with a fish from Loch Skerrols on 12th December 1984. There were eight sightings in 1985; one at Sgarbh Dubh south of Bholsa on 1st July 1986; and others of a bird around Gruinart Flats on 16th January 1987. Yellow, organge and white wing tags have been noted on these birds.

Pairs often hunt together, but these have still to be seen on Islay. Sometimes this eagle soars and searches over land, from heights of less than 200 m (650 ft), but prey is often located from a lookout rock, tree or post, or when the bird is standing still on the ground or in shallow water. The birds usually fly low over water, snatching fish from the surface, and also taking stranded or dying fish and carrion or offal. They may attack birds on water repeatedly until one is exhausted by many escape dives, and they may plunder seabird colonies or rob other birds of their food.

Marsh Harrier   *Circus aeruginosus*

A vagrant to Islay that breeds in most European countries and migrates to southern Europe and Africa. A few pairs nest in East Anglia, and it is reported in Scotland mainly between April and September, especially May. Female birds were seen on Islay in June 1974 and August 1979; males in May 1980 and April 1985. The 1974 bird was on Gruinart Flats and the others were in the Loch Gorm area. Several reports indicate that there was a juvenile/female in the Gorm and Gruinart areas during the summer of 1986; it was sighted at Foreland on 6th June.

Hen Harrier   *Circus cyaneus*

A resident that was virtually exterminated late last century but recolonised Islay from about 1960, becoming well established in the early 1970s. It is also a probable passage visitor in small numbers; there was an influx of 'considerable numbers' in August and September 1875. A male at East Carrabus on 3rd June 1975 had been wing-tagged at Banchory, near Aberdeen, in 1974. One flew out to sea southwards from Frenchman's Rocks on 31st October 1976, and a ringtail flew south-southwest from Port Wemyss on 28th January 1975. A male nestling was ringed near Kilchiaran on 4th August 1980 and killed in western Limerick, Ireland, on 1st October 1984; another nestling ringed near the same farm on 17th June 1984 was found freshly killed by a car in Saint Laurent de la Salle, south of Nantes in France, on 25th November 1985.

The Hen Harrier is found hunting throughout Islay except in the northern and eastern hills. It is most common in mixed habitat on the lower ground, on farmland with patches of rushes, gorse or scant scrub, or with walls or rocky mounds: anything that provides an opportunity for a surprise approach to prey. This species is also seen over saltings, machair, blanket and raised bogs, heather moorland and young conifer plantations. There were six breeding sites on the Gruinart Reserve in 1985.

About 40 per cent of a year's sightings are of males, but this rises to over 50 per cent for the last week of March to the first week of July, probably from when the spectacular sexual displays begin to when females relieve males of extra hunting duties. These birds fly low, often dexterously switching direction and changing from a glide with horizontal wings to brief soars with wings held in a V form. They take songbirds in faster flight and small animals and straying chicks in slower flight. Prey attacked on Islay includes voles, shrews, Rabbits, Rock Doves, Woodpigeons, Pheasants, Starlings, Redwings and Chaffinches. The larger species are probably taken only as unattended young. Males often hunt on

99

Hen Harrier (John Davies)

straighter courses than females and have been followed from Kilchoman to Leek 5 km (3 miles) on 13th November 1977 and from Knockdon to Carnducan 8 km (5 miles) on 1st June 1983. Adult males have larger home ranges than females.

Roosting takes place communally from July to March. Documented roosts are on the ground on slopes with good cover just above boggy areas: on the edges of Gruinart Flats, Foreland Marsh and the Tallant reedbeds, remote from roads. From two to 18 harriers have been noted entering these roosts, chiefly during the twilight period. Afforestation is likely to bring a temporary increase in the harrier population, because voles are their main prey and these increase considerably during the first few years after planting.

See pages 43–4 for further information.

Montagu's Harrier   *Circus pygargus*

A vagrant that bred in Scotland in 1950–5, is a rare summer visitor to England, and is declining on the Continent. It winters in Africa south of the Sahara and wanders to Scotland in some years, mainly in May. A first-year bird was seen at Kilchiaran in June 1983.

Goshawk *Accipiter gentilis*

A scarce and irregular passage visitor that is resident in very small numbers on the Scottish mainland and in central England. A few transatlantic vagrants have been recognised in Ireland from October to February. The first record of this visitor to the Inner Hebrides was of one at Ballygrant on 28th April 1959. A female was in the Bridgend area on 8th September 1975 and a male was at Ardnave Point on 5th March 1978. Others were identified in September 1973, September 1977 and April 1982. Since then it has become virtually annual, and in 1983 there were four sightings: at Skerrols on 14th May; Easter Ellister on 5th June; Bridgend on 12th September; and Sunderland on 16th September. This is a species that may be encouraged when the new conifer plantations mature.

Sparrowhawk *Accipiter nisus*

Sparrowhawk (John Davies)

A resident that was recorded in 1887, then in 1957 and subsequently. Some relaxation in keepering has probably allowed an increase in numbers in recent years. It is also a likely passage migrant in small numbers. There is limited evidence of movement: single birds were seen at Frenchman's Rocks on 14th and 28th August and on 4th, 14th and 27th September 1977; and two came in off the sea on 31st October 1976. On 6th April 1977, one flew across the Sound of Jura.

Records kept since the early 1970s indicate that there are home ranges attributable to about nine pairs, but not all are necessarily occupied each year. Four are around the principal wooded areas and four are further west, based on scattered copses and scrub areas. Virtually all woodland lies below the 90-m (295 ft) contour and only one record relates to this hawk above 90 m, travelling fast and high rather than hunting.

The Sparrowhawk waits in cover for birds to chance near, moving after some minutes to another perch, or uses other surprise tactics: flying low over hedgerows and slipping from side to side, along the edges of or through gaps in woodland, or between buildings or bushes. It seizes prey from a perch or gives chase and seizes in flight. The female takes thrushes and starlings, whereas the smaller male takes finches, sparrows, buntings and tits. Prey on Islay has been identified as Blackbird, Song Thrush, Starling, Chaffinch, Meadow Pipit, Pied Wagtail, Robin, Treecreeper, Water Rail and 'mouse'. Most roosting is solitary within woodland at night, the female being on her nest in the breeding season. When two went to roost near Knockdon, close to a Raven roost, on 2nd January 1986, there was much interaction between them and the Ravens. An apparently similar relationship was reported at Tallant Woods in October 1975 and August 1976.

Buzzard   *Buteo buteo*

This raptor has been resident since before 1800, but numbers were reduced by keepering from the mid-1800s to the First World War and by myxomatosis in Rabbits from about 1953 to 1973. It may be somewhat reduced again when the present extensive new plantations have grown. The Buzzard soars over slopes or on thermals, which are common on Islay from February to July and sometimes occur in other months. It may be seen travelling a few kilometres by alternate souring and straight gliding, or by gliding and flapping.

The Buzzard is to be found in open, usually rough country, with trees or other high perches. On Islay, it hunts over machair, sand dunes, heather or grass moorland, fields with rushes and farmland with warrens. It is most frequently seen from Cluanach to Bridgend, around Skerrols, and in the Lossit (Ballygrant) area, especially outside the breeding season. The numerous records, collected over 13 years, cluster into about 20 home ranges (Figure 11); some are ill-defined, and the range size varies from about 5 to 10 sq. km (2–4 sq. miles).

In the Inner Hebrides, the density of Buzzards is closely related to that of

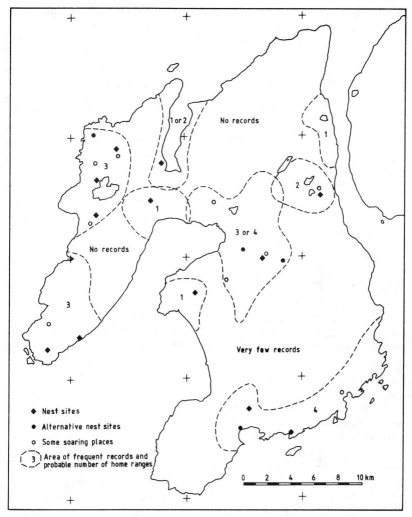

Figure 11: The distribution of the Buzzard on Islay, showing ranges and some nest sites

Rabbits. Other small mammals, birds, reptiles, amphibians, large insects, and earthworms are also taken. Islay records indicate that sheep and even Barnacle Goose carrion are eaten, as well as Rabbits and worms. Buzzards may walk around looking for small invertebrates, but the principal technique involves scanning from a vantage point and gliding steeply on to prey, sometimes using cover to increase the element of surprise. A vantage point may be gained by soaring or hovering, but is more often on telegraph poles, trees at the edge of a

103

wood, bushes or fences. They may roost solitarily but also in a family group, often in trees or on crags or cliffs.

Rough-legged Buzzard *Buteo lagopus*

A scarce winter visitor from Scandinavia and northern Russia that normally winters in a belt across central Europe from eastern Britain to Russia north of the Caucasus. Scotland's visitors probably come from Scandinavia; a few are reported each year. On Islay two were recorded in 1975: one on 15th January at Newton, and the other on 14th March at the Airport, where it was seen from 10 m (30 ft). Two were at Kildalton during the first week of January 1982. Other single birds were on the Rhinns on 24th April 1985, at Bridgend and Gruinart Flats on 16th November 1985, and at Easter Ellister on 11th and 12th October 1987.

Golden Eagle *Aquila chrysaetos*

Pennant appears to have seen this resident on Sanaig Cliffs in 1772, but it was persecuted during the 18th and 19th centuries and has been to a lesser extent since the First World War. There has been some recovery on Islay in the last decade, but increased afforestation will reduce its hunting area. Immigration from Jura or the mainland beyond is likely, while movement between Islay and Kintyre is less likely but possible; one flew in from the sea at Ardbeg on 16th August 1967. The Golden Eagle is adept at soaring over hill slopes or on thermals, and can manoeuvre well in hurricane-force winds. It hunts over heather and grass moors and the more barren high quartzite hills. Individuals visit the large dune tract near Killinallan and some sea cliffs. The scatter of records collected over eleven full years indicates a maximum of six or seven home ranges, but in most years only two to four are occupied in the breeding season; at least four have alternative eyries. Juveniles are often seen outside these ranges around the moorland-farmland borders, sometimes crossing a strath and occasionally hunting on lowland pasture. There is a small chance of spotting an eagle anywhere on Islay, but it is increased by walking along the Knockdon Lane or past Killinallan to Gortantaoid, especially just after a period of wet or misty weather, when hunting success has been reduced.

The Golden Eagle hunts solitarily, searching from low quartering flight or from a commanding crag or rock, striking with a swift glide or pounce. Prey is usually taken from the ground, the larger animals as carrion or when seriously incapacitated. Rabbits, hares, Fulmars, Rock Doves, Common Gulls, Hooded Crows, mice, lizards and dead sheep are recorded as taken on Islay; other seabirds, grouse and deer carrion are taken elsewhere. Pairs spend the night and poor hunting days on or close to the eyrie, in a situation that gives the best shelter under the weather conditions appertaining. Under the present reduced

Golden Eagle (John Davies)

keepering, the main threat to the Golden Eagle on Islay is excessive disturbance by birdwatchers.

Osprey *Pandion haliaetus*

The Osprey is an irregular passage visitor; one to three were seen annually on Islay in 18 out of 27 years to 1987, nearly half of them in May. Single birds or occasionally pairs from the Scottish mainland, or possibly from Scandinavia, pass through Islay to and from West Africa. There have been eleven sightings from mid-August to mid-October, but only five from late February to late April.

105

Sixteen records are from the Loch Ballygrant area, including Lossit and Cadhan Lochs; an Osprey was there on occasions from mid-May to the end of June 1969, and another from mid-May to mid-July in 1973. A further nine sightings were over coastal waters and twelve at other fishing lochs. One was on the Upper Laggan River and another at the River Sorn mouth. The Osprey takes medium-sized fish such as trout, pike and flounder from fresh or salt water, caught by a snatch during a shallow stoop to the surface of water or by plunging into the top metre of water with wings half closed and talons extended forwards. It hunts from an upwind powered flight, a glide into wind, a hovering position or a perch, usually at heights of 20–30 m (65–100 ft).

Kestrel *Falco tinnunculus*

A resident and passage migrant that was abundant around the turn of the century and common in the 1970s, but has declined in the 1980s. These variations, as elsewhere, are probably related to the availability of small mammal prey. The enclosure of ground for forestation allows a temporary increase in such prey, especially voles. There is a marked increase in sightings after the first week of September to the end of October as migrants pass through. An increase was also recorded in the third week of November in 1974 and 1979. The spring passage is less marked and mainly confined to the second half of March.

The Kestrel is found in most parts of the island, commonly on the Oa and Rhinns peninsulas and infrequently in the main wooded areas. It hunts especially over heather moor, peat moss, rushy fields, rough permanent pastures and saltings. Two were on Beinn Bhan on 15th June 1978. It has mastery of stationary flight; rapid tail movements and wing adjustments maintain the bird's stability in a gusty wind. After scanning the ground from hovering flight or from telegraph poles or pylons, it descends to its victim in swoops punctuated by hovering. It also seizes prey from trees and bushes, or in full flight. Voles, mice and shrews are its principal prey, supplemented by a few small birds and earthworms. On Islay it has been seen taking Rock Doves, Song Thrushes and Stoats. Usually the pair or a solitary bird roosts at night, at or near the nest site, in a tree or in a cleft in crags.

Merlin *Falco columbarius*

The resident Merlin (*F.c.aesalon*) is smaller and lighter in colour than the Icelandic subspecies (*F.c.subaesalon*), which is likely to be a passage visitor in small numbers; ringed birds from Iceland have been recovered in Scotland, and small increases in numbers sighted on Islay are recorded for mid-September, October, late March and much of April. It is probably under-recorded, and present afforestation may reduce numbers as the tree canopies close in. In 1986 there were at least eight, possibly 15, summer home ranges in open country on

Islay. These falcons occur particularly on heather and grass moorland, but also on blanket and raised bog, permanent and especially rushy pastures, sand dunes and saltings, young plantations and areas with scattered bushes. Their distribution is well known on the Rhinns but is unknown or poorly known in the east.

The Merlin uses low commanding perches, especially fence posts and walls, but also small bushes. This falcon hunts from a low swift flight, rising slightly before striking close to the ground or on the ground. It has been said to imitate the flight pattern of its prey, allowing a closer approach before alarming the victim. Moorland passerines and waders are typical prey; on Islay it has been seen taking Meadow Pipits, Starlings, Reed Buntings, Redwings and Rock Doves, as well as Rabbits, lizards and flying insects, and it may also take Skylarks and chats. The Merlin roosts at night on the ground, in heather, in scrub such as sallow, and on crags; sometimes in small groups in winter.

Hobby *Falco subbuteo*

A scarce vagrant to Islay, recorded thrice in 20 years to 1986. It bred near Perth in 1887 and now breeds in southern England and much of the Continent, visiting Scotland annually between May and September, often in May or June. It winters in southern Africa. One was shot near Foreland in 1966 or 1967; another was seen at Knockanbearach, near Bridgend, on 17th May 1973; and an immature was at Ardnave on 13th September 1977.

Gyrfalcon *Falco rusticolus*

A rare vagrant from Greenland and possibly Iceland; most winter in coastal areas of southern Greenland and Iceland, but a few sometimes wander to the British Isles, perhaps in years when many erupt from Greenland. Scottish records extend from September to May, particularly December to April. The earliest record on Islay is of a white-plumaged bird shot in 1862; in 1867 four were killed, two white- and two dark-plumaged; then in 1888 a single bird was shot. Two white birds were present in 1978/9. The first, a small one, was sighted several times on the Rhinns; it was at Easter Ellister on 22nd December 1978, and was last seen eating a Rabbit at Bruichladdich on 25th April 1979. The second, larger, bird was south of Bowmore at Loanbaan on 22nd February and at Loch Tallant on 2nd March. Then the two were together at Gruinart on 18th March before the large female was found poisoned alongside bait on Dun Nosebridge on 19th March 1979. A dark third bird was at Loch Lossit on 17th December 1979. Other dark birds appeared at Kilnave on 17th September 1982 and in the Loch Gorm area from 9th to 15th October 1987. In general, the dark birds breed at more southerly locations in Greenland and Iceland than do the light birds.

Peregrine *Falco peregrinus*

The Peregrine has been a breeding resident for centuries; there are records from Colonsay dated 1343 and 1549 and from Islay dated 1772 and 1892. In the present century there was a major decline of Scottish Peregrines in the early 1960s caused by pesticides; following controls, a slow recovery began in the mid-1960s, filling many sites by the mid-1970s. Up to 17 coastal and three inland eyries are known; six have nearest neighbours at less than 2 km (1¼ miles) which are not known to have been occupied in the same years. The maximum potential population is thus 14 pairs, but the maximum recorded was eight pairs in 1977; three might have been overlooked. Bridgend and Gruinart Flats, Bruichladdich Pier Starling roost and seabird cliff colonies are regularly visited by Peregrines. These birds have been recorded in most inland habitats but are probably rare over the large conifer plantations and the barren quartzite hills.

This falcon scans when soaring on updraughts and from hill, crag, cliff or tree. It stoops very fast at either steep or low angles towards bird groups, most prey being taken on the wing with a final snatch. On Islay it has taken Fulmar, Barnacle Goose, Mallard, Garganey, Pintail, Red Grouse, Pheasant, Moorhen, Oystercatcher, Ringer Plover, Lapwing, Dunlin, Curlew, Redshank, Common

Peregrine (John Govett)

Gull, Rock Dove, Woodpigeon, Swallow, pipit, Chough, Starling and finch. An individual Peregrine may develop a special skill, such as that of snatching Starlings as they gather at the Bruichladdich roost or Woodpigeons from the tops of trees as they settle down to roost in Bridgend Woods. Some take prey to special plucking places. Misty weather may restrict this fleet predator to pedestrian prey or to robbing nests or other birds. Peregrine roosts, like their nests, are often on cliff ledges. Protection from excessive disturbance is especially important for the well-being of this species.

Red Grouse *Lagopus lagopus scoticus*

A resident gamebird that is sedentary and supported by management. It was present in 1772, and since 1842 records show fluctuations between abundance and scarcity over cycles of about 20 years. The last steep decline was in the early 1970s, and sightings have been rare ever since. Periodic outbreaks of disease appear to be the principal cause; a lack of manpower owing to high costs, reducing the efficiency of heather management, may be prolonging the current period of low numbers. Furthermore, afforestation provides cover for Hooded Crows, which take grouse eggs and chicks. It seems unlikely that Red Grouse will recover in those parts of the island affected by these factors.

Red Grouse are usually found on heather moors and also on grassland, but five were recorded at Claggain Bay on 13th August 1985 and five were seen at Ardnave Point on 3rd February 1986. Most of their food is picked from the ground, but they also feed from low bushes and even from trees in winter. They will dig through snow to reach food, feeding principally on heather and selecting those parts, at heights and of such ages, that are most rich in nitrogen and phosphorus. Chicks also take insects and spiders. They mostly roost communally and at night, on the ground in small open sites sheltered by clumps of vegetation, rock or hillocks. A fresh site is used every night.

Ptarmigan *Lagopus mutus*

The Ptarmigan breeds on high ground in the highlands of Scotland and in the mountains of Skye, Mull and Jura. Pennant reported 'a very few' on Islay in 1772; one was shot in Gleann Leòra in 1846, and the keeper at Ardimersay saw one in 1850. There have been several records this century: one flew into a Port Ellen house in 1913; a brood was seen on the summit of Glas Bheinn in 1936; birds were said to be there in 1946; and one was shot on the same hill in 1967. Twenty years later, the status of this species on Islay is in doubt, but there were several sightings on the Paps of Jura from 1st to 20th December 1977. Thus the Ptarmigan appears to have been rare since at least 1772, and is likely to be so on the nutrient-poor areas of the quartzite outcrop.

Black Grouse   *Tetrao tetrix*

The Black Grouse is a sedentary, resident gamebird supported by management. Islay lies at the western extremity of this species' range, which extends right across northern Eurasia. Numbers have fluctuated owing to disease, over-shooting of males and re-introductions. The earliest record is for 1677; it was abundant in 1840; almost exterminated by 1919; recovered by 1926 and was again seriously reduced by 1948; it recovered again but has been at a low ebb since the early 1970s. It ranges from scrubby woodland, which is sometimes confined to the smallest glens, out onto moors and grasslands. Thirty were reported at Gruinart on 5th December 1982, and individuals are still occasionally seen in the Gorm area, as well as at other widely scattered localities, including Killinallan and the moors between Ardtalla and Proaig. Leks are not recorded, but a locality near Foreland House known as Carn nan Coileach, or 'Rock of the Cocks', is thought to have been the site of a lek.

This species is vegetarian; it eats catkins, berries, nutlets, new shoots on bushes and buds; chicks take ants and spiders. On Islay it has been reported feeding on birch, willow, hazel, heather and stubble. In 1874 it was reported that the stubbles of Islay were dotted with Black Grouse. It roosts in scattered groups at night on the ground, often among heather, or in trees and bushes.

Black Grouse (Brian Southern)

Red-legged Partridge *Alectoris rufa*

A species resident in France and Iberia that was introduced over 200 years ago to southeast England, where it is now feral. Many introductions to Scotland have resulted in a few self-supporting populations in the drier east. In 1953 or 1954, about 18 were hatched from imported eggs and set free in the sand hills near Laggan, but after a few weeks they could not be found. Several were introduced to sandy pastures at Kilchiaran in 1985 and were still there in the summer of 1987. They appear to have been crosses, probably between *A. rufa* and *A. chukar*, a species native to Turkey and regions further east.

Grey Partridge *Perdix perdix*

Probably extinct on Islay, but resident on mainland Scotland east and south of the Highlands. It bred well on Islay during the dry spring of 1969, but is seriously reduced by cold damp springs. The earliest record is for 1794, and it was plentiful at times between 1842 and 1969, helped by periodic introductions to the sporting estates. A series of failed introductions from 1971 to 1975 resulted in rare sightings and the last record is of one bird in June 1979.

Quail *Coturnix coturnix*

The Quail is an irregular and scarce migrant. It breeds sporadically in most parts of the British Isles but most rarely near western coasts. Most winter in Africa, but when birds breed in Ireland they may overwinter. From 1840 to 1849, the Kildalton Estate keeper saw three in autumn. Over the same span of years, three were recorded on the Islay Estate during the winter; one was shot near Bridgend on 1st February 1844. During the breeding season, one was reported on 18th June 1970 and another was heard on Gruinart Flats on 21st May 1978.

Pheasant *Phasianus colchicus*

A feral resident gamebird introduced about 1840; stocks are replenished yearly by artificial rearing. Hooded Crows and Hen Harriers are its principal predators, and the feral groups are likely to benefit from cover provided by further afforestation. This species is essentially a ground runner and is reluctant to fly. Flights normally extend only a few hundred metres, but very exceptionally a few kilometres across water. It is found in all parts of the island, usually not far from woods, copses or scrub, especially on farmland in rushy permanent pastures and arable fields, but also on heather moors and even occasionally in sand dunes. In 1876, it was reported to be surviving on the wildest moors without artificial feeding.

111

In winter, Pheasants retreat from open habitats to the shelter of woods and the sexes forage in separate flocks; Islay's relatively mild winters probably help feral birds to survive. To obtain food, it scratches with its feet and pecks or digs with its beak, excavating holes up to 8 cm (3 in) deep, sometimes rummaging among leaf litter or even dead seaweed for insects, spiders and other invertebrates. It may jump to obtain berries or scratch through snow and frozen litter. On Islay, Pheasants have been noted taking spilled grain from roads and lanes, at livestock feeding stations and in farmyards, and taking wild seeds, hazelnuts, blackberries, catapillars and other large insects or their larvae. They also consume acorns, the green shoots of grasses, roots, tubers and small arthropods. Their roosts are on the ground or in trees and are mainly nocturnal and communal.

Water Rail *Rallus aquaticus*

A scarce resident and irregular winter visitor and passage migrant that is probably much under-recorded. Records in game books and at the Rhinns Lighthouse suggest that it has been present for the last hundred years. Water Rails, presumably on passage, visit the lighthouse from mid-September to early November; a spring passage is not known. A wintering bird was at Easter Ellister from 28th October 1985 to 14th March 1986. One to three birds were recorded in most winters from 1971 to 1987, widely scattered through the island. Some were in wet rushy fields or overgrown ditches, but only Bridgend saltings has held this rail over several years, with eight sightings in six years from 1972 to 1982. These migrants and wintering birds probably come from Fennoscandia, as have ringed birds recovered in mainland Scotland and Northern Ireland.

The Water Rail breeds in extensive areas of aquatic vegetation. In 1897 it was said to abound at Foreland Marsh, where young with adults were seen in 1978. One was at Loch Tallant, Bowmore, where there is a very extensive reedbed, in the first week of June 1976, and another had two chicks by the small lochan southwest of Craigens on 15th July 1973. Grunting birds were at Loch Fada on 20th April 1974 and Loch Ballygrant, where there are further reedbeds, on 6th May 1974. The only other summer records are of a bird at Coullabus on 6th April 1975, perhaps just on Gruinart Flats, and another at Easter Ellister on 7th May 1987. This species feeds along set paths linking favoured localities, walking over waterlogged ground or soft mud, wading in the shallows or less often swimming. It takes insects, spiders, worms, small snails, crustaceans, small frogs, small birds or eggs, and also various water plants, seeds, berries or fruits; its diet on Islay, however, is not known.

Spotted Crake *Porzana porzana*

A scarce European visitor to Islay that is probably under-recorded. It arrives on the Scottish mainland in April and is most often recorded in May and June;

autumn passage birds are most common in August and September and probably come from Scandinavia. On Islay, one was shot in the 8 ha (20 acres) of Foreland Marsh on 29th September 1896 and was suspected of having bred. Another in a wet root field at Springbank, Bridgend, crossed the road to the saltings on 31st December 1973.

Corncrake *Crex crex*

A summer visitor that was said to be abounding in cultivated districts in 1849. Silage-cutting machines were introduced in the early 1960s and have increased in numbers, then spraying of herbicides began in the mid-1970s. A serious decline in Corncrakes was reported in 1978 and 1979, but surveys in 1985 and 1986 did not reveal any further decrease.

This species migrates at night from eastern Africa, south of the Sahara. Calling males are first heard during the last week of April or the first week of May. The most persistent and regular calling is heard in June during nights with

Corncrake (John Davies)

reasonable weather and especially between 01.00 and 03.00 hrs; some birds call at dusk and even in full daylight. Corncrakes are last heard towards the end of July or early in August, and departure for Africa probably takes place a little later. One was ringed on the Isle of Canna on 28th July 1980 and then noted at Port Charlotte on 30th June 1981. The birds are widely scattered throughout the farming districts, especially on pastures and in fields of hay or silage grass, but also occur in marshy areas with rushes, iris beds or reeds. All 23 calling sites located during the 1986 survey contained tall vegetation, 20 having silage grass or hay; 14 included a burn. These 23 sites were around Portnahaven (three), within 5 km (3 miles) of Port Charlotte (three), in the Loch Gorm Area (nine), within 5 km of Bridgend (four), and at Craigens, Sanaigmore, Kiells and Lagavulin. From 1960 to 1986, Corncrakes are known to have called from over 80 sites; adults have been seen occasionally and young very rarely. The Corncrake takes food from the ground and off plants; this includes insects, spiders, harvestmen, millipedes, earthworms, snails and slugs; also seeds, buds and some green plant parts. It probably roosts at or near the nest site.

See pages 42–3 for further information.

Moorhen   *Gallinula chloropus*

A resident that appears to have been common in the 1840s; numbers have fluctuated since. It was said to be at a low ebb in 1892 and 1948, probably as a result of excessive shooting. Counting is difficult owing to its skulking habit and its reluctance to take flight. It is certainly under-recorded, but there are probably over 25 pairs on the island.

This species requires dense aquatic vegetation for cover and nesting. Ditches or small pools with overhanging woody plants or a few tall aquatic plants suffice: places like Carnain Pond, the ditches alongside Cladville Lane, or the old river course across Gruinart Flats. On 16th December 1981, nine hid in a short culvert alongside the road southwest of Craigens to evade a Hen Harrier, and on 13th October 1986 there were 18 at the same locality. This latter is the largest number recorded at one site during the last 16 years. The Moorhen is also found on larger watercourses such as the Ballygrant Burn or the Sorn near Bridgend, and around inland lochs with some aquatic vegetation such as Loch Ballygrant, with its reedy north arm, and Loch nan Diol, Kildalton. It shuns the open waters of the larger lochs and usually chooses those with bordering farmland rather than moorland.

The Moorhen feeds while walking on land or floating plants, and when swimming it sifts from the surface, head-dips or up-ends. It usually finds the bulk of its food ashore, taking insects, spiders, worms, snails, small fish, birds' eggs and vegetable matter, including aquatic plants, cereals and berries. It is sometimes active on moonlit nights, and it roosts among reeds or similar plants, on specially built floating platforms or under ground cover.

Coot *Fulica atra*

The Coot is a resident and a winter visitor that is sketchily recorded. The visitors arrive in mid-September, presumably from the northeast, and build up to a maximum in November or December. There were over 100 on Loch Skerrols from 19th November 1973 to 4th January 1974, reaching a peak of 136 on 2nd December 1973. The first of the visitors appear to leave in February but others do not depart until late March, leaving a few residents, probably fewer than ten. This species prefers well-vegetated still waters, but tolerates some exposure and wave action. Eighty per cent of all records originate at Lochs Skerrols and Ballygrant; juveniles have been seen on these as well as on Loch Lossit and the small distillery pond at Port Ellen. It is also occasionally seen on some other fishing lochs or on the slow-flowing lower reaches of the Rivers Sorn and Kintour.

The Coot uses a wide variety of feeding methods: it scrapes algae (*Chara*) off stems and stones underwater; picks off the water's surface; breaks off young emergent stems; leaps up to bring down food; up-ends to reach down to 40 cm ($1\frac{1}{3}$ ft); dives to 1–2 m (3–$6\frac{1}{2}$ ft), occasionally deeper; grazes in flocks when driven off water by high waves; and parasitises conspecifics and other waterbirds. By these various means it takes algae, aquatic plants, grasses, cereal seeds, earthworms, invertebrates, molluscs and fish. It is often active on moonlit nights, but at other times it roosts on rocky islets, sandbanks, or low branches of trees and bushes at the water's edge.

Crane *Grus grus*

A rare vagrant to Scotland that has occurred with increasing frequency since 1950. It breeds from Scandinavia across Siberia and winters in Mediterranean countries. Accidentals arrive in Scotland in all seasons but especially spring, peaking in May; one was on Islay for a few days in late May and early June 1986.

Oystercatcher *Haematopus ostralegus*

A partial migrant, winter visitor and resident; changes in status have probably been associated with climatic factors. There was none from early autumn 1850 until early in 1851. Now there is a southerly movement, mainly in August, returning in late February and March; many stop over and numbers in Bridgend Bay have reached maxima of about 600 during both passages. One or two hundred are present in spring and summer. Birds found exhausted or dead had been ringed at Barrow-in-Furness, Orkney and Glamorgan; also, a bird ringed in 1981 as an immature on the Exe Estuary bred at Uiskentuie in 1986 and 1987. The winter visitors probably come from points north to Iceland. There were

1,014 counted at Upper Loch Indaal on 28th February 1984 and 568 at Loch Gruinart on 13th April 1984. Oystercatchers are found around all coasts at all seasons, but they are less common on rocky coasts; they also use inland loch shores as comfort stations and have been seen at 300 m (980 ft) on Beinn Uraraidh. Their nests are among pebbles and shingle on the higher shore, and inland on river gravels. There are probably in the order of 200–300 residents.

After hatching, many parents take their young into pastures, where they feed them on earthworms, leatherjackets and other items for up to a few weeks. When back on shore, the chicks may begin to learn a specialist technique from their feeding parents: either hammering mussels or cockles at the weakest point or stalking them in shallow water to stab between the gaping valves. Then, after clipping muscles and ligaments in a prescribed sequence while twisting and opening the bill to prise open the shell, the flesh is swallowed whole. Others learn to probe repeatedly, along hollows or low levels on sand foreshores, for shellfish. On Islay's beaches these probe holes have traces of a central partition left by an open beak. Three species are taken: *Cardium edule* (cockles), *Tellina tenuis* and *Macoma balthica*. A few birds learn to flip small crabs on to their back and stab them through their mouth to the brain. Other prey include dog whelks, lugworms and earthworms. On Islay many of the latter are obtained from sandy flat fields. Oystercatchers roost at sheltered points around the coast: some, for example, on the flats southwest of Islay House and others on the little delta known as Ard Chruaidh downstream from Gartmain.

Ringed Plover   *Charadrius hiaticula*

The Ringed Plover on Islay is both resident and a passage migrant. There are many weeks outside the breeding season when all flocks contain fewer than 50 birds. Yet isolated counts of 100 or 200 are spread throughout this period, suggesting that these are stop-over flocks rather than wintering flocks. The lowest numbers are found in June and July, when something of the order of 200 residents are present. Islay lies midway between two important stop-over sites, the Uists and the Solway Firth, on a flyway from northeast Canada, Greenland and Iceland down the East Atlantic seaboard to Africa. Most arctic Ringed Plovers on this flyway winter in West Africa, while others breeding at lower latitudes do not travel beyond Iberia. This is known as leapfrog migration. Some Islay birds may undertake short-distance migrations south for winter, but there is no direct evidence. Passage-migrant flocks have been seen at Ardnave, Loch Gruinart and especially around Upper Loch Indaal; they have also been seen flying southwest down Loch Indaal in the evening. Both migrants and residents occur on all but the more rocky and cliffed coasts, especially on sand or shingle beaches.

Ringed Plovers use visual cues to locate food during a stop-run-peck action. Less often, they are seen foot-trembling: standing on one leg while rapidly vibrating the other with toes just in contact with a sandy surface. It is presumed

116

that this simulates vibrations created by rain or an incoming tide, encouraging prey to emerge. The plovers take marine worms, small crustacea, and molluscs, sandhoppers or other invertebrates. To maintain energy requirements in midwinter, night feeding is at least as important as day feeding. They occasionally feed on grass near the beaches. In the non-breeding seasons they roost communally on saltmarsh, the higher parts of beaches, or adjacent grassland, including machair, when feeding opportunities are reduced around high tide. Ringed Plovers often nest on the storm beach in situations vulnerable to disturbance by humans and their pets. The agitated noisy displays of parent birds at any time between early April and late July should be heeded.

Dotterel   *Charadrius morinellus*

A scarce passage migrant that breeds high in the Grampians and northern Highlands, and also in Scandinavia and Siberia. It normally winters in North Africa, but two were shot at Ardimersay on the Kildalton Estate on 17th February 1843; then, in 1892, it was reported that Dotterels occurred on the watershed of Islay. The autumn passage through Scotland takes place mainly in August and September; one was seen on Islay on 9th September 1937, and eight flew south over Loch Cam and Loch Skerrols on 12th September 1974. A pair was a few miles north of Lealt, Jura, on 23rd March 1982, and two were on Beinn Bhàn on 13th May 1987.

Golden Plover   *Pluvialis apricaria*

Golden Plover (Brian Southern)

On Islay, this species is a winter visitor, passage migrant, and a breeder on a small scale. Most breed in Iceland, many are on passage, some stop over briefly, and others may stay for much of the autumn and winter. They first arrive in mid-August but do not reach peak numbers until October, or in some years November. The largest flock was of 2,000 birds at Killinallan on 2nd November 1981, but from 100 to 400 is more normal. From mid-November to mid-February fewer than 150 is the norm, then the northward migration peaks in the second half of March, with flocks of 100–350 birds; exceptionally, 700 were on Gruinart Flats on 18th March 1976. Birds ringed in Iceland have been recovered on Islay in December and January.

Winter visitors and passage migrants frequent low-lying, open, flat pastures that are mainly on sandy tracts: for example, northeast of Killinallan, east of Gruinart Post Office, southwest of Ballinaby, between Gartbreck and Ronnachmore, and east of Sanaigmore. Islay's population breeds on remote moorland and is scattered thinly in the north and east; finds of fewer than ten birds are usual. The Golden Plover takes a wide range of prey, mostly from the surface or by shallow probes, especially beetles, earthworms and some plant material. It usually roosts in flocks at night, on saltings or mudflats at the head of Lochs Indaal and Gruinart, and on ploughed fields. Like the Lapwing, the Golden Plover is the subject of piratic attacks by Black-headed and Common Gulls.

Grey Plover   *Pluvialis squatarola*

A passage migrant and winter visitor, found in very small numbers. It breeds in the Siberian Arctic between the White Sea and the Taimyr Peninsula, and migrates via the Baltic and North Seas to winter on the coasts of western Europe and Africa. The first arrivals on Islay are noted as single birds in late August and early September. On 21st September 1963 one was killed on passage at the Rhinns Lighthouse, and another was seen passing Frenchman's Rocks on 30th October 1977. Numbers build up to a peak between mid-September and mid-October; the highest count, of 29, was made on 4th October 1975. A decrease into November probably marks a small southerly movement following moulting. The few winter records are all of fewer than 15 birds; these most probably leave in late March or early April, but this is inadequately documented. A few birds in summer plumage were on poor pasture near Killinallan on 25th May 1984. Apart from the records already mentioned, nearly all are of birds on silt, sand or shingle around Loch Indaal, Loch Gruinart or the Ardnave Peninsula.

The Grey Plover detects prey movement visually and then captures it by a combination of runs, stops and pecks. Some individuals may establish feeding territories, and feeding at night is particularly important to this species. On shores it takes polychaete worms, molluscs and crustaceans. It assembles on coastal sites to roost by day or night, often with other plover species.

Lapwing *Vanellus vanellus*

A passage migrant, summer visitor and regular breeder that is rare or absent during some winters. Frozen ground inhibits feeding and initiates movement to milder locations to the south or southwest. Large flocks of 500 to 1,700, and one of 3,000, have been recorded from August to March and particularly in September and October. They probably stop over on their journey from Scandinavia to their wintering grounds. Also, there are periods in winter when numbers are depleted; there are no records for the first half of February, and during the exceptional cold spell from mid-January to early March 1986 the species was rare on Islay. British birds have been recorded in Iberia during the winter. Breeding pairs are very conspicuous in May and June; 108 pairs were on the Gruinart Reserve in 1985 and 121 in 1986.

When feeding, Lapwings select the older pastures where earthworms are most abundant. To maximise prey detection, they choose flat to gently undulating grassland, well grazed by Rabbits or sheep, giving open views of ground around themselves: on raised beaches and terraces, machair, pebble spreads as around Carnain, some loch margins as at Ardnave and some ill-drained rushy pastures. The largest winter flocks are around Upper Loch Indaal or at Gruinart. In spring these birds establish territories and breed on the same pastures, as well as on nearby tilled land.

The Lapwing is a soil-feeding wader, taking earthworms, insects, spiders, woodlice and other ground-loving invertebrates. Earthworms are the chief prey in winter and beetles are important among the insects. It relies heavily on visual cues to the activity of prey, and stalks with a slow walk, sometimes ending with a run and peck, but often pausing, sometimes crouching, and then probing to a maximum depth of 3 cm ($1\frac{2}{5}$ in). Foot-trembling, a technique thought to simulate the patter of rain on a damp substrate, is sometimes used to encourage prey to the surface. Freezing of the surface sends prey to deeper levels, as well as making probing difficult. Feeding may take place at staging posts en route to traditional roosts, and around full moon it may continue through the night, roosting being left until daytime. Lapwing roosting is communal in the non-breeding seasons. Roosts may be on saltings, rocky shores or islets, shingle shores by inland lochs, or sandbanks in rivers.

The Lapwing is often chased by Common Gulls or Black-headed Gulls. These gulls join flocks of plovers to steal food, and individual Lapwings try to distance themselves from attentive gulls. Chases are common and the gulls collect any dropped prey. While the gulls are scanning for potential targets, however, they are also the first to respond to danger from predators and the Lapwings benefit from this early warning. Because Lapwings nest on the ground they are often threatened by the unwitting approach of other birds, domestic animals or man; or by predators likely to take eggs or chicks. Defence may be by distraction display, feigning a broken wing, or by mobbing. Lapwings are frequently seen mobbing Pheasants, Redshanks, members of the crow and gull families, domestic cats and sheep.

Knot *Calidris canutus*

The Knot on Islay is a passage migrant, moult visitor and short-term winter visitor. The average annual flock size has fluctuated: it was eight in 1972, 41 in 1976 and seven in 1985; this variation may be related to weather conditions in the breeding areas. This wader breeds in northern Greenland and northeast Canada, and migrates via Iceland to the British Isles, Iberia and West Africa. Flocks of up to about 90 birds stop on Islay to moult from mid-August to early October. In late autumn and winter, flocks of a similar size stay for short periods: exceptionally, 300 were at Loch Gruinart on 12th October 1984. A sizeable return migration is not recorded, but the last few flocks pass through in mid-May.

The Knot likes sandy shores firmed up with a finer surface film, but is also found on low rocky coasts. Most records refer to beaches around Upper Loch Indaal from Bruichladdich to Gartbreck; a maximum of 90 was counted near Bowmore on 15th September 1983. A few small flocks have been noted by Loch Gruinart and at Traigh Nostaig, Ardnave. It probes, pecks and occasionally ploughs with its bill inserted to about 1 cm ($\frac{2}{5}$ in), taking intertidal shellfish such as tellins, cockles, periwinkles, *Hydrobia*, and other invertebrates. Roosting takes place chiefly at high tide. At 17.45 hrs on 26th March 1978, 20 Knots were on the saltings on the north angle of Bridgend Bay.

Sanderling *Calidris alba*

The Sanderling is a passage migrant and winter visitor in very small numbers. A few non-breeding birds in summer plumage have been recorded in June. It comes from the high Arctic of northeast Greenland and perhaps northeast Canada and Siberia, migrating to West and possibly South Africa. Passage flocks are recorded in late July and on 19th September 1985, but there is no evidence for a spring passage northwards. In winter, small flocks have been observed in successive weeks on the same beach.

This active bird is found on sandy beaches, especially those with strong breakers. It is often seen on the Atlantic beaches, as well as the open beach of Laggan Bay, where the largest count of over 100 was made on 23rd July 1972 and eleven, mostly in breeding plumage, were noted on 15th June 1973. It is equally often seen on the beaches of Upper Loch Indaal, but this is due to more intensive birdwatching; the largest flock there was of 40 on 28th July 1980. At Loch Gruinart, 94 were seen on 20th February 1983.

The Sanderling runs rapidly up and down a beach, following the very last swash line and picking up small washed-in items with great dexterity. It also probes at short intervals, making fast runs with occasional pauses between probes. Its food comprises insects, small crustaceans, seeds and many other small items, including carrion. In midwinter it may continue feeding at high tide and at night. When roosting, Sanderlings pack closely together above high-water mark.

Little Stint   *Calidris minuta*

A passage migrant that breeds in the high-arctic coastal tundra of Lapland and Siberia and winters mainly in Africa south of the Sahara. Fewer than ten are seen in most years, between mid-August and mid-October, in Bridgend Bay or on the mudflats of Loch Gruinart. It is also occasionally recorded in ones and twos at Machir Bay, Ardnave Point and Bruichladdich. Exceptionally, 50–60 very tame birds were seen on Gruinart Flats on 16th September 1937. The only confirmed spring record is of five on the shore of Upper Loch Indaal after a storm on 6th March 1980.

Baird's Sandpiper   *Calidris bairdii*

A scarce vagrant from northwest Greenland and arctic Canada that normally winters in South America. In Scotland it is usually recorded in September, but Islay has yielded one of very few British summer records: an individual was recognised at Ronnachmore at the end of May 1979 and confirmed on 3rd June.

Pectoral Sandpiper   *Calidris melanotos*

A scarce vagrant from arctic Canada that normally winters in South America; it also breeds in Alaska and Siberia, yielding possible vagrants west to Europe. It is recorded annually in Scotland, mainly between mid-August and late October but also in spring from late May to July. Spring sightings are probably the previous autumn's transatlantic vagrants returning from further south. A single bird was on the beach outside the Port Ellen Distillery warehouse on 13th September 1975, and another at Bun-an-Uillt on 22nd June 1981.

Curlew Sandpiper   *Calidris ferruginea*

A passage migrant, found on Islay in small numbers, that breeds in arctic Siberian coastal tundra from 80° to 150° E and winters in Africa. Some fly along a great circle route to West Africa, passing down the east coast of England. The adults migrate first, followed up to a month later by those in their first year. The latter are more likely to veer off course, and it is a few of these that in some years have been recorded on Islay between 10th August and 18th October. One seen on 16th May 1981 was presumably on northward migration. Most are found on the sand and shingle shores of Upper Loch Indaal and Loch Gruinart. They commonly associate with their close relative, the Dunlin, and feed in a similar manner. They also roost communally with other *Calidris* species.

121

Purple Sandpiper *Calidris maritima*

A winter visitor and passage migrant in small numbers, with single birds also occasionally recorded in summer. These are probably from Iceland or Greenland, travelling down western coasts to winter at various stations to northern Portugal. Presumed passage flocks have been noted at Frenchman's Rocks, including 50 on 30th December 1974 and 70 on 15th February 1976. Visitors arrive around mid-October and depart during the first half of May.

The Purple Sandpiper is found on rocky coasts and skerries exposed to wave action; less commonly on small beaches between rocks or by harbour walls, where seaweed is piled up by storms or mussel shells exposed. Half of the records of wintering birds relate to the rocky shores of Bruichladdich; 45 were there on 29th December 1977. This sandpiper often associates with Turnstones and feeds by daylight within the intertidal zone. It is interrupted by high tide and is much hampered by stormy conditions. However, it runs deftly over rocks and seaweed uncovered by the tide, dodging waves, sometimes by fluttering in the air for a second or two. It picks prey out of rock crevices, from between shells and from among seaweed, and takes small molluscs, crustaceans, insects and annelid worms. This species roosts gregariously at traditional sites on the seaward side of rocks or harbour structures.

Dunlin *Calidris alpina*

The Dunlin comes to Islay as a passage migrant and both a winter and a summer visitor. Three races appear to be involved: *C.a.arctica, C.a.schinzii* and *C.a.alpina*. The breeding birds (*schinzii*) leave in August. Others of the same race from southeast Greenland and Iceland pass through during the latter half of July and August, all of them on their way to West Africa; 120 were counted on 16th July 1974. In the latter half of August, birds from northeast Greenland (*arctica*) are also on passage; 300 were recorded on 21st in 1973. This passage continues into September and early October; 203 were noted on 9th September 1983 and a similar number on 7th/8th October 1972. In the latter half of October very few Dunlins are seen; a few may appear around the turn of the month, then from mid-November to the end of January winter visitors (*alpina*) call in. These come from northern Scandinavia and east to the White Sea and have been moulting in the Wadden Sea; on 15th November 1984 there were 480 at Loch Gruinart, and in January 1985 some 377 were there.

Return movements are underway in February and March. Very few Dunlins are recorded during the fortnight around the end of March, then Islay's breeders (*schinzii*) return, the earliest being three on Tais Bheinn and two on Beinn Bheigeir above Ardtalla on 8th April 1974. From the end of April to early June Icelandic and Greenland birds (*schinzii* and *arctica*) are on passage, counts including 200 on 29th April 1973, 150 on 21st May 1970 and 121 on 23rd May 1975.

Most migrants and visitors are seen on the soft shores of Loch Indaal, but some are found at the head of Loch Gruinart or around the Ardnave Peninsula. At Frenchman's Rocks small numbers have been seen during the late summer passage, but none has been recorded there in spring.

The local Dunlins nest on peat and heather moors, often near peaty lochans; they are probably well but thinly distributed and are known principally in northwest and central Islay, including those on Eilean na Muice Duibhe, northwest of Duich. A nest with four eggs was found near Beinn a' Chuirn, 3 km (2 miles) north of Balole, at the end of May 1972, and another nest on the marsh east of Loch Gorm had four eggs on 10th May 1978. Displaying or singing birds have been noted in June at Loch a' Gheoidh, Loch Eighinn, Sanaigmore and on Rubha Mor by Loch Gorm; also, chicks were seen at Feur Lochain, southwest of Sanaigmore, on 2nd June 1976. Some nesting Dunlins may associate with Golden Plovers, using them as 'sentinels'. The continued afforestation of moorland must decrease the habitat area available to the Dunlin for breeding.

This species feeds by pecking, probing, jabbing, and 'stitching', this last method being repeated jabbing at the surface while walking, leaving chains of shallow holes. It takes a wide range of small shellfish, bristleworms, amphipods, insect larvae and other invertebrates from muddy and sandy shores, and occasionally by hunting on coastal pastures. Dunlins roost on tidal flats, especially at the head of Loch Indaal, where they take up sheltered positions near Curlews, possibly using them, too, as 'sentinels'. The timing of roosting is governed by the tidal cycle.

Buff-breasted Sandpiper *Tryngites subruficollis*

A very scarce vagrant from arctic Canada and Alaska that normally winters on the pampas of South America. It is recorded annually in Scotland, mainly in September but also in May, June and August. One at Machir Bay on 28th September 1971 appeared incapable of flight and was the first record for the Inner Hebrides.

Ruff *Philomachus pugnax*

A rare passage migrant, recorded on Islay from mid-August to late October, more rarely in October and November, and usually as single birds but also in groups of up to 16. The spring passage is represented by singles at Loch Gruinart on 3rd April 1981 and on 16th and 24th April 1985. There were 22 records of birds on autumn passage between 1971 and 1981. Scottish migrants are probably mainly from Fennoscandia and Russia; they winter in West Africa and at points en route. The Islay sightings have been on saltings and wet fields round the heads of the two sea-lochs, with a minority on flooded fields near Port Ellen, Kilchiaran, Saligo and Ardnave Loch.

Jack Snipe *Lymnocryptes minimus*

A winter visitor noted in small numbers from September to April, but probably much under-recorded. Single birds are occasionally recorded on the Gruinart Reserve in winter. It breeds in Fennoscandia and northern USSR, British winterers coming from the western part of this range. Single birds seen on 6th August 1970, 30th July 1974 and 6th June 1976 were probably non-breeders. This species is found on marshy ground throughout Islay, but mostly recorded around the heads of the two sea-lochs, on the moors of the Oa and by Loch Corr. It feeds at night by pecking and probing to obtain insects and their larvae, snails, seeds and other plant remains. Consequently it roosts chiefly by day, solitarily and jn the vicinity of water.

Snipe *Gallinago gallinago*

A winter visitor, resident and passage migrant that has been very common for at least the last 100 years; now afforestation threatens to reduce its numbers. A high proportion of the records are of single birds put up accidentally; of these, many more relate to winter than to summer, in spite of the reduced cover by observers in winter. These facts, together with shooting returns, suggest a notable immigration of winter visitors. Ringed birds in Ireland have proved to be residents. Presumed residents on Islay are heard 'drumming' and 'singing' from mid-March to early July, especially at dusk or in damp overcast conditions. Sixty pairs bred on the Gruinart Reserve in 1986. Ringing has shown that a high proportion of Icelandic migrants winter in Ireland and, since the Snipe is not known in Greenland, Islay's wintering birds and passage migrants are likely to come from Iceland. The autumn passage commences in late August or early September and continues to at least the end of October. During this period, large flocks have occasionally been recorded and 'kills' have occurred at the Rhinns Lighthouse. A spring passage has not been noted.

The fast, erratic and high escape flight of the species, falling quickly back to ground, provides a challenge to shooting parties organised on the estates. These birds are found on soft soil as on Gruinart Flats or on other ill-drained fields with rushes, on the marshy areas adjacent to rivers and lochs such as Ardnave Loch, on saltings and in the slacks within machair, on blanket bogs and in ditches; all are common habitats on Islay. Snipe are widespread but secretive, yet can occasionally be seen perching on a wall.

Snipe probe in mud or ooze, often while wading in shallow water, sometimes while working slowly and sometimes in an arc while standing. Food is detected by touch with the sensitive bill, but occasionally a run is followed by an oblique lunge, suggesting detection of prey by sight. Insects, worms, crustaceans and plant material are taken. Feeding in roadside ditches sometimes leads to the death of these birds on the road. Snipe roost by night, or by day when active on moonlit nights, and show high fidelity to particular sites.

Great Snipe *Gallinago media*

A rare vagrant from Scandinavia that winters in Africa south of the Sahara, normally migrating directly south or north. Most Scottish records are dated between early September and late October. One was at the Rhinns Lighthouse on 27th November 1888 and another on the Oa on 11th September 1974, the latter being regarded only as probable by the *British Birds* Rarities Committee.

Long-billed Dowitcher *Limnodromus scolopaceus*

A rare vagrant that breeds in northern Alaska and nearby parts of Canada and Siberia, normally wintering from the southern United States to Guatemala. It has been seen in Scotland in all months except July, especially May, September and October. One was present at a pool just west of the Islay Airport from 3rd to 23rd June 1986.

Woodcock *Scolopax rusticola*

A passage migrant and winter visitor in small numbers that probably colonised Islay some time in the first half of the 19th century. Some may stay for the winter, but each immigration appears to be followed by a decrease up to two months later. Numbers are higher on Islay when feeding on the mainland is impeded by prolonged frosts. A decrease in numbers on the mainland since the 1950s has been attributed to extensive afforestation. The Woodcock does not breed in northwest Scotland, but a high proportion of Scandinavian birds winter in the British Isles. Some arrive in Islay in the second half of October but the main immigration is in November, concentrated into a period of favourable weather. Most leave again between mid-December and mid-January, probably bound for Ireland. Scandinavian-ringed Woodcock have been recovered in mainland Argyll and Antrim during January. The return migration is mainly during March, but is poorly documented on Islay. Summer visitors, probably from Ireland, arrive as the winterers depart; over three-quarters of British birds migrate within the British Isles.

This species occurs in woods with good ground cover, under rhododendron and gorse clumps, and less often among tall dense grasses, heather or bracken on moors. Two birds were put up on Am Miador, Sanaig, on 8th January 1987; but it is most predictably seen when 'roding' at twilight from March to July, usually alongside or over open woods around Bridgend. It feeds at night in damp or swampy places and ditches, but by day when the nights are frosty. It probes using a touch-sensitive bill and picks from under litter, taking mainly

125

earthworms and the larvae of insects. The Woodcock is very well camouflaged when roosting in dense cover.

Black-tailed Godwit   *Limosa limosa islandica*

The Black-tailed Godwit is a scarce passage migrant that occasionally summers; the maximum numbers recorded were seven at Port Charlotte on 20th June 1985, and 17 on Gruinart Flats on 16th August 1987. These birds breed in Iceland and pass through Islay in July to October, with a probable peak in September; five were at Craigens on 14th September 1980. They winter further south in the British Isles and at points en route to southwest Spain. The return passage is not well recorded but appears to be from mid-March to mid-May; four were at Loch Gruinart on 31st March 1981.

This wader prefers mudflats and wet pastures. Two-thirds of the 31 records come from Upper Loch Indaal; a quarter are from the head of Loch Gruinart and fields near Craigens, while other single records are from widely scattered localities. It feeds by vertical probing and pecking in mud and soft soil, taking insects, their larvae, worms, snails, small shellfish and seeds. Roosting is nocturnal, in compact flocks and often on grassland.

Bar-tailed Godwit   *Limosa lapponica*

The Bar-tailed Godwit is a winter visitor, passage migrant and non-breeding summer visitor. The years 1971 to 1982 yielded winter counts of up to 420 birds, and the largest migrant flock was one of 500 on the shore of Upper Loch Indaal on 15th September 1980. Fewer than 100 non-breeding birds summer on Islay. Birds of the race *lapponica* winter in the British Isles and breed in Lapland and arctic Russia east to the Taimyr Peninsula. They migrate via the Baltic and Wadden Seas, and some cross the North Sea to Britain, but many stop over on tidal flats to moult. Some of the latter then fly west to Britain. Others do not stop over until they reach the Wash or Morecambe Bay, and yet others continue on to moult on wintering grounds, some staying on and some passing through Islay. Thus Bar-tailed Godwits arrive on Islay in waves between late July and the end of January, on dates dependent on their migration itineraries and on the onset of severe weather at their staging posts. Numbers peak in late December or January, followed by departures through to late April.

The Bar-tailed Godwit is usually found on sandy beaches or silty, tidal flats. The largest areas of suitable habitat, the largest counts and the majority of flock sightings are all around Upper Loch Indaal. The only inland record is of five by Loch Gorm on 13th May 1976. This wader takes bristleworms, molluscs, and crustacea. It searches damp areas around the water's edge and shallows down to a depth of 15 cm (6 in), sometimes with both head and neck immersed. It probes while walking, sometimes 'stitching', that is making a rapid series of shallow trial probes close together to locate prey. It also picks from the surface and has a mowing action like that of the Redshank. Communal roosts form on the highest section of the beach, on saltings, or on coastal fields during high spring tides.

Whimbrel   *Numenius phaeopus*

A regular passage migrant seen in small numbers; maximum counts for both spring and autumn were in the mid-1950s, but at least 55 were at Coul on 5th May 1980. The subspecies seen on Islay (*N.p.phaeopus*) breeds in northernmost Scotland, Iceland and east across Lapland to beyond the Urals. Nearly all of Islay's birds are likely to be in the exodus from Iceland in August, but the earliest record is for 4th July and the latest 26th October; 20 were on Loch Gruinart in October 1985. They winter in tropical West Africa and some pass through Islay on their northward migration, chiefly from mid-April to late May. Exceptionally, single birds are seen on the island in March; these may have wintered in maritime Europe. Also, in some years, a few may linger until mid-June; perhaps these summer in northern Scotland.

Recorded localities are widely scattered on grassland, including the flats at the heads of the sea-lochs and machair; also on shingly and rocky coasts. The feeding actions of this wader include picking from the ground surface and, more rarely, shallow probing. It takes molluscs, small crustaceans and annelid worms from shores, and snails, slugs and insects from grassland. Feeding on the blanket bogs of Islay, where it may take berries as well as insects, awaits recording. It often associates with Curlews when feeding or roosting.

Curlew   *Numenius arquata*

A winter visitor in large numbers and a passage migrant; also breeds, probably as both summer visitor and resident. Breeding was first recorded in 1891; the species then became firmly established during the first few decades of this century as the range expanded through Scotland. About two-thirds of Scottish Curlews winter in Ireland, and these probably include birds breeding on Islay. As these leave in July, immigrants arrive mainly from northern Scotland and Norway. Most of the adults start a moult lasting two-and-a-half months soon after they arrive. A peak number of 1,086 birds was at Bridgend Bay on 15th September 1981, and 914 were there in August 1985. There is a temporary reduction of number in November and December, suggesting some midwinter movements. Most wintering birds leave by late March; from mid-March onwards others set up breeding territories, where their spectacular display flight can be seen, though with decreasing frequency through July.

This species can be seen throughout the island, breeding at low densities in open landscapes. It was originally confined to moorland but, concurrent with the range expansion early this century, it extended into rough and rushy pastures.

Forty-seven pairs bred on the Gruinart Reserve in 1986. During the winter months it is coastal, commonly gathering in flocks of 30–80 birds on stubbles, pastures and shores around the sea-lochs and on the Atlantic coast machair. A few birds remain in coastal areas during the breeding season, especially in May; these are likely to be first-year birds.

The Curlew uses three feeding methods: pecking at the ground surface, jabbing to half-bill depth, and probing to from half- to full-bill depth. Pecking and jabbing are quick, often exploratory actions, whereas probing is more prolonged and usually results in capture. It may invert its head to probe under objects with its strongly curved bill. Inland, it feeds on a wide range of insects, earthworms, spiders, woodlice, eggs, amphibians and plants, including moorland berries and grain from grasses and cereals. On the coast in the swash zone and shallows, it takes annelid worms, shellfish, crabs, crustaceans and small fish. On Islay, cockles, two other species of bivalve, lugworms and bristleworms are available to the Curlew in Bridgend Bay. Most males have bills under 130 mm (5 in) long, whereas the bills of most females are over 130 mm, permitting the latter to take food from depths out of reach of the former. Feeding sometimes takes place on moonlit nights and groups may be seen roosting during the day. Curlews form large flocks on grassy and rocky peninsulas, and on low rocky islets. At the head of Loch Indaal, counts of around 1,000 have been made in the months of July to October and January to April.

Spotted Redshank   *Tringa erythropus*

A scarce passage migrant from Lapland, wintering mostly in West Africa, while a few remain in Atlantic Europe, south of the Highlands of Scotland. Thirteen Islay records fall between 13th August and 6th December, six of these from mid-September to mid-October. Only one bird has been reported present in spring, on 10th May 1976. Most sightings have been around Bridgend Bay, with others at Machir Bay and Loch Gruinart.

Redshank   *Tringa totanus*

A winter visitor, passage migrant, breeding summer visitor and probable resident. The Redshank was reported common on shores from 1850 onwards and was found inland increasingly in the 20th century, but the population has decreased during the last decade. Towards the end of June and into July, the breeding birds (*T.t.totanus*) move to the coast; many migrate short distances into Ireland and along the Irish Sea coasts. One bird, killed on the road at Bridgend on 3rd July 1977, had been ringed in the Ogwen Valley near Bangor, North Wales, on 23rd March 1974. Winter visitors from Iceland (*T.t.robusta*) first arrive in late June, building up to over 200 in September; most depart again for Iceland during April. Summer visitors probably arrive in March; although smaller than the Icelandic race, they cannot be distinguished without capture. Twelve pairs bred on the Gruinart Reserve in 1985 and 1986.

The Redshank is found throughout the island in open habitats having ready access to wetland feeding. Half of the records relate to tidal flats and saltings; almost another third are scattered around the many sandy and shingle bays, even very small ones within rocky stretches of coast. The remainder are inland on marshy areas by the more productive lochs, at rain flashes in fields, on the damper parts of machair and at pools on moors. Counts of over 100 have been made only in Bridgend Bay and at Loch Gruinart during times of passage. The widely distributed moorland breeders are severely under-recorded.

This wader exploits almost any damp habitat, from tidal muds to rushy fields and rain flashes. It pecks, jabs and probes up to full-bill depth. The former actions are often exploratory, but may be followed by a short dash to capture. Jabs are made with the bill slightly agape, suggesting the use of a sense of touch, but more often these waders detect prey movement by sight. A side-to-side swishing movement with the bill slightly agape, performed as the bird walks slowly forward in shallows, enables the area to be searched for animals just below the surface. On the coast the Redshank feeds from wet areas and tidal pools, taking small shellfish, bristleworms and crustaceans, species of which are available in Bridgend Bay. Inland, it feeds on earthworms, cranefly larvae and adult beetles. This species roosts in loose flocks or individually on the coast, often on saltings, the timing being dependent on the tidal cycle.

Greenshank   *Tringa nebularia*

The Greenshank is present on Islay in small numbers as a passage migrant, winter visitor and summer visitor. Breeding is possible but not proved. It breeds in northern Scotland, Fennoscandia and eastwards across Siberia. Most of the migrants passing through Islay southwards in August and September probably come from northern Scotland; those from Continental Europe travel via the Baltic and North Sea to Africa south of the Sahara, and are seen mostly in the southeast parts of Britain. In the spring a northward movement cannot be recognised in Islay records, except that 'quite a few' in Bridgend Bay some time in May 1933 may have been passage birds.

The Greenshank favours quiet brackish or fresh waters in moderately open country. Half of the sightings have been in Bridgend Bay and another third in the Gruinart area. Only about 7 per cent were inland: one in a drainage ditch, one by a small stream, three on the shores of relatively productive lochs, and one on Beinn Tart a' Mhill. The largest group was of 26 in Bridgend Bay on 9th September 1973; nearly all sightings, however, have been of fewer than five birds and often only of one. This wader has been seen to use most of the techniques attributed to waterside birds: it wades to full-leg depth, pecks from standing, walking or running, 'mows' from side to side while walking, probes, and chases fish with a 'dash and lunge'. Less often it uses foot-trembling, flushes prey with a high-stepping dance, flips over objects with its bill, and swims to up-end like a duck. A wide variety of prey is taken, varying with habitat and season: insects, crustaceans, molluscs, small fish, worms and amphibians. It is sometimes active at night and roosts in various habitats close to water. On Islay, Greenshanks have been seen roosting with Curlews in Bridgend Bay, presumably on the saltings.

Greater Yellowlegs *Tringa melanoleuca*

A very scarce vagrant that breeds across sub-arctic Canada and normally migrates to the southern United States and places south to Tierra del Fuego. One was seen and photographed on grass overlooking the central part of Laggan Bay near the Uisge na Criche on 25th October 1985.

Green Sandpiper *Tringa ochropus*

The Green Sandpiper is a scarce passage migrant that breeds in Fennoscandia, Baltic countries and the USSR. Islay's birds are likely to be from Fennoscandia, and many from there winter in West Africa, Morocco and south of the Sahara. The main autumn movement through Islay is marked by six records in August and three in September. One representing the return migration of April and May was observed in Bridgend Bay on 20th April 1977; another was at Loch Gruinart on 19th May 1987. All sightings were of single birds.

This species likes fresh water: four have been reported from around the head of Loch Indaal; at least one in marshy ground; two were at Loch Corr, Sanaig; two flew over Easter Ellister; and one was at Bruichladdich.

Wood Sandpiper *Tringa glareola*

A scarce summer visitor and passage migrant, probably coming from Fennoscandia; most continue further south and winter at points en route to West Africa. Those passing through Scotland do so mainly in May, returning from mid-July to mid-October; a few nest in the Highlands. The spring passage is not truly represented by Islay records; the earliest were a single bird at Airigh Dhaibhaidh, Duich, on 7th June 1954 and two at Bridgend on 7th June 1963. Others that may have been non-breeding birds were one at a pool on the Bridgend saltings on 8th July 1962, one at Bridgend on 18th June 1977, and two near Bun-an-Uillt on 15th June 1986. The only birds noted during the autumn migration period have been singles southwest of Loch Corr, Sanaig, on 14th September 1974, and at Loch Gruinart from 28th to 30th September 1984.

Common Sandpiper *Actitis hypoleucos*

The Common Sandpiper is a regular summer visitor for which no passage has been detected, probably because of a nocturnal or high-flying habit. There are no records of birds from October to March. Most migrate to Africa, probably West Africa from the Gambia to Nigeria. Departure dates are poorly recorded; several appeared ready to leave from Dun Athad on 9th August 1976, and the last left Loch Gruinart at the end of August 1985. They arrive back on Islay mainly between 19th and 30th April. A bird ringed on Islay in June 1923 was reported 100 km (62 miles) southwest of Paris in late April 1925.

Pairs establish linear territories along rivers and streams, along the shore of a loch or along relatively sheltered coasts; always with shingly to rocky, rather than sandy or muddy margins. Three pairs were displaying along 1 km (0.6 miles) of river upstream of Kilennan Bridge on 3rd May 1986. On territory they fly in the lowest airspace, almost touching the water. The lochs occupied cover the range of biological productivity, from Loch Beinn Uraraidh on quartzite and surrounded by peaty moorland to Lochs Ardnave and Allan, the latter having an alkalinity of 124. This sandpiper feeds on a variety of insects and other small invertebrates. It stalks and picks from the ground, between stones and within cracks, and from the faeces of animals. The off-duty bird roosts in a sheltered place within its territory.

Turnstone *Arenaria interpres*

A possible winter visitor, probable passage migrant and summer visitor, though it is not known to breed. The complex movements of Turnstones are not fully understood. Islay's winter and passage birds probably come from Greenland and northeast arctic Canada; these birds may winter anywhere south to Morocco. The first Turnstones arrive on Islay in late July, but the main influx is in late August or the first half of September. There are ten weeks scattered through autumn and winter without records, so continuous presence is not proved. Around Upper Loch Indaal, however, there have been monthly maximum flocks of: 70 birds on 29th August 1977; 84 on 14th September 1980; 40 on 8th October 1976; 57 on 18th December 1983; 84 in mid-January 1972; 62 on 17th January 1974; and 50 on 6th March 1982. At Loch Gruinart, from 80 to 100 were seen during the 1984/5 and 1985/6 winters. There is an early passage or departure in late March or early April; flocks of 50 were seen at Port Ellen and Ardnave during this period in 1968, then in 1981 some 57 were at Loch Gruinart on 31st March, and 90 were by Upper Loch Indaal on 1st April. From mid-April to mid-July, eleven years produced 21 records which are likely to be of first-year birds from Greenland; all are of ten or less.

The Turnstone is found throughout Islay on shingly or rocky shores, especially where seaweed or mussel beds are present. Two-thirds of all records are from Upper Loch Indaal, but most other suitable coasts are under-recorded.

131

Sightings are likely on foreshores near working distilleries. The Turnstone specialises in hidden food; it bends its legs to insert its bill under an object and then jerks it up or flips it over. It searches in cracks in rocks and along the strand line; probes and pushes sediment aside; and opens shellfish with rapid blows at weak points followed by levering. These activities require the bird to work in close proximity to the waves and therefore feeding is limited by stormy days, driving it into confined sheltered locations, such as a corner of Bowmore Harbour, or onto coastal pasture. Two records are from a rain flash in a field near Saligo in March 1976 and 1977. The Turnstone's food is very varied, depending on the nature of the microhabitat searched. It includes shellfish, small crustaceans, insects and worms. It roosts communally near the first area to be uncovered by the tide, in shelter on a storm beach, low dunes or grassland. Timing is governed by the tidal cycle.

Red-necked Phalarope   *Phalaropus lobatus*

A rare passage migrant that comes from Iceland, the Faroes, Shetland, the Outer Hebrides or Tiree, and winters off coasts to the south, probably in the Arabian Sea. Most Scottish records of the northward migration occur in May and a bird was at Frenchman's Rocks, briefly, on 19th May 1974. Southward migration through Scotland occurs in August and September, and one was at a temporary pool near Saligo on 27th September 1974.

Grey Phalarope   *Phalaropus fulicarius*

A scarce passage migrant that breeds around the Arctic, including Iceland and Greenland, wintering off the West African and South American coasts. It flies well offshore but is driven to British coasts in westerly gales. On Islay, seven records in September, three in October and two in March are in keeping with this pattern. Grey Phalaropes have stayed for up to a few days around Upper Loch Indaal, and near Saligo, Machir and Claggain Bays, and have been seen briefly at Frenchman's Rocks. Typically they are found at small pools of fresh or brackish water; a brightly coloured female was at a temporary pool near Saligo on 11th June 1986 and stayed for about ten days.

Pomarine Skua   *Stercorarius pomarinus*

A scarce passage migrant seen on 14 occasions, especially in the autumn: six in September, four in October, and four in May and July. This skua breeds in the Arctic; its nearest sites are in northwest Russia and west Greenland. It migrates across the North Atlantic to the Caribbean or down the west coast of Africa. On

Islay it has been recorded at Frenchman's Rocks, Coul Point and off the south and east coasts. One penetrated Loch Indaal to Laggan Bay on 9th July 1973, and three reached Bridgend Bay during a gale on 13th October 1983. Four were seen from the ferry a few hundred metres off Texa on 10th July 1986, and an adult flew south down the Sound of Islay on 17th October 1986.

Arctic Skua *Stercorarius parasiticus*

A passage migrant that is said to have bred on Islay in the 18th century. There is no record from the 19th century, but in 1922 a nest was reported by a small loch on or near the site of the present airport; this Skua still breeds on Jura, but not on Islay. Of 93 records, 70 per cent relate to the period from mid-May, when eggs are laid, to mid-July, when the young first stray from the nest; 25 per cent are within the dispersal period during which movement has been detected off Frenchman's Rocks, the last one being in late October. There are no sightings through the winter to mid-May except of one at Uiskentuie, Upper Loch Indaal, on 21st March 1981. Most Scottish birds winter off South Atlantic coasts.

Arctic Skuas have been seen off all readily accessible coasts, but it is rare for one to penetrate the tidal Loch Gruinart. There are seven inland records, four of birds over fishing lochs; some over Loch Gorm in very stormy weather in September 1878 were part of 'considerable numbers' migrating south. On Jura, the breeding areas are on extensive moorland with countless small lochs. Arctic Skuas pirate on other seabirds to obtain fish; victims around Islay include terns, Kittiwakes and gulls, but they may also chase auks and Fulmars. They also strike small birds to the ground, take eggs and chicks of seabirds, and scavenge garbage.

Long-tailed Skua *Stercorarius longicaudus*

A scarce passage migrant that breeds in the Arctic; the nearest sites are in Norway and northeast Greenland. It migrates across the North Atlantic and south down both African and South American coasts. On Islay, single birds are usually recorded: as in June 1914 at Blackrock, in October 1967 at Coul, in August 1968 from the ferry east of Islay, and in September 1977 at Frenchman's Rocks.

Great Skua *Stercorarius skua*

A regular passage migrant in small numbers that breeds on the north and northwest Scottish mainland and islands, and in Iceland. One at Gruinart on 25th January 1976 was probably over four years old and wintering in British waters. This species is found around most of the North and tropical Atlantic, travelling widely in its first year but less so with advancing age. On Islay most records are dated from early June to mid-October, with maximum numbers between mid-August and mid-September; at Frenchman's Rocks, five were seen on 21st August 1977 and three on 14th September 1977. Single birds have been seen in most other months. The great majority of records are from seawatching at the Rocks, but there are also rare sightings from all coasts, including those of the Sound of Islay, Loch Indaal and Loch Gruinart.

The Great Skua feeds mainly on fish obtained by scavenging or piracy. It may dip-to-surface and pick or surface-seize at fish shoals, follow boats for rejected fish, take carrion, and hunt at seabird colonies for eggs and chicks. It chases food-carrying adult gulls, terns, auks and even Gannets, with intent to steal. On Islay, one has been seen chasing four Red-breasted Mergansers and another was eating from a Rabbit carcase. Outside the breeding season, it roosts at night on the sea.

Laughing Gull   *Larus atricilla*

A rare vagrant that breeds along eastern coasts of North and Central America, and in Caribbean islands. Some northern birds move south along these coasts in the winter. Single birds have been seen in Scotland in all seasons; one was on Islay at Knockanbearach on 21st April 1974. It is likely that sightings outside autumn and early winter are of birds that crossed the Atlantic during the previous hurricane season.

Little Gull   *Larus minutus*

An occasional vagrant that breeds mainly east of the Baltic in mid-latitude Eurasia; the nearest regular sites are in Jutland. Migrant flocks are regular in southeastern Scottish estuaries and the southern Irish Sea. An adult was at Lower Loch Indaal on 17th September 1973; an immature bird was at Claddach Reservoir from 8th May to at least 4th July 1976; and two other immatures at Frenchman's Rocks on 31st October 1976 were followed by an adult there on 14th November 1976. The last seen was an immature with a broken leg at Ardnave Loch on 18th May 1977.

Sabine's Gull   *Larus sabini*

A rare vagrant that breeds around the Arctic, with nearest sites in southeast Greenland and Spitsbergen. It migrates down eastern Atlantic coasts to South Africa and is regular in the southwestern approaches to British waters. One was at Frenchman's Rocks on 24th July 1977, and a second-winter bird was seen off the southeast coast in 1983.

Bonaparte's Gull *Larus philadelphia*

A rare vagrant from North America that breeds in central Alaska and western Canada and winters on United States coasts. An adult was near Bridgend on 26th and 27th June 1975, and one at Claggain Bay on 12th September 1975 was presumed to be the same bird.

Black-headed Gull *Larus ridibundus*

The Black-headed Gull is a resident and partial migrant; counts at most colonies in May 1979 suggested an Islay total of 750 birds. An inland survey on 20th March 1980 gave 441, and counts of those on the shores of Upper Loch Indaal gave 238 on 23rd March 1980, about 300 in September 1980 and 323 on 8th March 1983. There were 375 at the Bridgend roost on 3rd September 1980. There is probably dispersal, mainly towards Ireland in August, which appears to be balanced by immigration from the north. Breeding birds return to their colonies in March or the first half of April; many sites are on boggy moors, some on islets in lochans and a minority on flat coastal rocks. All are within 4 km ($2\frac{1}{2}$ miles) of good foraging on farmlands. There is much variation in numbers at individual colonies from year to year; competition from Common Gulls, flooding, habitat change and disturbance by predators, man and livestock are possible explanations.

Most Black-headed Gulls forage where the arable concentration is greatest, in Bridgend Strath, around Bowmore, at Rockside, Sunderland and Gruinart, in the Bruichladdich–Port Charlotte coastal strip, and also around the coast of Upper Loch Indaal. Few are found in the southern Rhinns or in the south, east and west of Port Ellen. They form flocks of up to 100 or so birds in Bridgend Strath, but often they are a minority in a Common Gull feeding flock, or in composite flocks that follow tractor-drawn equipment. They tend to feed in bared or tamped areas such as tractor turn-around places and tractor or livestock tracks, and avoid scrambles with larger gulls in deep furrows where they can be trapped by falling clods of soil. They also frequent livestock feeding stations, make search flights with steady flaps at heights of up to 2 m ($6\frac{1}{2}$ ft), and dip to pick from fields or beach swash lines, or hover over wave-agitated hollows. Below wind force 4, the Black-headed Gull swims and pecks or surface-plunges from a hovering position. Approaching upwind, and thus from behind prey, it pecks insects from cowpats or hawks swarming insects such as ants or craneflies. It also foot-paddles on muddy silts in 1–4 cm ($\frac{1}{2}$–$1\frac{1}{2}$ in) of water, leaving characteristic rectangular excavations, parasitises Lapwings and Golden Plovers, takes food brought to the water's surface by other waterbirds, and

135

scavenges. It takes insects and their larvae, worms, small crustaceans, seeds and many other foods. This species along with other gulls often uses the nearest freshwater shallows as a comfort station and loafing point. It roosts communally at night in Bridgend Bay, but a few stay with Common Gulls at lesser roosts.

Common Gull *Larus canus*

The Common Gull is a resident, passage migrant and winter visitor. The 'Seafarer' count of June 1969 gave 1,150; counts at most of the colonies in May 1979 suggested an Islay total of 1,800 birds; and eight inland surveys gave a minimum of 665 on 29th May 1985 and a maximum with visitors of 2,500 on 12 March 1983. Thirteen Bridgend roost counts gave a minimum of 350 on 3rd September 1980 and a maximum of 2,000 on 20th September 1983 and on 5th March 1984. Passages of Icelandic or Norwegian birds are probably indicated by the latter high counts. Two birds ringed on Islay in September 1960 were recovered in Donegal, one three months later and one 15 months later; and at Frenchman's Rocks on 16th September 1980 about 76 passed south in one hour. Young birds disperse in August, mainly to the Irish Sea and Ireland, and there is a temporary increase in the number of flocks as the breeding season ends.

Breeding adults arrive at colonies in March and April. A high proportion of these are on the west coast, particularly on the flattish rocks of minor headlands; some are on boggy ground by peaty lochans or on islets within a lochan, while others are on raised areas of permanant pasture and run the gauntlet of grazing livestock. There are also very small colonies on pebbly beaches and ruined walls of crofts on the east coast, and on river gravels, particularly in the Laggan Glen area.

Common Gulls often walk-peck in flocks of up to a few hundred on drained grasslands, sometimes further from the Bridgend roost than other gulls, extending northeast to Keills and east to Barr; also on the golf course and isolated fields around Laggan Bay and down the west side of the Rhinns to Portnahaven. They follow any tractor-drawn equipment, picking up disturbed worms and insects. They visit livestock feeding stations, make search flights at heights of up to 2–3 m ($6\frac{1}{2}$–10 ft), dip to peck from fields or strand lines, and hover over wave-agitated shallows. These gulls are able to swim and peck or surface-plunge in winds below force 4. They occasionally foot-paddle on muddy silts in 1–5 cm (up to 2 in) of water, leaving characteristic rectangular excavations, parasitise Lapwings and Golden Plovers, and scavenge. They take worms, insects and their larvae, small crustaceans, small fish, grain and other foods. On 29th July 1982, hundreds were in parties on Loch Indaal, which was 'full of Herring fry'.

Like other gulls, Common Gulls often use the nearest freshwater shallows as a comfort station and loafing point. They roost communally at night in Bridgend Bay or, if sheltered, at other bays or on rocky islets or low promontories near to the day's main feeding area. At Nerabus on 10th October 1981, about 200 roosted on grass. The majority, however, usually follow flight lines to and from the Bridgend roost which are centralised over farmland.

Lesser Black-backed Gull *Larus fuscus*

The Lesser Black-backed Gull is a breeding summer visitor, passage migrant and rare winter visitor. Icelandic and Faroese birds moving through Scotland, especially western Scotland, are joined by local birds of the same race (*L.f.graellsii*) soon after their breeding season has ended.This movement is protracted and there are records of such gulls passing Frenchman's Rocks from 11th August to 7th October. British birds are known to winter off Iberia and northwest Africa. The few records of the Lesser Black-backed Gull on Islay after 7th October are usually of single birds, but there were three on Bridgend Flats on 29th January 1986. Immigration commences in the first half of March, exceptionally in late February, and there is a gradual build-up into April; birds with very dark mantles have occasionally been seen during this period and are considered to be of Scandinavian origin (*L.f.fuscus*).

This gull breeds on broad rocky areas among cliffs on the Atlantic coast, especially on the Rhinns near Lossit and between Smaull and Sanaigmore, but is rare along other cliffed coasts. Small numbers are seen on shelving coasts and on farmland, but inland breeding sites are rare. Over 500 birds were breeding in 1980, and an incomplete 1986 count suggested that this number had fallen to near 300.

Since only small numbers are normally seen feeding on land, it is likely that the majority feed at sea. They may be seen aggregating over shoals of fish, following fishing boats, or feeding solitarily, using a variety of methods: dipping from searching flight to snatch food from the water's surface; surface-plunging from a height of 8 m (26 ft); submerging to take slightly deeper prey; or practising 'food-piracy'. On land this agile species is not so versatile as the Herring Gull. However, it captures insects in aerial pursuit, follows the plough and sometimes rummages for food among root crops, but does not visit the refuse tip. It takes fish, small mammals, chicks, shellfish, worms and insects. It is active on some moonlit nights, and roosts at the breeding colony or in the 'club' or loafing group nearly.

Herring Gull *Larus argentatus*

The Herring Gull is a resident and winter visitor. The 'Seafarer' count of June 1969, adjusted for complete coverage, gave about 1,250 birds; counts at the end of May 1979, 1980 and 1981 similarly gave 1,600 individuals. In the early 1980s, three autumn surveys averaged 505, three in winter averaged 670, and two in spring averaged 1,055 birds; each survey excluded 100 to 500 at the Gartbreck rubbish dump. After breeding, some of Islay's birds are likely to disperse to Northern Ireland or the Central Valley, especially Glasgow. In the late autumn, immigrants probably arrive from points north to Iceland.

This gull breeds colonially on flattish rock expanses among cliffs, especially on the west coast of the Rhinns, around the Oa, near Laggan Point and on Texa and

137

Nave Island; a few pairs are scattered along the north and east coasts, and 50–60 pairs bred on the moss near Duich in 1987. It forages on the sea, on soft coasts and inland, but few are seen on moorland. The Herring Gull searches from heights of 100–200 m (325–650 ft), taking advantage of updraughts on thermals and at slope soaring sites. It obtains food on and around Islay by many means: it walk-pecks on grassland, sowings, and stubbles, and at livestock feeding points; follows tractor-drawn equipment, especially ploughs; scavenges at the Gartbreck rubbish dump; takes seabird eggs and chicks and road carrion; rummages among turnip crops and fresh seaweed on beaches; wades in tidal pools and combs beaches, dropping well-protected items from heights of 4.5–7.5 m (14–25 ft) to crack them open; pirates on other seabirds; dips to the surface of water to pick; surface-seizes and surface-plunges from heights of 5–6 m (16–20 ft); is attracted to diving seabirds and follows fishing boats; also hawks insects; and occasionally foot-paddles. One or two Herring Gulls sometimes accompany groups of Eiders on Loch Indaal and try to seize food brought to the surface by these ducks. Feeding is curtailed on the open sea during a gale, but food becomes more plentiful on storm-swept beaches. These birds take: starfish, sea-urchins, shellfish, crabs, fish, eggs, chicks, rats, young Rabbits, frogs, earthworms, insects, grain, carrion and edible refuse. A human presence may cause parent birds to vacate a nest, allowing other Herring Gulls to steal the contents.

This gull roosts at night with other gull species on the saltings or mudflats in Bridgend Bay and in smaller groups at the mouths of some rivers and burns. It uses all these places as comfort stations and loafs there during the day, as well as in the shallow bays of some inland lochs. The number roosting at Bridgend is very variable: 650 on 6th September 1974; 250 on 3rd September 1980; and 80 on 5th September 1982.

Iceland Gull   *Larus glaucoides*

A scarce dispersive migrant that breeds in Greenland (*L.g.glaucoides*) and Baffin Island (*L.g.kumlieni*). It has been noted on Islay since the mid-1800s and may be regarded as annual. Sightings are possible in every month, but of 19 records between 1970 and 1986, three were in January and February, ten in March and April, one in May and five from July to October. None has ever been reported in November or December. All records are of single adults or sub-adults. They have been seen off the Atlantic coast, especially at Frenchman's Rocks, in Port Ellen Bay and Upper Loch Indaal, and occasionally inland on farmland.

Glaucous Gull   *Larus hyperboreus*

A scarce dispersive migrant, visiting Islay more often than the Iceland Gull. It has a circumpolar arctic breeding distribution and probably arrives in Britain from the Barents Sea northeast of Scandinavia, or perhaps from east Greenland. Over about twelve years, immature birds have been seen on Islay in all months, with 36 records from mid-January to mid-April and a peak in March; four birds were near Bridgend on 14th March 1982. Seven have been recorded in October, but in each of the other months there have been fewer than four records. About half have been found in Bridgend Bay or along the very accessible north coast of Loch Indaal; others have been seen in Port Ellen Bay or off the Atlantic coast, especially at Frenchman's Rocks. About one-fifth have been inland, often with other gulls on farmland. Occasionally, one visits the Gartbreck rubbish dump. Seven were around the island on 10th February 1984.

This dominating gull is omnivorous and is a predator, scavenger and pirate. It takes food from the sea, from seabird colonies and from the land, including fresh food, offal, carrion and refuse, using techniques similar to those of the Herring Gull. It roosts and loafs with other gulls.

Great Black-backed Gull *Larus marinus*

The Great Black-backed Gull is a resident and winter visitor in small numbers; data collected in late May and early June from 1976 to 1981 suggested an Islay total of about 150 birds. After breeding they disperse, and many go south; Scottish birds have been found wintering in Ireland. Most visitors are probably from points north to Iceland, but one shot on the Laggan Estate in 1945/6 was said to have had a Moscow ring. The larger flocks occur in autumn and spring: over 50 were at Loch Gorm on 3rd September 1974; 36 were there on 3rd October 1976, 31 were at Ballinaby on 17th November 1981; and 35 at Rockside on 23rd November 1981. The maximum numbers seen were 80 off Knockangle Point in Laggan Bay on 3rd April 1981 and 160 at Loch Gruinart on 31st August 1984. This gull nests solitarily on stacks and rocky headlands, especially on the west coasts of the Oa and the Rhinns, and also at Rhinns Point, Laggan Point and a few other locations. It forms small colonies on Sanaig Cliffs and Nave Island. The latter appears to contain 80 adults at a maximum, but has regularly been persecuted. Foraging birds are usually thinly scattered over the whole island.

Usually the Great Black-backed Gull is seen foraging in ones and twos, except that up to 30 are at the Gartbreck rubbish dump daily and small groups may quickly assemble around fishing vessels or groups of other seabirds, such as Gannets, diving on a shoal of fish. It dominates other gulls at beach, farmland and road carrion, and is capable of dismembering prey by tossing, stabbing, shaking, pulling, tearing and banging it on the ground. A single bird sometimes waits by a warren for a careless Rabbit to come close.

Like the Herring Gull, it often searches at heights of about 100–200 m (325–650 ft), taking advantage of updraughts on thermals and at slope soaring sites. It robs other seabirds; rummages among seaweed; wades in tidal pools just isolated by the receding tide; combs beaches, dropping well-protected animals to crack them open; and even occasionally hawks insects. Food taken includes seals and sheep as carrion, Rabbits, rats, incapacitated adult seabirds, eggs, chicks, offal, edible refuse, dab fish, starfish, shellfish, crabs, worms and insects. It roosts and loafs with the Herring Gull. Numbers at the Bridgend roost range up to the 70 seen on 5th September 1982.

Ross's Gull   *Rhodostethia rosea*

A rare vagrant that breeds in northeast Siberia and is presumed to approach Britain from Scandinavian waters. Most Scottish records are from the Shetlands, where it has been seen in all seasons, especially winter. An immature bird, however, reached Frenchman's Rocks on 15th August 1976.

Kittiwake   *Rissa tridactyla*

The Kittiwake is a summer visitor to Islay and a passage migrant. It feeds on the open ocean, some traversing the full width of the North Atlantic, but during the breeding season adults at colonies range only 65 km (40 miles) out over the sea. Rafts on Loch Indaal and small groups on the breeding cliffs have been seen from 20th March. At 09.45 hrs on 26th March 1980, 80 were resting in Bridgend Bay in linear formation; heading into the wind, they flew down loch with a snake-like undulating flight pattern, passing Bruichladdich at 10.15 hrs. Breeding cliffs lie between Lossit and Tormisdale, and to the northwest of Sanaigmore; in May/June there were about 200 occupied nest sites on Sanaig Cliffs in 1954, 220 in 1976 and 615 in 1986. The Lossit Cliffs held about 350 in 1986, and ten nest sites were found on the Beinn Mhor Cliffs at the Oa on 22nd June 1987. One bird was still on its nest on 24th August 1980; and large rafts were seen at Claggain Bay on 26th August 1957 and between Islay and Gigha on 23rd August and 6th September 1980. Thus Islay's Kittiwakes frequent the breeding cliffs from late March to late August. Passage south off Frenchman's Rocks becomes significant early in September—it reached peaks of 2,000 per hour in late September 1975 and mid-October 1976 and 1984—and is again at low ebb early in November. Kittiwakes are rare in winter, but over 100 were at Bridgend on 12th January 1976. The spring passage is poorly documented, but it is probably irregular from early March to late May.

This species feeds off the surface or from near the surface of the sea, by picking while flying or swimming, or surface-plunging to less than 1 m (3 ft). It takes small crustaceans and small fish of the cod family or sand-eels. It also scavenges at fishing vessels for offal. All the birds roost and loaf communally on the sea when away from their breeding grounds, and during the breeding season non-breeders roost on a cliff near a colony.

Ivory Gull   *Pagophila eburnea*

A rare vagrant that breeds around the high Arctic; the nearest sites are by the Denmark Straits in Greenland. In winter it moves south with the limit of the pack-ice. Most Scottish records are from the Shetlands and are dated November or December. In January 1867, one reached Islay and was found dead on a loch after a heavy gale. Ivory Gulls have been found on Islay on one or two occasions (Gray 1871).

Sandwich Tern   *Sterna sandvicensis*

An occasional, probably annual, dispersive visitor whose nearest breeding grounds are on the north coast of Ireland. The majority migrate to West Africa, leaving in September and returning in April. On Islay, most sightings have been in May or June, but three were in September and adjacent months. One to three birds were recorded on each occasion, half around the shores of Upper Loch Indaal and half scattered widely on the outer coasts. In addition, three were at Loch Gruinart on 24th July 1985.

Roseate Tern   *Sterna dougallii*

A rare dispersive visitor that breeds in very small numbers elsewhere in southwest Scotland and in the Belfast district, and migrates to West Africa. Most arrive in Scotland in the second half of May and two were seen at Frenchman's Rocks on 25th May 1975. They leave by the end of September; one was still at Traigh an Luig, Upper Loch Indaal, on 28th September 1976. Five were at Port Mias-sgeire, Portnahaven, on 2nd June 1975.

Common Tern   *Sterna hirundo*

The Common Tern is a summer visitor, breeder and passage migrant; colonies of up to 1,000 birds were known in 1848 and 1907, but in recent years 200 has been exceptional. Only 23 breeding pairs were found in 1986 and only one in 1987. Dispersal north and south is chiefly in late August and September, when movement has been recorded off Frenchman's Rocks; one bird was found resting on grass by Loch Indaal in a storm on 8th October 1976. Southward migration strengthens in October, and from November they winter off West Africa, mainly from Mauritania to Ghana. The return to Islay is largely in May, the earliest record being for 4th, and colonies are well established by mid-June.

During the last decade or so, a few pairs have bred on the shingle and pebbles of beaches subject to frequent disturbance. The main colonies, however, have

141

been on a few small low rocky islands. Eilean Mhic Coinnich off Portnahaven and Castle Island in Loch Gorm have been important breeding places in the past; twelve nests were at the latter locality in 1976.

These terns feed chiefly on small marine fish obtained by hovering and then plunge-diving from heights of 1–6 m (3–20 ft). They also dip to the surface in flight, picking up fish, crustaceans and other small invertebrates. More rarely, they hawk insects or parasitise other terns carrying fish. When conditions are unsuitable for fishing, they loaf or roost communally on sandbanks, mudflats or isolated rocks.

Arctic Tern *Sterna paradisaea*

A summer visitor, regular breeder and passage migrant that appears to have expanded on Islay since early this century, at the expense of the Common Tern. About 1,000 Arctic Terns were on Islay in June 1969, and nearly 400 breeding pairs were counted during a complete census in 1987. Dispersal is chiefly to the south in August, three travelled south past Frenchman's Rocks on 10th September 1980 and the latest record is for 12th September. Many migrate to southern hemisphere oceans but a few winter off the west coast of Africa. The return passage is largely in May and the earliest record is of two birds in Bridgend Bay on 9th May 1976. At Frenchman's Rocks, 49 were seen travelling south on 12th May 1975.

Colonies are well established by mid-June. Some nest on shingle beaches, but the main colonies are usually on low rocky islets and promontories just out of reach of stormy seas. These localities are scattered around most of Islay's coastline except that of the Oa and the southeast Rhinns. In June 1969, Castle Island, Lock Gorm, was occupied by 100 Arctic Terns, but none was there in 1986. Foraging birds search upwind, often hovering before plunge-diving from heights of 1–6 m (3–20 ft) to take fish. They dip to the surface in flight, picking crustaceans or insects from the water's surface, catch insects in aerial pursuit, and occasionally parasitise other birds carrying fish. The Arctic Tern loafs and roosts communally in open coastal areas, often on the water after a bout of feeding.

Little Tern *Sterna albifrons*

A regular summer visitor that breeds on Islay in small numbers. It was thought to be absent in 1878, but in 1925 it was said to have nested; one nest was reported in 1949 and four in 1954 and 1957. Thirteen pairs were counted in 1969 and 20 in 1982, but in the 23 years to 1985 the population was normally less. In 1986 and 1987, there were about 26 and 16 breeding pairs, respectively, at four sites.

The Little Tern arrives between late April and mid-May; two were at Gortan,

Bruichladdich, on 25th April 1974 and 32 were seen flying east at Blackrock on 11th May 1974. Nest sites are established on the upper parts of sand and shingle beaches; prior to 1978 a few were reported near the entrance to Loch Gruinart, but the majority of records come from Laggan Bay or the beaches of Upper Loch Indaal. These birds leave during the first half of July and migrate coastwise to the west coast of Africa. The latest date of a bird on Islay is 24th July 1985, when one was on the Gruinart Reserve.

The Little Tern usually forages close inshore, taking small fish, crustaceans and insects. It quarters a likely area, hovers and plunge-dives, or less often skims the water to take prey with a backward flick of the bill. Insects are taken off the surface or in aerial pursuits. Dives may be into shallower water than those of other tern species, and strong winds reduce the fishing success rate. There is no information on roosting, but, like daytime loafing, it probably occurs in small groups on shingle banks or spits.

The continued presence of Little Terns on Islay depends on minimal disturbance from humans, horses, cattle, sheep and dogs. It is unfortunate that this species chooses to nest where such disturbance is likely.

Black Tern *Chlidonias niger*

A rare vagrant to Islay that breeds on freshwater marshes throughout much of Europe. The nearest breeding grounds are in Holland and Denmark, from which it migrates to tropical West Africa. Movement through eastern Scotland occurs in May to June and mid-August to mid-October, reaching the Hebrides only rarely. Two were at Loch Gruinart in late May 1974 and again on 18th May 1985.

Guillemot *Uria aalge*

The Guillemot is a summer visitor, regular breeder and passage migrant. Guillemots leave Islay in mid-June and the first-year birds disperse widely to waters between southern Norway and the Bay of Biscay. In 1975, some 803 flew south past Frenchman's Rocks as early as 6th June. Adults stay within British waters and may visit their breeding ledges after the flightless moult period from late July to mid-September. Rafts were seen between Gigha and Islay on 23rd August and 6th September 1980 and are commonly present during these months. Large numbers of auks pass mainly southwards by Frenchman's Rocks from September to November, especially in October (Verrall and Bourne 1982). About 100 birds were back on their ledges of Sanaig Cliffs by 21st March 1972. There are no records of birds at colonies in winter as elsewhere in Scotland in recent years.

This auk breeds on cliffs betweeen Sanaigmore and Smaull, between

Tormisdale and Lossit, on Texa, and on the southern Oa. About 1,600 birds were at colonies on Islay in 1969; of these 1,000 were on the northwest cliffs. In 1981 the population was 1,962, and in 1986 this had increased again to 2,626. About 370 were counted around the Oa on 22nd June 1987; these were probably under-represented in the previous counts. Some 10 per cent of Islay's Guillemots are of the bridled form.

Guillemots head-dip to spot prey, then surface-dive and swim underwater using both feet and wings; they may also crash-land over fish shoals, diving immediately. They pursue prey within 20 m (66 ft) of the surface and catch shoaling fish such as sand-eels and sprats. They also take crustaceans, worms and shellfish. Groups of Guillemots may swim in line abreast when hunting, and occasionally encircle and herd fish shoals. Feeding efficiency is affected by the state of the sea, less food being brought back to the ledges when the sea is rough. They do not fly at all in hurricane-force winds. Guillemots roost on the sea outside the breeding season and when they are off duty from the ledge site. Oiling is a potentially serious threat to this species and oiled birds have been found on Islay's beaches from time to time.

Razorbill   *Alca torda*

The Razorbill is a summer visitor, regular breeder and passage migrant. It disperses southwards in winter, immatures moving further than adults. From September to November, especially in October after their moult, large numbers of auks pass by Frenchman's Rocks, mainly southwards; 90 per cent are too far out to be identified, but 15 per cent of those identified were Razorbills (Verrall and Bourne 1982). A similar northward passage has not been detected, and there is no winter record of colony attendance. These birds breed on ledges beneath rock overhangs and in small caves and crevices, on sea cliffs between Smaull and Sanaigmore, between Tormisdale and Lossit and in places around the Oa. About 1,800 birds were at these colonies in 1969; of these, 1,000 were at the northwest cliffs and 200 near Lossit. In 1986, only 1,325 birds were counted. About 150–175 birds were seen around the Oa on 22nd June 1987.

The Razorbill feeds on inshore waters in the breeding season, up to 15–20 km (9–12½ miles) from the colony. It searches for prey by head-dipping while swimming, then surface-dives and swims underwater using both feet and wings; it may also crash-land over shoals, diving immediately. It dives to 2–3 m (6–10 ft), exceptionally more, and is submerged for up to about 45 seconds. It takes mainly fish, especially sand-eels and sprats, and also small shrimp-like crustaceans, worms and shellfish.

Razorbills roost and loaf at sea outside the breeding season, but early in that season they loaf on their nest sites. Later, off-duty birds and non-breeders form a 'club', loafing on a flat area of rock near the colony, but at night they may still roost in a raft on the sea. Oiling is a potential hazard; oiled birds have been found on Islay's beaches from time to time.

Great Auk *Pinguinis impennis*

The Great Auk was a large flightless penguin-like bird weighing about 5000 gm (11 lb). It is now extinct but was eaten by Mesolithic Man and bones have been found in his kitchen middens in North Argyll on the island of Risga in Loch Sunart. Bones are also known from Mesolithic middens on Oronsay, 8 km (5 miles) north of Islay, and it is likely that the species once lived on Islay. These middens have been shown to be 5,000 to 6,000 years old. The last Scottish Great Auk was killed at Stac an Armin, St Kilda in 1840 and the last pair on earth was killed on Eldey, Iceland in June 1844.

Black Guillemot *Cepphus grylle*

The Black Guillemot is a resident that was first recorded in 1848. Ringed birds recovered in western Scotland have usually moved less than 50 km (31 miles), but Darling (1947) gave an example of movement away from the 'oceanic island' of North Rhona in winter. They were numerous in the Sound of Islay on 5th November 1977, while none was found on the Atlantic coast. The few records for December to February are from Sanaigmore Bay, Upper Loch Indaal, Kilnaughton Bay and the 'south side of the Oa'.

This auk nests among boulders on beaches or in crevices low down on cliffs, and can be seen off most of Islay's rocky shores. There were some 200 at Bagh an da Dhoruis, Islay's most northerly beach, on 15th June 1971. In recent years there have been 300–500 Black Guillemots around the island; about 23 nesting pairs were found around the Oa on 22nd June 1987. Perhaps the most convenient place to see this species is around Laggan Point. They feed in shallows close inshore, surface-diving for 30–60 seconds and mostly down to 2–8 m (6–26 ft). They swim using both wings and feet, taking prey found on or near the bottom: chiefly small fish, crustaceans, shellfish, worms and seaweed. These birds roost on the sea or near the nest site, according to season and duties. The Otter is a potential predator on the boulder beaches, and the Black Guillemot is also susceptible to death through oiling; a few were found oiled after the Loch Indaal incident in October 1969.

Little Auk *Alle alle*

The Little Auk visits waters northwest of the Hebrides in winter and is a vagrant to Islay. It is usually seen when storm-driven to land and is often found dead or in a weak condition. Reports are dated from 1st November to 6th March, but it has not been found alive after early February. This auk breeds from west Greenland eastwards to the Soviet arctic islands. On Islay it is found both on the coast and inland, particularly on or near west-facing coasts. Exceptionally, one was on the sea off Lagavulin Distillery on 11th July 1985.

This small bird feeds on crustaceans obtained by surface-diving and

145

swimming just below the surface. It is vulnerable to oiling, and as a result of this one was in a poor condition at Lossit Bay in 1956.

Puffin   *Fratercula arctica*

A passage migrant and also a summer visitor in very small numbers; it formerly bred and possibly still breeds in some years. Puffins were reported breeding near the Mull of Oa in some numbers last century, and also in 1914 and 1937; they were last seen there in 1967. Some bred at Sanaig Cliffs during the first half of this century and birds were reported there in 14 summers from 1962 to 1986; up to twelve in the 1960s but only one or two in the 1980s. Most pairs nest in burrows, but a few nest in crevices in cliffs or under boulders or screes. One was seen leaving a hole in Sanaig Cliffs in 1953 and again at Port Carraig Sgairn on 25th May 1979; another visited a cave there on 25th May 1977. Seven were off the Mull of Oa on 26th June 1985. These figures contrast with the 'vast concentrations' fishing off Portnahaven on 19th August 1885 and the 'thousands' there on 9th October 1887.

Most Puffins disperse widely from Scotland in August, ranging well over the Atlantic through the winter; many migrate south to waters off France, Iberia and Morocco, avoiding rough seas and the associated reduced feeding rates. Most of these migrants return to Scotland in March, and Puffins are occasionally washed up on west-facing shores. Puffins forage chiefly for fish, but also for crustaceans, by dipping their heads in search of prey, surface-diving down to a maximum of about 15 m (50 ft), and swimming underwater propelled by their wings.

Rock Dove   *Columba livia*

The Rock Dove is a resident which appears to have been very abundant in the west prior to 1777, when droppings were collected from caves for use as fertiliser; in 1839 there were 'myriads' at Kilchoman. It probably declined into this century, and flock sizes have decreased again since the harvesting of barley has become more efficient.

Feral pigeons, also *C. livia*, were noted in a Rock Dove flock in the Bruichladdich area in 1979 and 1981. The species is very sedentary, most recoveries being at less than 10 km (6 miles) from the ringing site. However, there are local movements to and from feeding sites outside the breeding season. The largest flock on record was one of 400 birds by Eresaid on 26th November 1977; in recent years, the largest was one of 86 at Gruinart in January 1986, and again one of 100 at Coullabus in October 1987. In April and the first half of May, when the first broods are fledged, flocks are rarely seen.

Nesting takes place in coastal caves and crevices, and in old barns and ruined buildings. Feeding is on open farmland to which these birds commute by swift low flight, often following the undulations of the ground; they visit stubbles in the early autumn and livestock feeding stations in the winter. Two-thirds of all records relate to farmland, and a major part of the remainder cite localities on rocky coasts. None has been noted on the east coast from Rhuvaal to Ardbeg. Rock doves feed by walk-pecking, taking chiefly seeds of cultivated cereals, legumes, grasses and a wide variety of other herbs. They occasionally take earthworms, small snails, slugs, spiders and insects. They roost where they breed, in coastal caves.

Stock Dove *Columba oenas*

A dispersive visitor to Islay that first bred in Scotland in 1866 and in Ireland in 1877, reaching Argyll the same year. It is now resident throughout the Scottish lowlands and Ireland, with nearest sites in east Kintyre and Antrim. Over 20 were at Sunderland Farm on 27th November 1973 and eight at Craigens Farm on 19th October 1979; single birds were reported from Portnahaven on 19th June 1977 and in the Loch Gorm area on 14th February 1981.

Woodpigeon *Columba palumbus*

A resident that appears to have been introduced some time in the first half of the 19th century, was abundant and increasing in 1892, and remains plentiful to the present day. It is likely to increase considerably as new conifer plantations close their canopy; its most favoured conifer is Sitka spruce. In Scotland dispersal is minimal, and birds on Islay usually commute less than 2 km (1¼ miles) from farmland feeding areas to woodland roosts or nests. Temporary small flocks may form in September, or even August if cereals ripen early, but winter flocks assemble in early October and break up in early April as the breeding season starts. The largest flocks recorded contained 250 birds, near Sunderland in December 1979 and at Skerrols on 22nd October 1986.

The Woodpigeon is common in the Bridgend, Ballygrant and Foreland Wood complexes, and is found in smaller woods near the richer arable areas, especially in those not far removed from the complexes. It is less common in southeast woods, including those at Kildalton, presumably because there is a lower proportion of arable land in their vicinity. Like others in the same family, it obtains food by walking and pecking on the ground, but it also collects food in trees, where it is quite agile. It takes leaves, seeds, nuts, berries, buds, flowers and root crops. On Islay, grain from ripening barley and stubbles, hazelnuts, turnips and probably clover are important food sources. The Woodpigeon feeds on cereals for less than 10 per cent of the daylight hours. At night it roosts communally outside the breeding season, mainly in trees, often in conifers.

Collared Dove   *Streptopelia decaocto*

The Collared Dove is a resident that was first reported in Islay at Aoradh Farm in 1961; five were there in March 1962, and others were at Port Ellen in that year. It was still spreading in 1968, and flocks of over 50 were seen in March 1972 at Laphroaig and near Port Ellen in August; 80 were at Bowmore on 5th November 1977. By 1979, however, double figures were unusual, and very few were seen in 1983 and 1984. From November 1980 to September 1981 the seven distilleries reduced production and far less grain was spilled on the roads; this probably contributed to the decline in numbers. A small recovery was apparent in 1986 and 1987, with 28 at Bruichladdich on 9th July 1987 at a householder's feeding point.

This dove nests in Bridgend Woods, where some were shot during each of its peak years. Other nests have been found in a bush at Aruadh, Sunderland, in sheds at Bridge House and Sunderland, and at Bruichladdich Garage and Pier. In the spring of 1980, pairs and groups of up to six were noted in small woods throughout the island. From 1962, there has been a tendency to flock in the autumn and winter at villages and distilleries, and at the larger farms and other places where grain is spilled or birds are fed; the only clear exception was a flock of 20 at Laggan Point on 23rd December 1981. A 'white' dove was reported near Port Ellen Distillery in late August 1973, and pale birds were also seen on Colonsay on 25th March 1973 and 30th April 1974. The Collared Dove feeds mainly by walking and pecking at ground level, taking cereal grain, the seeds and fruits of other grasses and herbs, bread and some insects. It also takes berries from bushes and trees aided by rapid wingbeats. It has learnt to feed among poultry and on birdtables, and prior to 1980 collected much spilled grain from roads. It usually roosts communally and nocturnally in trees and buildings, including for example the cubical sheds at Coultorsay and Sunderland Farms. It has also been seen with Starlings going to roost at Bruichladdich Pier.

Turtle Dove   *Streptopelia turtur*

A passage migrant recorded in most years in Islay in very small numbers; it is said to have bred in Carnmore Wood in the spring of 1919. The nearest regular breeding haunts are in Lancashire and County Durham, southeast from which the main food plant, common fumitory (*Fumaria officinalis*), is readily available. Turtle Doves winter in scrub south of the Sahara and most returning migrants enter Britain from the southeast; those reaching Islay have overshot the breeding range and may be inexperienced birds. They are first seen in early May and records peak in the first half of June. All have normally passed through the island by mid-July, but there was one at Bridge House on 25th July 1973. A total of six records from mid-September to mid-October could relate to single non-breeders that summered at points northwest of Islay as the breeding *Atlas* suggests. Islay records are of birds in ones and twos, widely scattered through the island, sometimes with Collared Doves.

148

This species takes food, mainly the seeds and fruits of weeds and cereals, almost entirely from the ground. The seeds of common fumitory normally form 30–50 per cent of its diet, but, although the birds are on Islay when these seeds are in season, the seeds are rare and secondary foods such as cereal grain found in farmyards, on poultry runs and scattered on roads must be utilised; they also take the fallen seeds of Scots pine. The Turtle Dove roosts communally in dense trees, probably with Collared Doves.

Cuckoo   *Cuculus canorus*

The Cuckoo is a summer visitor and Britain's only regular brood parasite. It arrives in the latter half of April; the earliest date is 13th, when one was at Ardmore in 1979. Records from late June are sparse, but a juvenile was being fed at Ballimony on 3rd August 1970, and the latest sighting was of a juvenile at Laphroaig on 24th August 1976. Adults leave first and juveniles later, bound for Africa south of the equator.

Islay's Cuckoos are widely scattered, especially in Meadow Pipit habitats; they are often seen to be mobbed by Meadow Pipits, which appear to be their main host. Other hosts are Grey Wagtails, Reed Buntings and possibly Yellowhammers. Trees, telegraph poles and electricity pylons are used as song and lookout posts. Cuckoos feed on caterpillars, including species bearing warning colours and avoided by other birds; some beetles are also taken. They search for food on the ground and from a perch. There is no record on Islay of a Cuckoo roosting, but it is known that they use the same site throughout the season, and that it is often in a bush.

Barn Owl   *Tyto alba*

The Barn Owl is a rarely seen resident. Records date back to 1907, and a decrease in numbers is indicated by the greatly reduced frequency of sightings since the mid-1970s, although the species is probably under-recorded. Nine pairs were located in 1987, and there were possibly twelve or more widely distributed throughout the agricultural areas. No movements apart from dispersal are known, and the 90 records are fairly well distributed throughout the year. Many records come from the Port Ellen area and the distillery belt through to Kildalton, around the conifer plantations by the middle reaches of the Laggan River, and around the partially wooded areas stretching from Bridgend to Port Askaig. Some autumn and winter records are more widely distributed: eight are from Gruinart and the eastern Rhinns and seven from Bowmore and around Island House; one bird was seen near Carnduncan in 1986; and another was on the Gruinart Reserve in most months from August 1984 to September 1985. Nests have been found mainly in abandoned buildings, but also in caves, in holes and crevices among rocks, and even under a tree root.

Barn Owls on Islay hunt over farmland, rough pasture, grassy moorland and around woods, and also along the inner edge of Bridgend Flats and over sand dunes. They are usually seen at dusk, sometimes following ditches, hedges or verges; their hunting flight is low, slow and buoyant, descending to prey with quick changes of altitude and direction. Less often, they hunt from a series of perches or from repeated hovering positions. They take mainly Short-tailed Voles, but also mice, shrews and a few small birds from their roosts. They roost solitarily during the daytime in well-concealed sites in buildings or less often in dense evergreen tree cover, and are also found loafing on the ground. One fell down a chimney in Bowmore on 14th February 1976.

Snowy Owl   *Nyctea scandiaca*

An irruptive migrant that reaches Scotland from the Arctic at irregular intervals. It has a circumpolar distribution, the nearest regular breeding grounds being in northeast Greenland and on the northern Scandinavian mountains. An adult male was trapped on Sanaig rocks on 15th April 1870.

Tawny Owl   *Strix aluco*

The Tawny Owl is resident in small numbers and was first reported in 1871 (Gray). It is highly territorial and sedentary, more than 80 per cent of recoveries in Britain being within 10 km (6 miles) of the place where they were ringed as nestlings. These owls are found in the more extensive mixed woodlands at Bridgend, Ballygrant and Kildalton; they are also reported from smaller woods at Carnmore, Laphroaig, Gruinart, Eresaid, Tallant, Foreland and Laggan Bridge, but are probably irregular at some of these. The Laphroaig Woods have a high proportion of conifers and three eggs were found in a nest at the foot of a pine there on 3rd June 1971.

The Tawny Owl hunts at night, often perching on a pole or tree listening for activity on the ground, then gliding on to prey, but sometimes pouncing from flight. It takes a variety of small animals: voles, mice, young Rabbits, shrews, birds, earthworms and beetles. This owl roosts by day, often on a branch close to the trunk of a tree, in a hole and even in a chimney. One roosted by the trunk of a spruce in Ballygrant Woods in June 1975, and another came down a chimney at Aoradh on 1st February 1977 and was probably roosting there.

Long-eared Owl   *Asio otus*

An under-recorded resident that has been seen or heard in all months except January and November. It is likely to be sedentary, except for the dispersal of young and short-distance movements caused by food scarcity in autumn and winter. It typically occupies small copses or plantations surrounded by open country and it is at such locations that it is said to have bred on Islay: Foreland House Wood in 1875, Carnmore Wood in 1907 and a conifer wood near Island House in 1953. In the latter half of the 19th century it was also of 'daily occurrence in Kilchoman Forest', many remnants of which are shown between Kilchiaran and Kilchoman on the ordnance plan of 1900. One stayed at Easter Ellister for over seven months in 1975, and others were in the Kilchoman School House Wood, Gruinart, in 1979, near Bruichladdich in 1982, and more recently at Olistadh Woods.

The Long-eared Owl hunts mainly at night with a slow, steady, searching flight at heights of 0.5–1.5 m (1½–5 ft), with alternate wingbeats and glides and occasional hovering. In windy weather, it may hunt in sheltered areas from low perches. It takes shrews, moles, Rabbits and bats. The bird at Easter Ellister in 1975 took chickens. During the day, outside the breeding season, it roosts communally in trees or bushes.

Short-eared Owl   *Asio flammeus*

A resident, partial migrant and nomad, first reported in 1871 (Gray) and now breeding regularly. Numbers vary in relation to prey availability, especially that of voles. In July 1973 several were on and around Gruinart Flats; during most summers, however, only one is seen there or none at all. Within Scotland there is a tendency for this owl to move southwest in winter, some crossing to Ireland. In 1913 (Ross) it was said that considerable numbers arrived on Islay about the end of October. Only a fifth of all sightings, however, have been recorded from September to April, suggesting that most birds pass through. Those few that remain disperse widely.

A high proportion of sightings since 1970 have been during the breeding season, from April to July; they are well clustered into six to nine ranges of 10–15 sq. km (4–6 sq. miles), at least five of which were occupied in 1985. Two nest sites are reported in each of two ranges, and frequent sightings in the vicinity of Easter and Wester Ellister suggest that one home range covers only 5–7 sq. km (1.9–2.7 sq. miles).

Nearly 60 per cent of the records relate to the Rhinns, where four to six of the ranges are located. The remainder are mainly in the strip of low country between Bowmore and Port Ellen. These birds are found in open grassy moorland, rough grazings, harvested fields, root crops and sand dunes. The recent extensive planting of conifers on the Rhinns will eventually reduce the area covered by wild grasses and hence the area of good vole habitat, in turn reducing the area of Short-eared Owl habitat. This owl hunts by day and night, with a slow flap-and-glide flight; it may hover before pouncing and occasionally uses a perch. It takes mainly voles, but also mice, rats, shrews and small birds. One attacked a Stoat carrying a rat. Outside the breeding season it roosts in good cover, often on the ground.

151

Nightjar   *Caprimulgus europaeus*

A summer visitor, arriving in May and leaving in August to winter in Africa south of the Sahara. Birds were heard 'jarring' near Kildalton at 20.00 hrs on 15th July 1907; breeding probably occurred at Torr na Carraige, Kildalton, in 1927. Two singing males and a female were in Bridgend Woods in 1954; another was seen on Gruinart Flats in August 1963; 'jarring' was heard on the moss between Coullabus and Carrabus during the same summer, and again on 3rd July 1973; and lastly one was heard at Kildalton after 23.00 hrs on 24th and 25th June 1974. A bird was found dead in the Foreland district on 11th May 1970. There have been no records since 1974 and the species has generally declined in Britain during the last half century, but it is probably under-recorded and may still visit Islay.

Swift   *Apus apus*

This species is a passage migrant. A nest was reported on Islay in 1927. It currently breeds throughout Northern Ireland and may do so again on Islay, just as it did on the Mull of Kintyre in 1981; two stayed at Ardbeg in July 1986 for at least a week. It is first seen in mid-May, the earliest record being on 8th May 1981 at Proaig. Maximum numbers are seen in June or July, and most depart late in the latter month; the latest was seen on 19th October 1975, at Gruinart. British-ringed Swifts have been found wintering in southeast Africa.

Half of the 56 sightings were on or near the south coast; five are of 10 to 44 birds at Port Ellen and on the Oa Peninsula. Many, however, are of individuals scattered throughout the island. The Swift, with its wide gape, hunts in flight for a large variety of airborne insects and ballooning spiders up to the size of an 8-mm ($\frac{1}{3}$-in) hoverfly, but avoids stinging insects. To maximise the catch, Swifts fly in a low airspace in windy, cold or wet weather and in a high airspace on warm summer days. They roost on the wing or at the nest site.

Kingfisher   *Alcedo atthis*

The Kingfisher is a dispersive visitor that breeds as near as Antrim but with no firm record of breeding on Islay. There are 24 records of individuals seen this century, distributed fairly evenly throughout the year, suggesting occasional exploration of Islay by birds dispersing from points south. Since 1969, 14 records have been from the River Sorn and its tributary the Daill Burn, four from Bridgend, and two along the southeast coast of Upper Loch Indaal. In 1980, one was seen on the Sorn from early July through to November; it may have bred there in 1984, and one was on the Daill Burn on 15th April 1985. Another was on the Gortantaoid River in July 1985.

Prior to 1969, the records suggest a more widespread occurrence on the

Dunlossit Estate, on the Laggan as well as on the Sorn. Records from Loch Allan for 1903 and Loch Ballygrant for 1954 are surprisingly the only ones from fishing lochs. The Kingfisher feeds by diving from a perch or from a hovering position, taking small freshwater fish supplemented by aquatic insects and, when driven by circumstances, marine fish. It roosts solitarily in dense cover near water.

Bee-eater   *Merops apiaster*

A rare vagrant, in Scotland usually recorded from May to August. It breeds around the Mediterranean and in southeast Europe, and its wintering areas are along the Cold Coast and in southeast Africa. Two were photographed on wires near Knocklearach on 3rd June 1981, and one was seen by Portnahaven Hall and in the nearby Lith Gleann on 3rd July 1985.

Roller   *Coracias garrulus*

A rare vagrant, recorded in Scotland from May to October. It breeds around the Mediterranean and in eastern Europe and winters in East Africa and in small areas on the Gold Coast. An immature was at Cladville Farm on 29th September 1968, and an adult was near Sanaig and Loch Gorm from 25th September to 12th October 1983.

Hoopoe   *Upupa epops*

An annual vagrant to Scotland that breeds in southern and central Eurasia and normally migrates to Africa. Most are seen in April-May or September-October and are considered to be diverted from their migration by warm winds associated with unusual developments of anticyclonic conditions. On Islay individuals have been found: between Foreland House and Loch Gorm on 9th May 1978; at Nerabus on 10th October 1981; on Gruinart Flats on 22nd April 1983; at Ardtalla on 8th June 1984; and on the Gruinart Reserve on 9th May 1985.

Wryneck   *Jynx torquilla*

A very rare passage migrant normally moving through eastern Scottish counties, and probably wind-drifted to the west while migrating between Fennoscandian breeding grounds and the western Mediterranean area or tropical Africa. Passages occur from April to mid-June and from mid-August to the end of September. There are records of Wrynecks seen in the grounds of Kildalton House in 1913 (Ross) and 1927, but months are not given.

Green Woodpecker *Picus viridis*

A dispersive visitor that first bred in Scotland in Selkirk in 1951, and has gradually spread through much of the mainland. On Islay, single birds were found at Kilchoman School House, Gruinart, in the third week of May 1978, at Laggan Bridge on 5th and 6th January 1979, and calling at Ballygrant on 11th July 1979. Two or three pairs bred on Mull in 1981.

Great Spotted Woodpecker *Dendrocopos major*

A dispersive visitor that recolonised the Scottish lowlands in the 1890s and was first reported breeding in Argyll in 1921. It is now well established as a breeding species throughout mainland Argyll, including Kintyre, and has bred on Mull from 1946 and on Jura since 1953. Ten birds have been recorded on Islay in eight years from 1954 to 1985; these sightings are dated from April to November. The first record was of a bird shot a Ardmore in 1887; in April 1959 one was in a wood at Ardbeg and later near Loch Lossit; a bird was at Kilchoman, Bruichladdich and Portnahaven from 22nd to 24th October 1962; another was north of Craigens on 21st and apparently near Erasaid on 22nd November 1979 (both localities have small woods next to Gruinart Flats); one was photographed at Machrie in the autumn of 1972; and in April 1982 an adult stayed from at least 12th to 18th in Kildalton Woods. The most recent record is of one at Port Askaig on 10th April 1985. All the major mixed woodlands and some copses have been visited; perhaps one day this species will breed on Islay.

Skylark *Alauda arvensis*

A summer visitor, passage migrant and winter visitor or resident that has been common on Islay since at least 1892. In 1913 (Ross) large winter flocks were reported. Flocks seen at Sunderland since 1970 include over 200 on 21st November 1973, about 400 on 17th December 1975, and 300 on 27th December 1980. Some 300 were still at Kilchoman on 21st March 1981. Only a few Skylarks are seen on the Gruinart Reserve during the winter, but they are plentiful in spring and summer; 345 pairs bred in 1986. The visitors arrive during March and April; some were singing at Ballimony on 11th March 1977, and about 50 birds were at Craigens on 12th March 1986. The spring passage continues into April, and from 10th to 17th April 1963 they were numerous everywhere, including 200 near the Machrie Hotel.

The autumn passage and departure commences in mid-September, when flocks of up to 112 birds have been noted, and continues through October. Rushes were recorded at the Rhinns Lighthouse on 16th October 1885, 19th October 1887 and 23rd October 1962. Large flocks on the Rhinns include over 200 at Portnahaven on 10th October 1974 and 450 at Easter Ellister on 8th

October 1975. It is probable that Islay's birds winter in Ireland and that the passage migrants come from further north in Scotland and Fennoscandia.

Based on the Gruinart Reserve, the Islay population in summer is likely to be between 5,000 and 8,000 pairs. Skylarks were on the summit of Beinn Bhàn in 1953, and are found in most open habitats with low vegetation: heather moors, pastures, leys, machair, saltings, and arable land. They are seen on sowings and stubble, and at livestock feeding stations; they take spilled grain, wild seeds, soil invertebrates, leaves and frost-damaged vegetables. They nest and roost on the ground in rough grass or heather, or in furrows on ploughed land.

Shore Lark   *Eremophila alpestris*

A rare passage migrant; the race concerned breeds in Fennoscandia and across northernmost Siberia. It winters from Britain south to the Mediterranean and usually arrives in October or November in Scotland, where it may be sighted in any month through to May. Three in summer plumage were at Bowmore on 18th October 1976 and then at Ardlarach on 19th.

Sand Martin   *Riparia riparia*

A summer visitor first reported in 1913 (Ross) at several localities, known at five places in 1954, and occupying 120 holes in Laggan River cliffs in 1972. Since then numbers have decreased, until in 1986 only twelve holes were found in the Laggan cliffs and three were in a dune overlooking Traigh Mhachir, Kilchoman. The island population is probably between 15 and 25 pairs.

The first Sand Martin arrives between mid-March and mid-April, the earliest date being 19th March 1986, when one was on the Gruinart Reserve. The majority arrive around the turn of the month. They soon prospect for nest holes in weakly coherent sands which are found primarily in river cliffs, but also in high dunes and at lenses in aggregate-quarry faces. It is likely that dune sands tend to be too loose, and the sand lenses are liable to contain unwanted pebbles.

Sand Martins set off on autumn migration in late August or the first half of September; 25 flew west past Carnmore on 26th August 1974 and presumably followed the coast to the southern Oa cliffs before heading for Ireland. Young were still being fed at Laggan Bridge on 14th September 1972, and four stragglers were at Bridgend on 1st October 1977. Ringing records have shown that Scottish birds winter in West Africa, especially Senegal.

The diet of this aerial feeder is largely flying insects, including some aphids and beetles, taken at low to moderate heights over rivers such as the Laggan, lochs including Skerrols, Gorm and Ardnave, and saltings. They are often with other aerial feeders over Bridgend saltings in the evening. Sand Martins commonly roost in reedbeds in late summer, but this habit has not yet been recorded on Islay.

Swallow *Hirundo rustica*

A summer visitor and passage migrant that was noted at the Rhinns Lighthouse on 2nd May 1887. The main influx takes place during the second half of April, but the earliest birds on record were 'a lot' at Easter Ellister on 6th April 1976. Prior to autumn migration, flocks assemble in the second half of August; 200 birds were on the Gruinart Reserve on 12th August 1986, and many were near Bridgend over the saltings at 19.30 hrs on 29th August 1986. A well-documented passage starts about mid-August and departure is mainly in September, continuing into October. The latest sighting was at Gruinart Flats on 4th November 1981. A juvenile ringed in Cumberland in July 1934 was recovered at Portnahaven on 8th May 1935. Most passage birds are presumed to originate further north in Scotland or in Scandinavia. British Swallows travel to South Africa to winter.

Swallow nest sites are scattered all over the island in farm buildings, derelict houses, and other places with open access at the distilleries or in the villages. Twenty pairs bred at three locations on the Gruinart Reserve in 1986, but in 1980 an average of three pairs per farm was counted in the Stirling district and, using this as a basis, the Islay population probably lies between 150 and 300 pairs. These birds catch insects while flying at low levels. In high winds they often fly back and forth in the lee of woods or in other sheltered places where insects are likely to collect. On 9th September 1976 a flock was feeding, mainly within 50 cm (20 in) of the road surface, in the lee of the wood near the old Gruinart Post Office; the next day similar behaviour was seen over the road by Laphroaig Wood; and on 16th Swallows were flying under the very low bridge that spans the main drain southeast of the Gruinart Post Office. These autumn flocks establish communal roosts, but to date these have not been recorded on Islay.

House Martin *Delichon urbica*

A summer visitor and passage migrant that usually arrives in the first week of May, but occasional birds are seen in April, the earliest record being of one at Sanaig Cliffs on 2nd April 1985. Passages were noted at Carnmore on 29th April 1973 and 8th May 1974. Records indicate nesting at a minimum of 16 localities since 1974; the largest colony, comprising 23 nests, was at Balole Farm on 28th May 1980, and a similar number were there in 1987. Most groups nest on buildings in the villages or at isolated farms, but there were three nests on a ruin at Ballimony in 1976 and several pairs on Sanaig Cliffs on 14th May 1979. Nesting probably occurs at ten to 20 localities in most years, suggesting a breeding population of 50–100 pairs. Success is decreasing owing to the destruction of nests during maintenance work.

Flocks build up in late August and early September: 75 were at Skerrols and Bridgend on 1st September 1974; about 80 were on the Gruinart Reserve on

12th August 1986, with 160 at Blackrock on 24th; and a large number were flying over the Bridgend saltings near roadside trees at 19.30 hrs on 29th August 1986. It is likely that these flocks include passage migrants. Most birds have left the island by late August or early September, but a straggler was still at Bridgend on 20th October 1970. This species winters in tropical and southern Africa.

The House Martin preys on insects while flying at low to moderate heights over land and water; there are several records of birds over Loch Skerrols. It probably roosts in colonies.

Richard's Pipit *Anthus novaeseelandiae*

A rare vagrant that breeds in western Siberia and Mongolia and erupts westwards into Europe. A few reach Scotland each year, mainly in September and October and very rarely in winter and spring. Three have been found on Islay: one near Kilchoman Coastguard Station on 28th September 1971, one on the Oa on 10th September 1973 and another there on 30th October 1987.

Tawny Pipit *Anthus campestris*

A vagrant that breeds in most of mid-latitude Eurasia and around the Mediterranean. The European population winters in Africa south of the Sahara. A few are sighted in Scotland almost annually in late spring or early autumn; two, however, have been in July and one of these was on the Oa at Lower Killeyan on 16th July 1985.

Tree Pipit *Anthus trivialis*

A summer visitor that was said to be 'not common' in 1906 and probably colonised Islay late in the 19th century during a general expansion in Scotland. The earliest known arrival on the island was on 30th April 1984 at Kildalton, but most probably reach Islay during the first half of May. Many records are dated May or June, when the males are singing most frequently; a pair was feeding young in Bridgend Woods on 7th June 1954. Departure appears to take place mainly in August or early September; one was still on the Gruinart Reserve on 2nd September 1986. There may be a small passage in September and the first half of October; three flew east over Loch Skerrols on 8th September 1973 and two flew south over Bridgend on 12th October 1974. They winter in northern tropical Africa.

Tree Pipits require fairly high songposts and they are typically found in open woodland or parkland. On Islay, 70 per cent of all records are from the edges of woods near Kildalton and Bridgend, or from the shelter belts north of Lagavulin, between Tallant and Avenvogie and on the Gruinart Reserve. Five were at Kildalton on 21st June 1986. The Islay population is probably between ten and 20 pairs. Other possible habitats include young conifer plantations preferably with some tall trees nearby, grazed native woods, and scattered tall scrub. Three records provide probable examples: a pair in a young larch plantation near Bridgend on 7th June 1954; a bird at Coille nam Bruach on the Ardmore Estate on 26th May 1978; and another in the Loch Gorm area on 21st August 1986. Foraging occurs mainly on pastures adjacent to trees, and a variety of insects and spiders is taken.

Meadow Pipit *Anthus pratensis*

A summer visitor, passage migrant and winter visitor or resident that has been common on Islay since at least 1892. In 1913 (Ross), it was reported to have become less common in winter. On the Gruinart Reserve, 530 birds on 18th July 1985 and 325 breeding pairs in the summer of 1986 were both reduced to 20 birds by December. If the latter are immigrants, the resident status is suspect. In 1978, birds were arriving at Carnmore on 5th March and on 16th a flock of 80 was on the Oa, where 200 on 8th April is the largest spring count on record; by mid-April movement appears to cease. During summer, the island's population probably lies between 4,000 and 8,000 pairs.

The autumn passage starts in the second half of July or early August; birds were 'abundant all over' the Oa on 25th July 1976. A peak is reached between mid-August and mid-September; 600 flew south by Frenchman's Rocks on 9th September 1973, and 2,000 were on the Oa on 11th September 1980 while many hundreds were setting off south over the sea. Exceptional numbers were noted during this period in six years between 1973 and 1982; they probably went unrecorded in other years. These movements die down in mid-October. Ringing recoveries suggest that Scottish birds winter in southernmost Ireland, Iberia and Morocco, and that most immigrants to the Hebrides come from Ireland.

On Islay, Meadow Pipits breed from mid-April to mid-July and are the principal hosts to visiting Cuckoos; they are seen harassing Cuckoos during the latter half of May. They are found on open ground and are often the most common species on moorland and rough pastures. They also feed on stubble fields, sown fields, beaches with dried seaweed, machair, roadways, and occasionally in riverine habitats: one was catching insects from, and bathing on, floating vegetation in the Uisge an t-Suidhe, near Lyrabus, on 16th September 1976. Their diet includes a variety of insects, spiders, small worms, seeds, spilled grain and a few berries.

Rock Pipit *Anthus (spinoletta) petrosus*

This resident appears to have been common around all rocky coasts since at least 1871 (Gray). It normally nests in rock crevices, but one pair had chosen a wall at

Crosshouses, Carnain, on 12th April 1978. Frequent 'parachute' display flights were performed at Laggan Farm on 25th May 1984. Fifteen pairs bred along 4 km (2½ miles) of coast with low rocks on the Gruinart Reserve in 1986. Islay has about 220 km (137 miles) of coast of which about 180 km (112 miles) are probably suitable, suggesting that the population lies between 500 and 1,000 pairs. Three records indicate that there may be an autumn passage: on 13th September 1973 about 30 were at McArthur's Head; on 13th October 1976 they were very common; and on 20th September 1986 there were 72 on the Gruinart Reserve.

The Rock Pipit finds food chiefly in the intertidal zone and especially among seaweed, but it takes prey from coastal pastures when feeding young. Its diet includes small periwinkles and crustaceans, midge larvae, kelp-fly larvae and other insects.

Blue-headed Wagtail   *Motacilla flava flava*

A rare passage migrant, this race of the Yellow Wagtail breeds in southern Scandinavia and central Europe from France to the Urals, and winters in northwest Africa. It is most frequently seen returning north through Scotland in May but is even rarer on autumn migration. One was at Proaig in eastern Islay on 7th May 1981.

Birds resembling the Continental Blue-headed Wagtail have been found in Ayrshire breeding with yellow-headed birds typical of Britain, rendering the true origin of a vagrant in southwest Scotland difficult to establish.

Yellow Wagtail   *Motacilla flava flavissima*

A rare vagrant to Islay that breeds throughout much of England and Wales and in parts of central and eastern Scotland; regular breeding occurs in mainland Strathclyde. The principal winter quarters of British birds are probably centred around Senegal. There are eight records of single birds on Islay between 1971 and 1987. Four are in spring, between 28th April and 27th May, and the others in autumn: two on 17th September, one on 15th October and the latest on 16th October. The 1986 and 1987 birds were both found on the Gruinart Reserve. A pair is said to have bred in 1922.

Grey Wagtail   *Motacilla cinerea*

A resident, summer visitor and passage migrant that breeds on Islay in small numbers, probably between 50 and 100 pairs. From 1st November to 15th March records are sparse and mainly of individuals; numbers increase during the second half of March, when summer visitors arrive and there is possibly a small passage. Pairs and singing birds are first noticed during this period. The Gruinart Reserve maximum count for 1986 was five in March. Dispersal and migration commences again early in July; for a few days from 5th July 1973 a passage was noticed at Carnmore. Movement is most pronounced between late July and mid-September; eight birds set off from the Oa towards Ireland on 11th September 1980, and there were still a few passing Carnmore on 23rd September 1973. Some of Islay's birds probably winter in Ireland or southern England, but others from further north in Scotland may continue south to France or Iberia.

The Grey Wagtail breeds and feeds along rivers and streams, particularly on fast-flowing reaches with a little cover of scrub, tall heather or ferns along the banks. It has been found along many watercourses, such as those at Ardtalla, Bruichladdich, Daill, Lagavulin, and Kilnaughton. It also visits the shores of both freshwater and saltwater lochs and bays, and occasionally joins Pied Wagtails in their habitats away from water.

When feeding, it uses the run-and-peck technique and also hawks insects on small aerial sallies from both ground and branches. It preys on aquatic invertebrates, flying insects in the vicinity of water, beetles, midge larvae, amphibian larvae, small fish, small molluscs and worms. Many items are taken from the strand line, but, since water freezes first at the edge, this source is the first to be lost in a hard winter.

White Wagtail   *Motacilla alba alba*

A passage migrant that breeds in Iceland and winters in Ireland, France, Iberia or northwest Africa. It is recorded on Islay from late March to mid-May and again from late August to late September; 16 per cent of 230 records of the species refer to this race and it is likely to have been overlooked. Eleven were at Frenchman's Rocks on 1st May 1977 and ten at Bridgend saltings on the following day. Thirteen were between Bowmore and Laggan Point on 14th September 1980, and 14 were at Bridgend saltings on 20th April 1982.

Single birds are occasionally seen in summer; one paired with a Pied Wagtail was feeding young at West Carrabus on 3rd June 1972, and a mixed pair was at Storakaig in June 1976. The habitat and feeding of the White Wagtail are very similar to those of the Pied Wagtail.

Pied Wagtail   *Motacilla alba yarrellii*

A resident and passage migrant first recorded in December 1900 and common from at least 1913 (Ross). It is present in small numbers from November to early March, when a maximum of ten has been found on the Gruinart Reserve; some birds probably leave the island temporarily during the coldest weather. Numbers increase some time in March; on 18th in 1975 there was 'a sprinkling all over', and some came into Carnmore on 7th March 1977. There was a spring maximum of 38 on the Gruinart Reserve on 8th April 1984, and eleven pairs bred there that year, as did six in 1985 and ten in 1986. A pair nested on a lobster boat anchored off Tayovullin in May 1974 and 1975.

The autumn passage commences in late July: there were 'a lot' at Port Askaig on 26th July 1971 and 'lots all over, mainly juveniles' on 31st July 1975. Migrant flocks are noted through to early October, reaching a maximum in September: 40 were at Sanaigmore on 14th September 1973; 50 at Bridgend on 17th September 1976 and 120 there on 21st; and 75 were on the Gruinart Reserve on 28th September 1984. On Rathlin Island, Pied Wagtails appeared to arrive from Islay and Jura between 20th August and 27th September 1960; these migrants presumably originate further north in Scotland and travel to Ireland or still further south.

These very active birds appear to require a fairly flat area with clear views allowing hunting by a run-and-peck technique, supplemented by jerky swerves, leaps and some hawking. They are found on well-grazed moorland, around farm steadings, on short-cropped pasture, saltings, machair, beaches, roads, farm tracks and roofs, as well as on the shores of some lochs and rivers, on ploughed fields and at livestock feeding stations. They are scattered widely on these specialised habitats, making the population difficult to estimate, but possibly 150–250 pairs are resident on Islay.

Pied Wagtails have a diet that includes beetles, flies, midges, insect larvae and caterpillars, small worms, small molluscs and seeds. They roost in thickets or reedbeds: some were apparently going to roost on 'Castle Island' in Loch Gorm on 11th August 1976; 15 entered a roost at Loch Tallant, Bowmore, on 18th March 1978; and 55 flying east at Kilchoman on 31st August 1979 were probably going to roost.

Waxwing *Bombycilla garrulus*

An irruptive visitor from the forests of Fennoscandia, arriving annually in eastern Scotland and penetrating westwards when in large numbers or when food has been depleted by thrush invasions. The largest numbers to reach Islay were in November 1970, when 18 were at Kildalton on 4th, 20 at Bridgend on 7th and five at Carnmore on 16th. Birds were sighted in nine years out of the 23 to 1986, and the first record was of one with a damaged wing in 1922. Three Waxwings were at Bunnahabhainn on 7th March 1980, but otherwise all records fall between the last week of October and 5th December, when one was at Bowmore in 1985. These records are from widely scattered locations; the birds search out berries or buds on rowan, cotoneaster, hawthorn, sea-buckthorn and rose bushes.

Dipper *Cinclus cinclus*

A resident reported as common in 1871 (Gray); then, in 1913 (Ross), it was found on the Rivers Laggan and Sorn and on the burns at Callumkill and that issuing from Loch Kinnabus. The River Sorn yielded 34 sightings from 1975 to 1986. In 1954 there were several pairs found along the Sorn and a sighting on the Abhainn Bhogie; then, on 1st April 1973, one was on the Doodilimore River 4–5 km (2½–3 miles) northeast of Killinallan. Others were near Octofad on 15th August 1973, Kilchiaran on about 25th October 1977, Glenmachrie Lots on 28th March 1980, Easter Ellister on 3rd November 1981 and Tormisdale on 31st May 1985. The strong bias towards the Sorn is likely to be due mainly to the easy access open to birdwatchers; other watercourses are probably under-recorded.

Even the Sorn sightings decreased from six in 1977 to nil in 1985, territory in Bridgend was apparently unoccupied after 1981, and no Dippers were found at the Wool Mill in the summers of 1985 and 1986. They were, however, seen near the mill on 19th August, 12th September and 28th November 1986, and they bred successfully there in 1987. A decline in Dipper populations elsewhere in Britain has been attributed to various human activities that increase the acidity of rivers, including afforestation. Dippers like fast-flowing streams with rocky or gravelly beds; they prey on crustaceans, the waterborne stages of insects, fish spawn, small molluscs and small fish. They roost singly or in small groups and in sheltered places including crevices in rocks. Favoured sites for both roosting and nesting are in gorges and beneath bridges. A pair nested near the road bridge in Bridgend in April 1977 and produced young.

Wren *Troglodytes troglodytes*

A resident that has been common on Islay since at least the turn of the century. A few may pass through on autumn migration; some were killed at the Rhinns Lighthouse on 23rd October 1962. The Wren is scattered throughout Islay wherever there is low cover such as well-grown heather, gorse or other shrubs, stunted trees or untidy hedges. It also occurs in overgrown ditches, ungrazed native woods, shelter belts and the shrubbery of estate woodlands. More unusually, it was recorded along the cliffs near Rhuvaal in 1954, high on gully walls at Sanaig Cliffs on 15th May 1978 and 25th May 1986, on cliffs below Beinn Mhor, the Oa, on 5th April 1981, and on an ivy-clad cliff south of Braigo Wood on 21st May 1986. In these situations it takes cover among fallen rocks or in crevices on bare cliffs.

The Wren also occupies conifer plantations at the establishment stage, moving to the wood edges at the thicket stage. The death of suppressed trees, and the thinning and windthrow of others, lead to a more open wood which will again attract Wrens if fallen trees, brushwood and ground vegetation are allowed to accumulate. Peak numbers of Wrens were recorded on the mainland in 1975, after a series of mild winters, and they appear to have been even more numerous than usual on Islay. There were twelve singing males around Bun-an-Uillt in April 1981, and 36 pairs bred on the Gruinart Reserve in 1985, 35 in 1986 and 39 in 1987. At this density, the Islay population may be around 1,000 pairs.

The Wren feeds mainly on small insects, but also on spiders and occasionally on wild seeds. It usually roosts singly, but in hard weather tens of birds may huddle together in a confined space.

Dunnock   *Prunella modularis*

A resident that is very under-recorded, but was reported to be common in 1892, 1913 (Ross) and 1954, and still appears to be so in 1987. Scottish Dunnocks are very sedentary and will not cross water when there is a wind of more than force 3, but they are known to erupt over short distances after good breeding seasons. Scandinavian birds migrate to southern Europe, and a few ringed in Scotland have been recovered in Norway during the breeding season. Two caught at Bridgend on 26th March 1977 had wing lengths corresponding to those of Continental Dunnocks, and there is a small peak in the numbers of sightings in September and October, suggesting a passage. Six, the largest count, were at Carnmore on 3rd October 1972.

The Dunnock requires ground cover for its skulking habits. It is found in those parts of estate woodlands, shelter belts and gardens that have much undergrowth or shrubbery, and in conifer plantations at the thicket stage; it is absent from grazed native woods. Some occur in scrub or overgrown ditches. On the Gruinart Reserve, eight pairs bred in 1984, seven in 1985, nine in 1986 and eight in 1987. Unusually, two were found in a cave at Port nan Gallan, the Oa, on 27th January 1977. There were rather fewer Dunnocks than Goldcrests caught for ringing in estate woodlands at Bridgend from 1973 to 1977, but, taking into account the wider habitat spread of the former and the Gruinart numbers, the Islay population may be between 200 and 300 pairs. The population is likely to increase as newly planted conifers grow, and to be locally high after trees are felled by storms, adding to the ground cover.

This active species takes its food from the ground, sometimes turning over small leaves; it takes weed seeds, beetles, spiders, flies, springtails and insect larvae, concentrating on seeds in the winter and occasionally added cereal grain to its diet.

Robin   *Erithacus rubecula*

A resident and probable passage migrate that has been common since at least the turn of the century. However, numbers are reduced for a few years after a severe winter, and they were at a low ebb in 1976. A small spring passage probably occurs and there is some evidence for one also in October, when the main influx of Continental birds occurs on the Scottish east coast. There was an unusual abundance on 1st October 1976 and on 29th of that month over 20 were in one field at Portnahaven and another observer reported Continental birds. Larg numbers were on the island between 26th and 29th October 1979. Twelve wer at the Rhinns Lighthouse on 24th April 1987.

The Robin is widespread on Islay, frequenting the estate woodlands, shelte belts and copses adjacent to farms, and also the richer native woods with som undergrowth. It visits well-stocked gardens and is even seen along scrubb ditches. It is attracted to plantations at the pre-thicket stage and was in lov conifers 0.5 km (547 yds) southeast of Loch Allan on 22nd May 1978. Presen afforestation is likely to increase the population. On the Gruinart Reserve, wher there are shelter belts and a little scrub, 14 pairs bred in 1985, 16 in 1986 and 1 in 1987. In general, the density is likely to be lower than on the mainland, bu there are probably 400 to 600 pairs on Islay.

These attractive birds feed mainly on the ground and at birdtables, but the may also perch on a fence or wall and dart to collect any prey spotted or briefl hawk flying insects. Their natural food includes a wide variety of so invertebrates and also moths, gall-insects, small fruits and berries. They ofter roost communally in dense vegetation.

Nightingale *Luscinia megarhynchos*

A vagrant that breeds in southeast England, central and southern Europe an northwesternmost Africa; it winters further south between the Sahara and th equatorial forests. Some individuals have been found in Scotland from mid-May to June and a few from mid-August to the end of October. On Islay, one san from a thicket near Loch Skerrols on 28th April 1973 and another was heard an seen at Kilnaughton Bay on 2nd May 1984.

Black Redstart *Phoenicurus ochruros*

A rare migrant visitor that breeds in southeast and central England and in mucl of central and southern Europe. Most winter in the southern part of this range o in Africa north of the Sahara. It is possible that some birds migrate west out of th harsh Continental winter to Britain; one ringed on the Isle of May on 12th Apr 1953 was caught in East Germany the following June. On Islay, a female was at th Machrie Hotel on 23rd and 25th October 1977 and then at Bowmore Pier on 9t November; an adult male was alongside the highest part of the Kilbride Lane or 31st March 1981; and a male was at Kilchoman on 26th October 1987. Both winte and summer visitors are known in the Outer Hebrides.

Redstart *Phoenicurus phoenicurus*

A passage migrant and irregular summer visitor that was recorded in ten year from 1969 to 1986; no more then two breeding pairs have been found in any one year. The first birds arrive in May; a male was at Bushmill on 15th in 1973 and four were at Sanaig on 14th in 1979. Three arrivals on Colonsay have been in May; one was there on 15th in 1982. A female was feeding young in a stone wall at Port Askaig on 12th June 1953, and there was a nest with young at Kildalton as well as a pair at Ballygrant in June 1969. Three males were found singing between Port Askaig and Ardnahoe on 7th June 1974. Departure is from late August on the mainland; one was at Laggan Bridge on 28th in 1957 and another was on the Gruinart Reserve on 26th September 1986. Two late passage visitors have been seen: a male in winter plumage at Easter Ellister on 31st October 1976 and again at Bridgend on the same day, and a female behind the Lochside Hotel, Bowmore, on 6th November 1985. These probably came from Fennoscandia and, like the Scottish birds, winter in the Sahel of West Africa.

The Redstart favours woods with oak and pine and is attracted to the estate woodlands when on Islay. The male often hawks insects, but the female usually feeds on the ground. They take caterpillars, flies, aphids, ants, earwigs, grasshoppers, woodlice, very small snails, berries and fruits.

Whinchat   *Saxicola rubetra*

A summer visitor and passage migrant that is widespread but somewhat scarcer than the Stonechat; probably from 100 to 200 pairs breed on Islay. They arrive in late April or during the first half of May, the earliest sighting being of a male at

Whinchat (Brian Southern)

Kinnabus on 25th April 1976. A male was seen with food at Avenvogie on 13th May 1980; twelve pairs bred on the Gruinart Reserve in 1986 and 19 in 1987. Food was still being given to young alongside Kintra Lane on 13th August 1972. Movement commences about this time and continues into September; all have normally departed at the end of the month, but a male was still at Carnmore on 29th September 1973. Late passage migrants that may have been of Scandinavian origin were at Portnahaven on 29th and 31st October 1976. There was a male at Grulinbeg by Loch Gorm on 26th November 1973 and two further birds were recorded on 26th November 1983. Two overwintering birds were seen in the Port Ellen area on 4th January during the *Atlas* survey of 1981/2 to 1983/4. The species normally winters in tropical bush country south of the Sahara.

The Whinchat's habitat is scattered across moorland, especially where there is tussocky grassland. It requires metre-high perches as lookout posts and songposts and is found on bushes including gorse and sallow, on tall thistles and on fences by ditches with brambles, as well as on the edge of thin native woods and young plantations. It is most readily found around Loch Gorm, and is likely to be encouraged by recent conifer plantations. It picks insects from herbage, heather and flowers, and by sallying forth from perches and occasionally hawking them. Food from the ground is of minor importance; beetles, flies, larvae, earwigs, spiders and occasional worms and small molluscs are eaten. Roosting is presumably within territory.

Stonechat   *Saxicola torquata*

The resident population of Stonechats is greatly reduced in severe winters but is capable of quick recovery. This species was said to be scarcer than the Whinchat in 1892, and was at a low ebb after the 1947 and 1978 winters; conversely, it was common in 1945, appeared to have been common before 1953 (Baxter and Rintoul), and was well distributed in 1985 and 1986. Eight pairs bred on the Gruinart Reserve in 1986 and ten in 1987. When numbers are normal, Islay probably holds from 150 to 250 pairs.

A small passage seems to occur between mid-August and mid-October: some were at Carnmore with other migrants on 15th August 1972; a passage was reported there on 3rd September 1974; there were many juveniles and adults assembled between Portnahaven and Cladville on 12th September 1976; and 30 were counted on the Gruinart Reserve in August 1985. Very few sightings are reported from late November to mid-February and it may be that some of Islay's birds spend the winter in Ireland.

The Stonechat requires rough pasture or heather, often with some short-cropped grass, and also a few perches that serve as songposts and points from which to scan for potential food. Sparse scrub or gorse, mature heather over 15 cm (6 in) high and a stone wall, plantations of conifers less than ten years old, a bushy watercourse, and even a ditch with a few brambles may be occupied. It often feeds by dropping on to prey from a perch, and takes ants, small beetles or flies and their larvae, butterflies and moths, spiders, small worms and a few wild seeds; caterpillars and larvae are fed to the young.

Wheatear *Oenanthe oenanthe*

A summer visitor and passage migrant that consistently arrives in late March or early April; the earliest record is of a male sighted near Balulive gate on 18th March 1977. The spring passage continues until late May and birds of the larger and brighter Greenland race (*O.o.leucorrhoa*) were at Limekiln Cottages, Bridgend, on 17th May 1974 and at Sanaig on 27th May 1975. Most passage birds continue north to northwest on an approximately great circle route to the Faroes, Iceland, Greenland or arctic Canada; the further along this route they summer, the more likely they are to differ from the British race (*O.o.oenanthe*). The return passage begins in late July, but Islay's birds depart mainly in

Wheatear

167

September and the first part of October; most have gone by mid-month, but single birds were at Easter Ellister and Ballimony on 31st October 1976, at Coultorsay on 7th November 1976 and on the Gruinart Reserve on 19th November 1985. A male of the Greenland race was near Loch Gorm on 20th October 1978. Their wintering grounds are in the savannahs south of the Sahara.

The Wheatear is well distributed throughout Islay, mainly in open country with herbage less than 10 cm (4 in) high, cropped by Rabbits, sheep or feral goats, allowing these birds uninterrupted view of potential food. Rocks, outcrops, drystone dykes or shielings are essential for songposts and nest or roost sites. Twenty-six pairs bred on the Gruinart Reserve in 1987.

These birds are insectivorous, using a run-and-peck technique to take beetles, flies, bumblebees, ants, moths, grasshoppers, insect larvae, spiders and centipedes; they also take small snails and occasional berries. It has been suggested that the Wheatear's ability to hover enables it to scan for prey.

Ring Ouzel *Turdus torquatus*

The first reference to this passage migrant being on Islay is dated 1871 (Gray); it was considered to be scarce then and still is, with only one recorded in some years. Exceptionally, there were seven sightings in 1976.

Ringing recoveries show that these migrants are likely to originate in the Scottish Highlands or Scandinavia. The earliest autumn date of a sighting on Islay was 15th August 1885; nearly all others fall between 18th October and 6th November; three were on Beinn Mhor, the Oa, on 20th October 1976. They winter chiefly in southern France and northeast Spain. The spring passage is represented by only one occurrence, at Kilchoman School near Gruinart on 13th April 1980.

It has been reported that the Ring Ouzel once bred on Islay, and a few pairs bred on Jura until recently but the last firm record was dated June 1977. This species prefers open moorland with steep rocky hillsides and is likely to be excluded by afforestation. It is unlikely to return to Islay in the foreseeable future.

Blackbird *Turdus merula*

It is probable that Blackbirds in the estate woodlands are resident; others breeding in open country visit Ireland from November to February, and yet others are winter visitors to Islay from Fennoscandia. Although this is based on an understanding of this species on mainland Britain, data collected on Islay do indicate a marked autumn passage. Blackbirds were noted in 1840 and 1892, and again as abundant in 1913 (Ross) and before 1953 (Baxter and Rintoul). Selected densities of this well-studied species, including that on the Gruinart Reserve, suggest that nowadays there are probably between 400 and 700 pairs on the island in the breeding season.

The autumn passage begins in August or the first half of September and was especially marked in the 1970s: on 13th, 15th and 16th October 1974 flocks were said to be 'flying west over the whole island'; more than 100 were at Sanaigmore on 31st October 1975; large numbers were at the north of the island, on the Oa and on the Rhinns on 16th, 17th and 18th November 1975; and 350 were on the southern Rhinns on 30th October 1976 when there was again a concentration at Sanaig as well as flocks elsewhere. Occasionally loose flocks are seen during the winter, but all signs of movement end by late March or early April; the spring passage is small or absent.

The earliest nest noted was on 19th April 1923 in the wreck of a lifeboat at Port an Eas, the Oa. On the Gruinart Reserve, 17, 16, 11 and 15 pairs bred in the years 1984 to 1987 respectively. This species breeds in all parts of Islay, except on the high ground devoid of a tree or shrub. It is most common in estate woodlands, shelter belts and well-stocked gardens, but is thinly scattered over other habitats with some woody vegetation. Pairs nested in a hedge by Cladville Lane on 1st June 1977 and foraged and sang in 200 sq. m (240 sq. yds) of sallow scrub near Gearach on 1st and 4th June 1986.

Blackbirds feed on a wider variety of animal and vegetable foods than any other thrush. They forage on the ground, in bushes and trees, on bare soil and grass, and rummage among leaf litter on woodland floors and in hedge bottoms. They take earthworms and other soil invertebrates, turning to grain, wild seeds, berries and fruits in season. One at Port Charlotte was 'persistently eating new putty' from windows in December 1976.

These thrushes roost singly in territories or communally in evergreen shrubs, hedgerows or thickets. A pair went to roost in a small patch of birch scrub by Loch Lossit on 31st January 1986.

Fieldfare   *Turdus pilaris*

A winter visitor and passage migrant, having an eruptive nature. A maximum of six was reported in 1913 (Ross) but large flocks on passage were common during October in the 1970s, reaching over 2,000 individuals in one group flying over Leorin at 08.30 hrs on 1st November 1975. A flock of 178 was on the Gruinart Reserve in October 1985, and many large flocks were scattered over the island in October 1987. These birds come from Fennoscandia, many continuing on to Ireland; on 11th October 1974, at Kinnabus on the Oa, 'several dropped out of the sky from a great height'. A few may arrive in September, but the main influx usually commences during the first half of October and has passed south by early November, after which parties of only a few tens are normally reported through to the end of the winter. The spring passage, usually in flocks of less than 100, begins late in March, most flocks leaving by mid-April; however, 100 were near Port Ellen on 21st April 1977. There are a few summer records; one was at Easter

Ellister on 1st June 1975 and six were singing there on 6th May 1981. Three were heard passing over Carnmore on 8th August 1977. Breeding occurs in most years on the mainland and has been suspected on the island of Mull.

The Fieldfare is found scattered throughout the island on open pastures and arable farmland, often taking wild fruit from trees and bushes. It feeds in loose flocks, sometimes accompanied by Starlings or a few Redwings, and takes berries, earthworms, slugs, snails and other ground invertebrates. It roosts communally in cover varying from heather and scattered scrub to evergreen shrubs and dense woodland. At dusk on 30th October 1975, about 500 were roosting in heather on Creag Mhor, Kilchoman.

Song Thrush   *Turdus philomelos*

A mainly migratory breeder that was first recorded as a native of Kilchoman parish in 1840. It was absent from Islay during the severe winter of 1878/9, was reported in 1913 (Ross) as common, and was stated to be very numerous in 1953 (Baxter and Rintoul). Flocks of presumed migrants are seen chiefly in October and November: some were at Carnmore on 27th September 1974; 56 were scattered throughout the Rhinns on 30th October 1976; and over 50 were in fields around Cladville on 29th November 1980. A bird ringed as a juvenile at Heligoland on 2nd October 1974 was killed at the Rhinns Lighthouse on 19th October 1976 along with twelve other Song Thrushes. The Outer Hebridean race (*T.p.hebridensis*) has been seen several times on Colonsay in the autumn and may be among migrants passing through Islay; it is darker-backed and more strongly spotted than the usual British race (*T.p.clarkei*).

Twenty were on the Gruinart Reserve during the first three months of 1986, but in general there are few winter records; many probably winter in Ireland, as ringing studies suggest for some Highland birds. Returning migrants are usually seen in March, and a large number arrived on about 22nd March 1971. Nests are noted from 2nd April, when in 1972 one at Carnmore contained three eggs. Eleven pairs bred on the Gruinart Reserve in 1985 and twelve in both 1986 and 1987, but in general the Song Thrush appears much less numerous than the Blackbird. Between 250 and 400 pairs breed on Islay and are widely distributed except on the moorlands.

This thrush requires trees or a few bushes near farmland or gardens; it nests in the estate woodlands, shelter belts and copses, and in young conifer plantations or even gorse bushes and heather. It feeds mainly on the ground, taking earthworms, snails, slugs and a wide range of invertebrates, including caterpillars, beetles, flies, ants, aphids, spiders, centipedes and millipedes; also wild fruits in the autumn, such as haws, blackberries and elderberries. The Song Thrush uses a stone or other hard object as an anvil on which to crack open snail shells by hammering. It often roosts singly or in small groups in bushes and shrubs.

Redwing *Turdus iliacus*

A passage migrant and winter visitor that was at the Rhinns Lighthouse on 12th April and 17th October 1885. The first immigrants arrive in late September or early October; the earliest arrival was in 1973, when a small flock was at Laggan Bridge on 20th September. This influx often continues until mid-November, the largest numbers passing through during the second half of October. Exceptionally large passages were noted in the mid-1970s: over 1,000 went southeast over Carnmore on 28th October 1975; thousands passed over the Oa on 20th October 1976; and thousands were at Kintra on about 24th October 1977. Many large flocks were scattered over the island in October 1987. Normally groups of a few hundred are found alternately feeding and flying as they work across Islay; many are probably on the island for only one day. On 19th October 1976, at the Rhinns Lighthouse, 336 dead Redwings were counted; they included both Icelandic (*T.i.coburni*) and Fennoscandian or Russian birds (*T.i.iliacus*). In general, most birds passing through the Hebrides are Icelandic, the darker and slightly larger of these races; 420 were killed at the lighthouse on 2nd October 1977. These migrants probably winter in Ireland, France or Iberia. Only a few are found on Islay during the winter; 95 were at Easter Ellister on 14th December 1977, and 60 were on the Gruinart Reserve in February 1986.

The northward migration occurs in March and April but is rarely spectacular; 400 birds were west of Newton School, Bridgend, on 10th March 1977. The last groups usually leave the island during the second half of April; the latest departures were on 22nd April in 1978 and 1980, but one stayed on the Gruinart Reserve until 2nd and another until 8th May 1986. Occasionally birds are seen during the breeding season; one was near Nerabus on 25th May and 2nd June 1973.

Redwings sometimes flock and feed with Fieldfares. They take rowan and hawthorn berries and small invertebrates, including worms, beetles, the larvae of moths, earwigs, flies, snails and slugs. In bad weather they turn to stubble and root crops. They roost in dense leafy cover, such as rhododendron bushes; 40 entered a roost in Kildalton Woods on 26th March 1980.

Mistle Thrush *Turdus viscivorus*

A partial migrant that extended its breeding range over most of Scotland and Ireland during the first half of the 19th century. It was reported on Islay in 1822, and was apparently still rare but said to be breeding in 1839; by the early 20th century it had become frequent. Ringing recoveries have shown that the Scottish Mistle Thrush is highly migratory, and it is very sparsely distributed on Islay through the winter. A large number was recorded about 22nd March 1971 and pairs have been noted at this time of year. On the Gruinart Reserve, eleven pairs bred in 1985 and twelve in 1986; this suggests that two pairs per sq. km (five per sq. mile) breed in suitable habitat, giving an island population of about 80 pairs.

Flocks of ten to 20 are seen from late June to late October; 30 flew south into Scots pines in the Avenvogie roadside shelter belt on 17th September 1976 and fed on rowan berries. Evidence of a southward passage includes reports of an abundance in late June 1976 and many throughout the island on 18th September 1978. Most birds in these 'rushes' are probably from further north in Scotland and are en route to France, though the evidence is sketchy.

Mistle Thrushes prefer the edge of woodland adjoining farmland or occupy parkland. They are most frequently seen around the estate woodlands and some plantations; observations are widespread except in the Rhinns, where the only record is from Easter Ellister. A pair was nesting in gorse at Laggan Bridge on 23rd May 1977. This species feeds on earthworms and other ground invertebrates for most of the year but takes fruit and berries in the autumn. Individuals sometimes defend a tree in berry against other birds. The invertebrates eaten include beetles, weevils, earwigs, centipedes, millipedes, flies, spiders, slugs and snails. Small roosts may be sited in conifers.

Grasshopper Warbler   *Locustella naevia*

A summer visitor that is present in most years. It leaves in late July or early August to winter south of the Sahara, probably on the northern fringes of the tropical forests, and returns in late April or early May. Extreme dates on Islay are 30th April 1985, when it was recorded on the Gruinart Reserve, and 9th August 1977, when one was at Bridgend. Five pairs bred on the reserve in 1986 and two in 1987.

This warbler requires rank ground vegetation, and is found in sedges, reedbeds, dense tall grasses with some brambles, isolated bushes, or conifer plantations at the establishment stage. The 'reeling' that gives this species its English name is usually heard at dusk, morning or evening, especially on drizzly, cloudy days. Four pairs bred on the Gruinart Reserve in 1985, five in 1986 and two in 1987. Singing birds have been reported alongside the old Loch Gorm road in several summers and one was heard in a conifer plantation between Cluanach and Avenvogie Cottage from 19th June to 2nd July 1977. In total, birds have been reported from 14 widely scattered localities and it is likely to be under-recorded. Probably over ten pairs breed on the island in good years.

The food of the Grasshopper Warbler comprises a wide range of insects and their larvae, especially flies, aphids and small moths and their caterpillars, also small dragonflies, mayflies, beetles, woodlice and spiders.

Sedge Warbler   *Acrocephalus schoenobaenus*

A summer visitor that winters in Africa south of the Sahara; British-ringed birds have been recovered in tropical West Africa. Relatively few summer north of Islay and the species is not detectable as a passage migrant. A few Sedge

Warblers were reported on Islay in 1871 (Gray), and they were still said to be uncommon in 1913 (Ross). The species was then reported to be common in 1947, 1954 and 1963, but it suffered a decline in Britain after the onset of the Sahel drought in 1968/9. Twenty-two pairs bred on the Gruinart Reserve in 1986 and 39 in 1987, indicating densities of 1.7 and 3.0 pairs per sq. km (4.4 and 7.8 per sq. mile) on fairly typical Islay moor and farm, and suggesting an island population of between 500 and 1,000 pairs.

These very active birds normally arrive in the first half of May, but several were at Easter Ellister on 24th April 1987 and another was seen and heard in reeds near Kilchoman Coastguard Cottages on 3rd April 1981. Sedge Warblers are found throughout Islay and are reported at a large number of localities. They stay in reeds, rushes and sedges, especially where there are isolated bushes, in damp scrub, roadside ditches with ample cover, and some conifer plantations at the pre-thicket stage while the ground cover is still dominant. Emigration occurs mainly in August or in the first half of September, the latest date being 16th September 1976 when one was at the 'canal' bridge on Gruinart Flats. One ringed at Bridgend on 4th August 1975 was recovered at Radipole Lake, Weymouth, on 1st September 1975.

These birds often feed low down in vegetation but rarely on the ground. They take a variety of 'flies', including midges, craneflies and dragonflies, and also aphids and beetles.

Reed Warbler *Acrocephalus scirpaceus*

A scarce vagrant that breeds in England and much of Europe and migrates via Iberia to winter in tropical Africa. Scottish records range from April to October. It traditionally nests in *Phragmites* reeds and has been found at three localities with reeds on Islay: at Foreland Marsh on 1st July 1976; at the Springbank road junction early in August 1980; and in the Loch Gorm area on 26th June 1981.

Icterine Warbler *Hippolais icterina*

A rare vagrant that breeds across central Eurasia and winters in eastern tropical Africa. It does not breed in Britain but a few extend their northeastward migration into the British Isles and coastal Scandinavia, breeding in the latter area in recent years. It has been seen in Scotland from mid-May to early July and from August to October. One was at the Mull of Oa on 28th August 1978.

Lesser Whitethroat *Sylvia curruca*

A scarce vagrant whose breeding density decreases southwestwards from an irregular few in Ayrshire to become more common than the Whitethroat in

Kent. British birds winter in northeast Africa, returning northwestwards across Europe; a few overshoot the breeding range to the Hebrides, arriving mainly in May and June. Single birds were singing at Easter Ellister on 26th May 1974 and Bridgend on 27th May 1975. Other Hebridean records are in September and October.

Whitethroat   *Sylvia communis*

A summer visitor that was once very common on Islay; it was reported as frequent in 1913 (Ross), and as on moors among bushes and bracken in 1954. Baxter and Rintoul (1953) said that it was a common visitor and a passage migrant, but there has not been a record suggesting a significant passage since 1970.

The earliest arrival of these visitors to Islay was on 20th April in 1974, but they are not normally present until early May. They occupy scrub, bushy ditches and burns, ground cover on the edge of woods or in clearings, and conifer plantations less than ten years old. There were four singing males in Gleann Osamail on 17th June 1976, several by the burn and path leading to Loch Allan on 28th May 1977, and one with a metal ring on its right leg in a conifer plantation near Stone Cottage, Bridgend, on 25th May 1981. Six pairs bred on the Gruinart Reserve in 1984, and one was singing in an isolated bush alongside the main road near Eorrabus Smithy on 24th June 1986. Emigration commences in July but continues into the autumn, the latest bird on record being one at Easter Ellister on 24th October 1976. Migration takes them to the Sahel and the northern fringe of tropical Africa. A severe drought there in 1968/9 reduced the British population by 77 per cent, accounting for the fall in numbers on Islay since 1954. The present breeding population on the island is probably between 50 and 100 pairs.

The food of Whitethroats is primarily insects and their larvae, especially moths and butterflies, and also ants, flies, aphids, wireworms, dung beetles and spiders.

Garden Warbler   *Sylvia borin*

A scarce summer visitor which has never been proved to breed on Islay. Single birds are usually seen, but two were in a birch clump at the Allt nam Gamhna bridge near Catterdale on 21st May 1978. Only 23 records cover the fifteen years to 1987. During this period the earliest arrival was on 25th April 1972 at Dunlossit; nine records dated May might include birds on passage; and the latest bird was at Skerrols on 12th November 1980. Most winter in tropical or southern Africa.

During the breeding season these warblers occupy thickets, hedges, scrub or brambles, including rhododendrons and conifers at the thicket stage. One was in brambles and scrub on the edge of Loch Indaal saltings in July 1962, and another stayed in a bush at the Aoradh junction from 4th to 14th May 1986. Nine records are from estate woodlands. The Garden Warbler feeds primarily on insects, taking the caterpillars of small moths and butterflies, small beetles, flies, ants, aphids, spiders and occasional small worms. It turns to fruits and berries in late summer.

Blackcap   *Sylvia atricapilla*

A summer visitor to Islay that has probably bred and an autumn passage migrant. Only one male has been recorded in winter, at Whin Park, Bridgend, on 21st December 1973. The migrants have been found between late September and mid-November, especially in the latter three weeks of October; 15 males and 15 females have been recorded. It has been suggested that they come from Scandinavia and that the majority winter in Ireland. One ringed at Bridgend on 29th September 1976, however, was controlled at Beachy Head, Sussex, on 29th October of that year. British breeders are known to winter mainly in Iberia and northern Africa.

From 1970 to 1987, only 17 birds were noted in spring and summer. The earliest and latest of these were on the Gruinart Reserve on 7th April 1985 and 29th August 1986. A pair collecting caterpillars at the footbridge upstream of Bridgend on 23rd June 1985 was probably breeding. This locality satisfies the Blackcap's requirements well: it prefers deciduous woodland with a good understorey, and estate woodlands with rhododendron bushes are often selected in Scotland and Ireland. Half of Islay's sightings were in such woodlands.

These birds are omnivorous; they take insects and their larvae from trees and bushes, small worms and beetles from the ground, an increasing proportion of a wide range of fruit as the summer progresses, and any berries available in autumn and winter.

Bonelli's Warbler   *Phylloscopus bonelli*

A woodland warbler that is a rare vagrant to Scotland; it breeds in southern Europe and winters in tropical Africa. Its nearest breeding grounds are in northern France and the Netherlands. The several Scottish records fall between 5th September and 3rd October, apart from one on Islay, at Easter Ellister on 21st and 22nd May 1976.

Wood Warbler   *Phylloscopus sibilatrix*

A summer visitor that probably reached Islay late in the 19th century; in 1907 it was common in Kildalton estate woodlands, but now the understorey is too dense in many parts. It winters in tropical Africa and normally arrives on Islay in early May, but one was already singing at Kildalton on 30th April 1984. The two songs of this species are heard until mid-June; in recent years birds have sung close to the Wool Mill and at other places within 1 km (0.6 miles) of there. Singing birds can give a false impression of the breeding population; it is known that there is often an excess of males and that polygamy may occur. Thus the number of pairs is difficult to determine, but it is likely that 20–30 individuals visit the island annually.

Wood Warblers prefer a partially closed canopy with only a little ground cover, and on Islay they are mainly in open beech woods in the estate woodlands, but ocasionally in sycamore copses or groups of native oaks. An adult and juvenile were in the Kilslevan shelter belt on 31st July 1986. Departure takes place late in July or early in August, the latest record being on 3rd August 1907 at Lagavulin.

These birds forage among foliage and hawk flying insects. They take midges, aphids, beetles, mayflies, small moths and the eggs and larvae of insects, including caterpillars of small moths and butterflies.

Chiffchaff   *Phylloscopus collybita*

A regular summer visitor that overwinters in very small numbers in some years. Around 1950 the species' range was extending in Scotland, and by 1953 (Baxter and Rintoul) it had been noted several times on the Rhinns of Islay; breeding was first proved in the Inner Hebrides in 1959. From about that time it has been found in all estate woodlands on Islay and in some broadleaved shelter belts and copses. Nine birds were around Loch Skerrols and Bridgend on 28th April 1973, and four were in Kildalton Woods on 9th April 1985; a pair bred on the Gruinart Reserve in 1986. The poorly known distribution suggests a population of from 30 to 100 pairs.

The first arrivals are normally in late March or early April, the earliest recorded being on 24th March 1977. Three probable Chiffchaffs flapped wearily over the stern of the ferry southeast of Islay, heading for the island, on 29th March 1980. The song that gives the species its English name is commonly heard in April and May but rarely thereafter; two were singing at Kildalton on 21st September 1977. They most likely leave between mid-August and the end of September to winter in a Mediterranean country or tropical West Africa. The mild Scottish winters of the early 1970s are thought to have been reflected in peaks in the numbers of Chiffchaffs that stayed behind in 1975 and 1976. On Islay there were four winter sightings in 1975, three in 1976, and two in 1980 and one on the Gruinart Reserve in 1986; all fell between 30th October and 13th December.

These birds like dense undergrowth for nesting and prefer tall trees interspersed with shrubs; those estate woodlands with rhododendrons are often occupied. They tend to feed among twigs and foliage at higher levels than

Willow Warblers, taking flies including midges, aphids, beetles, moths and spiders, as well as the larvae and eggs of insects.

Willow Warbler *Phylloscopus trochilus*

A summer visitor and passage migrant that in 1871 (Gray) had not been reported in the Hebrides. One was found dead at the Rhinns Lighthouse in 1887 and the species was established on Islay by 1892; it was said to be abundant in 1913 (Ross). In the mid-1980s, it summered in all woodland and shrub except where there is a closed canopy. One was in just 200 sq. m (240 sq. yds) of sallow scrub near Gearach on 11th June 1986. Using a woodland density of 50 pairs per sq. km (130 per sq. mile), rather less than that determined on mainland Argyll (Williamson 1972), and taking account of the relative frequency of capture of this species during ringing operations, an island population of 800 to 1,100 pairs is suggested. On the Gruinart Reserve alone, 36 breeding pairs were counted in 1985, 64 in 1986, and 41 in 1987. Throughout the island there is likely to be an increase in numbers as new conifer plantations grow, but they will leave each wood as the canopy closes following about 15 years' growth.

The first Willow Warblers of the year normally arrive during the first half of April, but the earliest record is of one near Gruinart Farm on 31st March 1981. Abundant birds on passage were noted at Carnmore on 14th April 1971 and on 24th April 1974. Breeding commences early in May and is usually completed by the end of June. Assemblages of migrants have been seen from late June to early September: they were abundant in the trees at Carnmore on 25th June 1977, and 4th September 1976 was described as a day of passage. There are many similar records for this time of the year, and the latest straggler was on the Gruinart Reserve on 28th September 1984. Three birds ringed at Bridgend on 24th August 1973, 5th July 1976 and 12th July 1977 were on Skokholm in Pembroke on 25th April 1975, at Silverdale in Lancashire on 16th August 1976, and on the Calf of Man on 17th August 1977, respectively. Most Scottish Willow Warblers winter in tropical West Africa, with some further south.

These agile birds feed by pecking small insects from leaves and twigs, taking a few berries, or hawking flying insects. They occasionally feed on the ground, adding small worms to their diet. Invertebrates taken include small flies, moths, aphids, beetles, weevils, ants and spiders.

Goldcrest *Regulus regulus*

Islay's Goldcrests are residents and passage migrants; they were reported in 1871 (Gray) as frequent, and scanty records suggest that they have been common since. A few migrants from northern Scotland or Scandinavia move south through Islay during September and October, peaking in mid-September. One ringed at Bridgend on 13th September 1976 was found near Tamworth, Staffordshire on 5th February 1977. The largest gatherings are seen in the early autumn; 26 were in a wood by Loch Skerrols on 20th September 1980, and many were in trees on the south coast at Carnmore on 15th September 1971. A probable migrant was killed at the Rhinns Lighthouse on 14th October 1963, and another was at Easter Ellister on 15th and 16th October 1985. One in a gorse bush at Ardnave on 11th April 1979 was presumably on northward migration.

The residents breed in mixed estate woodlands and mature conifer plantations, scattering more widely in winter to occupy some broadleaved shelter belts and copses. From one to nine were in small woods on the Gruinart Reserve from October 1985 to May 1986. Calculations using low summer densities suggest that the island's population is between 150 and 250 pairs. This is supported by the number caught for ringing in Bridgend Woods from 1973 to 1977, which was similar to that of Blue Tits. The species is very much under-recorded. A population expansion has occurred on Mull as a result of afforestation; this is likely to be repeated on Islay as the new plantations mature.

This tiny bird is very agile on the smallest twigs and is able to extract insect larvae and springtails from conifer needles with its very fine bill. It also takes small flies, moths, ants, aphids, bugs, weevils, beetles and spiders, by searching closely among, under and in twigs, cones, bark, moss and lichens.

Spotted Flycatcher   *Muscicapa striata*

For at least a century the Spotted Flycatcher has been a regular summer visitor to Islay. During the period 1971 to 1976, small assemblies of passage migrants were recorded near Port Ellen from 7th August, with a maximum in the third week; the latest bird was seen on 5th September 1976 at Carnmore Cottage. This species migrates from Britain to Africa south of the Sahara, some to the southernmost parts; their late return, starting in the first half of May, is timed to harvest an abundance of flying insects. Isolated pairs are found in sheltered but open glades or on the edges of each estate woodland, including some small broadleaved copses such as those at Carnmore, Easter Ellister, Foreland and Avenvogie as well as the larger areas. This distribution suggests that in most years the Islay population probably lies between 15 and 30 pairs.

The breeding season extends from late May to early August: in 1974 the first of three eggs was laid at Carnmore Cottage on 25th May, the nest was robbed on 13th June, a second clutch was commenced on 11th July, three eggs were hatched on 26th July, and the juveniles were fully fledged on 7th August. There have been a few records of birds in birch scrub between 18th May and 1st June; presumably these had not established territories.

These flycatchers feed almost entirely on insects which they hawk during sallies from particular branches overlooking open areas; trees on the wooded banks of the River Sorn are particularly favoured. Their catch includes craneflies, small butterflies, moths, ants and beetles.

Red-breasted Flycatcher   *Ficedula parva*

A vagrant or dispersive visitor that breeds from Germany and Austria east to the Pacific, and normally winters in southeast Asia. The European population migrates to western India, but a few sometimes travel in the reverse direction to arrive in the British Isles in autumn. Nearly all Scottish records fall between 17th August and 15th November. Single first-year birds were at Easter Ellister on 1st November 1974 and from 10th to 17th October 1975.

Pied Flycatcher   *Ficedula hypoleuca*

The Pied Flycatcher is a rare passage migrant that arrives in the Hebrides from mid-May. Spring passage on Islay is represented by single males that were at Kildalton on 9th June 1976 and Loch Ballygrant on 10th June 1976, and also by a bird in a woodland fragment on the north coast on 24th May 1985. The southward passage peaks in August and one was just north of the Airport on 9th in 1963, a second was outside the Port Charlotte Museum on 24th in 1978, and an adult female with five juveniles were at Easter Ellister on 15th in 1980. Perhaps these five young had been raised on Islay! The remaining records are of late migrants, one at Barr Farm on 16th October 1977 and two juveniles at Easter Ellister on 15th October 1981. A few of Islay's passage birds may summer in Scandinavia, and the wintering grounds are on the savannahs of central Africa. The species breeds on the mainland but only sporadically in the west. These birds could be encouraged to breed on Islay by placing suitable nestboxes in broadleaved woods.

Long-tailed Tit   *Aegithalos caudatus*

This species is a resident particularly susceptible to severe winters. It was reported in 1871 (Gray) as fairly common, in 1915 as of doubtful occurrence and as very numerous in 1971. From 1971 to 1986 sightings varied from none to seven per year, and it was seriously reduced by the bad weather of 1981/2. A low breeding density, as found by Williamson (1972) in North Argyll, and a maximum flock size of 15 in each occupied woodland suggest an Islay population of between 25 and 50 pairs in normal years.

Long-tailed Tits are found in all the estate woodlands. Fifty counted at Loch Skerrols on 14th June 1971 was exceptional and probably represented combined flocks from all woods within 3 km (2 miles) of Bridgend. Flocks are found outside the breeding season from June to early March and may combine with Blue Tits or Great Tits. Thirty per cent of all records are widely scattered and dated October; these include twelve birds in a conifer plantation near Avenvogie on 29th October 1975, 16 in scrub by Loch Gorm on 21st October 1979 and twelve in a native wood at Braigo on 23rd October 1979. From September to November, dispersal sometimes extends to Scottish islands not having residents.

These very active birds forage high in trees on the smaller branches and twigs, often pecking in and around buds. They take grubs, flies, spiders and other insects all the year around. Unlike the *Parus* tits, they do not hold food firmly underfoot but hang from one foot while holding the item in the other foot to peck it. They also differ by huddling together with tails pointing outwards when roosting.

Marsh/Willow Tit *Parus palustris/montanus*

These two sibling species are possible vagrants to Islay; both breed in the southern uplands of Scotland, the Willow Tit reaching the Firth of Clyde coast and the Marsh Tit being confined to the Borders Region. There are five Islay records between mid-July and mid-November; three do not identify the species, but two observers claim to have heard a Marsh Tit in Loch Skerrols woods on 6th September 1975. A major part of this locality is well-drained beech wood with some undergrowth and is therefore a suitable habitat.

Coal Tit *Parus ater*

A resident that was rare or absent in 1871 (Gray) and 1892, and was first reported in 1913 (Ross) as frequent. Two birds with the pale primrose-yellow cheeks of the Irish race (*P.a.hibernicus*) were shot in 1913 along with a third having white cheeks as found in the British race (*P.a.britannicus*). It is likely that there is a periodic movement between Ireland and Scotland in response to food shortages, and Irish birds may be overlooked on Islay. The population is difficult to estimate, but it is probably between 200 and 400 breeding pairs and is likely to increase as additional conifer plantations reach the thicket stage.

On Islay, the Coal Tit is found in native broadleaved woods and mixed estate woodlands, as well as in conifer plantations. It occasionally leaves these woods, making forays along hedges and into gorse clumps. Outside the breeding season it may flock with Blue Tits, Goldcrests and Treecreepers; up to 20 have been seen together in estate woodlands.

Having a slender bill, this species is better adapted to conifers that harbour tiny invertebrates in their needles and cones, and it takes more insects than the Great or Blue Tits. It forages among leafy twigs and branches, and on the ground, taking mainly insects in the summer and a mixture of seeds and insects in the winter. In times of glut it is prone to store food at ground level. This species roosts singly in dense foliage, especially in clumps of conifers, and may also use the discarded nests of other birds.

180

Blue Tit *Parus caeruleus*

The Blue Tit has probably been on Islay since the first estate woodlands matured in the mid-19th century, and possibly earlier in those native woods containing oak or hazel. It is still common in many broadleaved woods but is rare or absent in conifer plantations. About 2.5 times as many Blue Tits as Great Tits were caught for ringing in Bridgend Woods from 1973 to 1977, even though they tend to feed and fly at higher levels. On this basis, an island population of 150–250 pairs is suggested. Sightings are most frequent when many juveniles are present in flocks from mid-August to mid-October. These birds are, however, uncommon in the Rhinns, except around Port Charlotte and Bruichladdich.

Outside the breeding season, this species sometimes ranges out from woods along hedgerows or between scrub patches and into gardens, feeding on a variety of insects, seeds, nuts and birdtable food. In the woods its agility enables it to feed among the leaf canopy, often on the outer branches and twigs that are beyond the reach of the Great Tit, harvesting the caterpillar crop during the breeding season from May to July. Both nesting and roosting take place in holes, mainly in the woods.

Great Tit *Parus major*

This species has been a resident on Islay since at least 1892; it extended its range on the mainland during the first half of this century and probably increased in numbers on Islay. It is now thinly distributed in the major deciduous woodlands and has been recorded in 22 small woods, some of which contain hazel or oak trees and are remnants of native woodlands. On a basis of one pair in each small wood and three to four pairs per sq. km (eight to ten per sq. mile) of the larger woodlands, there are from 50 to 80 pairs on the island. The few birds found on farmland and in gardens are probably from nearby groups of trees.

The Great Tit forages mainly on the lower branches of trees and on the ground, and has a longer, more powerful beak than other tits. In autumn and winter it sometimes accompanies related species in the search for food. It is primarily insectivorous in summer, but in winter it takes seeds and nuts along with a few invertebrates. Many caterpillars are collected from oak trees and nuts from the ground below beech and hazel; the nuts are held underfoot, allowing them to be hammered with the beak, splitting them open. Individuals roost separately, mainly in holes.

Treecreeper *Certhia familiaris*

A resident, said to have been rare in 1913 (Ross) and not uncommon in 1937. Records indicate its regular presence in the estate woodlands at Port Askaig,

Ballygrant, Bridgend and Kildalton; it has also been found in smaller woods a
Foreland, Gruinart, Tynacoille and Carnmore and visits some native wood
such as those near Rockmountain and Airigh nam Beist at Ardbeg. Severe winte
weather is rare on Islay and is not likely seriously to reduce the population. Fror
the distribution of records through about 10 sq. km (4 sq. miles) of suitabl
habitat, it seems likely that the island's population is fairly steady at about 20–2
pairs. This may increase as 6 sq. km (2.3 sq. miles) of conifer plantation in th
Avenvogie-Kynagarry area grow tall and when many other square kilometre
planted in 1986–7 reach a suitable stage. One pair bred on the Gruinart Reserv
in 1984 and 1985 and two pairs in 1986.

Outside the breeding season Treecreepers on Islay have only rarely been see
associating with flocks of tits and Goldcrests. Feeding individually or in pairs
they search in upward and outward spirals on tree trunks and branches. Thei
decurved beaks are adapted to probing into insect-inhabited tunnels an
crevices, seeking food there or under moss, lichens and flakes of bark, an
occasionally making quick movements to catch escaping prey. They take th
eggs and larvae of insects, as well as adult insects and spiders.

Treecreepers roost in crevices in trees and also excavate hollows where sof
bark is available; they are well known for their habit of using Wellingtonia tree
for this purpose. In 1976 roost hollows were noted in a Wellingtonia nea
Kildalton House.

Golden Oriole   *Oriolus oriolus*

A vagrant to Islay that breeds throughout much of Europe and western Asia an
normally winters in Africa or India; a few pairs breed in southern England. *
scatter has been recorded annually in Scotland from early May to early July an
from September to early November; one was at Kildalton on 22nd Septembe
1965. Two males were exceptionally early at Keills on 15th April 1987, and on
was seen again on 17th at the Caol Ila Lane end.

Red-backed Shrike   *Lanius collurio*

A vagrant to Islay that breeds throughout most of Europe and east to centra
Asia; it normally winters in Africa and countries bordering the Indian Ocean. *
few bred in North Lancashire in 1850, but the range limit in England ha
gradually receded until now consistent breeding is confined to southeaster
counties. A few pairs, however, have bred in eastern Scotland since 1977, an
passage birds are recorded on rare occasions from early April to early July an
from early August to mid-November. A male, probably a first-year bird, was a
Portnahaven on 5th June 1954.

Great Grey Shrike *Lanius excubitor*

A scarce winter visitor that has a circumpolar breeding distribution including Norway and the Low Countries. It arrives in Scotland in the autumn from mid-September and leaves mostly during April and May. Single birds have been recorded on Islay: one was shot at Kildalton in October 1909; one flew from a hawthorn tree near Kilchoman on 1st April 1960; and another was at Port Ellen on 19th October 1965. In 1976, one took a Wren at Island House on 12th February, and one was seen at Laggan Bridge on 2nd December and at Avenvogie on 27th.

Jay *Garrulus glandarius*

An irregular dispersive visitor to Islay that is gradually colonising the mainland, including nearby parts of Argyll. One was at Port Charlotte in July 1969 and another was at Kildalton in early June 1970. A third was reported in the garden of Carnmore House on 1st and 8th November 1970 and another was there on 30th April 1982.

Magpie *Pica pica*

A dispersive visitor to Islay and a common resident in the lower-lying parts of the Scottish mainland, but rare in the Kintyre-Knapdale Peninsula. Nineteen sightings on Islay since early 1965 have all been in the first half of the year, especially April, May and June; nine in 1977 were between 4th April and 8th June, and four in 1979 were in January, April and June. Large time gaps between sightings of this conspicuous bird suggest that three individuals were probably involved in 1979. Records from the gardens at Carnmore on 5th April 1977, Easter Ellister on 8th May 1977 and Surnaig at Lagavulin on 15th May 1977 also suggest the immigration of three birds, probably from Ireland where this species is common. Recently there have been individuals at Conisby in November 1985, at Blackrock on 8th February 1986, at Glenegedale on 1st August 1987, and at Bridgend on 16th August 1987. Most other records were at or near the more extensive woodlands.

The future of the Magpie on Islay is uncertain; reduced keepering and increased afforestation may encourage breeding. It can live around conifer plantations and is doing so increasingly on the mainland.

Chough *Pyrrhocorax pyrrhocorax*

A resident that has probably been on Islay for at least two centuries and was said to be common in 1851. During a long run of severe winters in the 19th century, the Chough abandoned inland sites on the Scottish mainland and the last mainland pair bred in Kintyre in 1983. It is reported that at the end of September 1918 'quite a number' of Choughs were blown from Islay to the Mull of Kintyre, and in 1947 Fraser Darling suggested that birds from Rathlin Island replenished stocks on Islay. Many observers reported a marked decline in numbers on the island after the bad winter of 1963, but usually the population benefits from the mild maritime climate. The largest flocks of the year were commonly of 50–60 birds up to 1985. Estimates of numbers during the breeding season have suggested an increase from about 160 in the mid-1970s to 300 in 1986. Some 53–61 breeding pairs were located in 1981, 59–67 were found in 1985 and 84 in 1986. Most of their nests are on sea cliffs, often in caves, a few are on inland cliffs and many are in abandoned buildings. A high proportion are sited in western Islay or western Oa and others are widely scattered in central Islay and on the north and south coasts, but it is very rare for a site to be found on the east coast.

Choughs frequent coastal heathlands or the short turf of the machair, old dunes and permanent pastures well grazed by Rabbits or sheep. They are usually seen in pairs, and when in flocks these are often clearly composed of loosely aggregated pairs. An odd pair may turn up almost anywhere, especially along or near the coast, but the greatest densities are along cliffed sections, backed by pastures, or on stubbles near the coast; they are readily seen at all seasons.

Choughs have a decurved bill adapted for probing and twisting into intricate pathways, scraping backwards and pecking. Three nestlings at Rockside in 1980 had deformed bills with crossed mandibles and would be seriously handicapped when foraging for themselves. Normal birds often search around rock outcrops.

Chough (Brian Southern)

184

turn over cowpats, root-mats, stones and seaweed; jab and flick to break up dung; or occasionally run and lunge at prey. By these means they obtain leatherjackets, craneflies, blowflies, kelp-fly maggots and scarab beetles; also other flies and beetles and their larvae, sandhoppers, earwigs, millipedes, ants and spiders. Choughs rely on these soil invertebrates but supplement their diet with oats and barley obtained from stubbles, livestock feeding stations and other places where grain is spilled.

The main roost is on the ledges and in the crevices of a cliffed gully in Creag Mhor, south of Kilchoman; 165 birds were counted there on 23rd February 1986. In addition, a few birds have been seen going to roost at their breeding sites on sea cliffs or in buildings. These observations appear to support recent population counts.

See pages 41–2 for further information.

Jackdaw *Corvus monedula*

A resident and winter visitor that colonised Islay in the mid-19th century during a general increase and advance to the north and west, becoming common on Islay by 1888. Ringing has shown that immigrants enter Scotland from Scandinavia; some join flocks on Islay in late July and August and depart again in March. Thereafter the aggregations are reduced to a few tens of birds; a maximum of 50 was at Woodend, Ballygrant, on 5th June 1986. Winter flocks are normally 100 to 500 strong.

These corvids nest in holes and crevices in cliffs, including those at Port Askaig, on the south side of Kilchiaran Bay and 1 km (0.6 miles) inland near Kilchoman House. In recent years they have occupied similar accommodation in ruins at Mulindry Mill, chimney pots on inhabited cottages, and holes in tall dunes and trees; they have even built in trees where holes are in short supply. Individuals have been seen pulling hairs out of a cow's back to line these nests.

Foraging flocks are found on the short grass of leys and permanent pasture, including machair and old dunes, and on dead seaweed, piles of manure and the rubbish dump at Gartbreck. Jackdaws may follow 5–10 m (16–33 ft) behind a plough, visit livestock feeding stations, scatter cowpats in search of insects, and jump after or hawk flies. When on pasture, they may walk-peck close to livestock or ride on the backs of these animals searching for parasitic insects; at other times they feed away from livestock, as a loose flock or less often leapfrogging in a close flock like Starlings. They take farmland insects, other small invertebrates, grain, weed seeds, berries, the eggs or young of open-ground nesting birds, and human leftovers. They hold food underfoot, freeing their beaks for tearing, and carry food in bulging crops.

Small groups that roost in woods during the summer build up and unite through the autumn, and are often joined by Rooks. Pre-roost flocks often have 500–800 birds and at Bridgend 1,000 were recorded on 10th February 1976 and 1,200 on 25th December 1979. If an extra large flock forms well away from the roost site, the birds fly across country in a long snaking ribbon, either hedgehopping against the wind or at a fair height with the wind. Roosts containing a few hundred birds have been recorded at Creag Mhor, Kilchoman, in conifers near Knockdon, Bridgend, and in deciduous trees at Keills and Mulindry. There are alternative sites to the latter two at a wooded island in Loch Lossit and in conifers at Cluanach, where there were 800 birds in the 1985/6 winter. In 1984/5 over 600 Jackdaws roosted in conifers at Kildalton, moving to deciduous trees between Kilbride and Callumkill in 1985/6. These roost counts indicate that there were about 1,800 Jackdaws on Islay during the 1985/6 winter. They travel up to 12 km ($7\frac{1}{2}$ miles) from feeding grounds to roost (Figure 12).

Jackdaws occasionally associate with Oystercatchers; they were found roosting together near the mouth of the River Laggan on an isolated sandbank at 20.30 hrs on 4th April 1981 (Ogilvie and Ogilvie 1984), and flocks of these species were engaged together in spectacular aerobatic flights at Kilchiaran on 20th March 1978. At other times Jackdaws are accompanied by Common Gulls in similar displays.

Rook   *Corvus frugilegus*

A resident, occupying twelve rookeries in 1985, with a total of 211 nests counted from mid-April to late May. Eighteen rookery sites are known, all in small woods of which many are groups of sycamores close to farms or other buildings. Five sites are in the west: one near Gruinart Farm dates from 1857 and in 1985 had 44 nests; in a few years this has had an 'annexe' at Aoradh. On 9th February 1982 about 80 birds were already over the Gruinart rookery. A rookery at Ballinaby has been disused for about two decades; other small ones are at Rockside and Port Charlotte. Four rookeries are near Port Ellen: one at Tighcargaman had 54 nests in 1985, and in succession to the west there were 24 at the distillery, 14 at Carnmore House and four at Cornabus, this last dating back to 1818. Another four are south and southeast of Bridgend, at Cluanach, Mulindry, Gartmain and Tallant; these have been recorded only in recent years and contained a total of 23 nests in 1985. The remaining five include those at Eallabus and Loch Lossit; these have not been occupied in recent years and there are no counts. The others are at Esknish, Ballygrant Quarry and Keills, which is the largest, having 42 nests in 1978 and 29 in 1985.

Foraging flocks are found mainly on mixed farmland, but also on machair and in small numbers on beaches with rotting seaweed. Some birds visit livestock feeding stations and large flocks accumulate in barley and stubble. At Corsapol, 51 were in barley on 26th August 1985, and at Keills 100 were on stubble on 15th October 1977. Rooks feed by pecking, probing and digging, sometimes breaking up cowpats or hawking insects. They take grain, waste root crops, animal feedstuffs, many field invertebrates including earthworms, voles, and the eggs or young of field-nesting birds. They hold food under their feet to facilitate

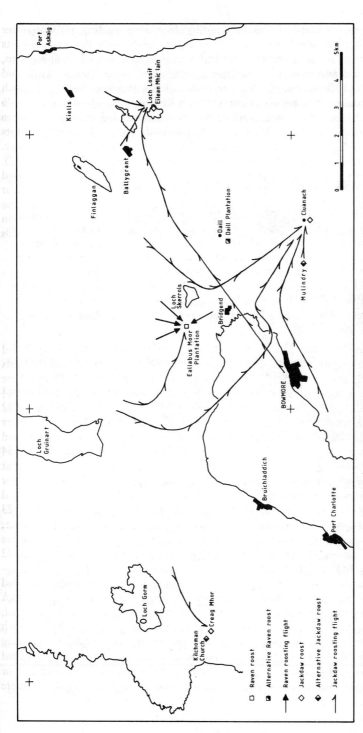

Figure 12: Jackdaw and Raven roosts in central Islay during the winter of 1985/6. Some Rooks roost with the Jackdaws

preparation and may store food in a hiding place or a specially dug hole, carrying it in a bulging crop.

From mid-July to about the end of February birds from several rookeries attend a communal roost. On Islay they roost at Tighcargaman, Mulindry, Lossit and Keills rookeries but often move to join Jackdaws forming roosts in Islay House woods, between Callumkill and Kilbride in deciduous trees, or near Cluanach and Kildalton in conifers. Flight distances from feeding grounds to roosts range up to 5 km (3 miles) and exceptionally 8 km (5 miles) (Figure 12).

Carrion Crow   *Corvus corone corone*

An annual vagrant or dispersive visitor that breeds east of a hybrid zone running north to south from Caithness to the Mull of Galloway. The nearest breeding pairs are on the Isle of Arran. It is recorded on Islay in ones or twos in every month, but is very rare from mid-April to mid-August; it is probably under-recorded. Flocks are occasionally seen: ten were at Lyrabus on 13th August and beyond Killinallan on 3rd October 1972; 28 were around Bridgend Bay on 8th September 1973 and 14 were there on 7th September 1974; 18 flew over Craigens on 23rd October 1980; and 60 were at the Rhinns Lighthouse on 25th January 1986.

Three-quarters of all records are from the low ground between Port Ellen and Island House, around Bridgend Bay or in the Gruinart or Loch Gorm districts. Feeding and general behaviour are similar to those of the Hooded Crow. A hybrid Carrion × Hooded Crow with all-black upperparts and grey, blotched black, underparts was recorded on 8th September 1974, and a second was seen during the *Winter Atlas* survey in the early 1980s. A Carrion Crow was paired with a Hooded Crow at Duich in 1973.

Hooded Crow   *Corvus corone cornix*

A resident and winter visitor whose numbers have been kept low by gamekeepers. During the two world wars it became common, but in 1939 it was said to be almost exterminated. It became common again as the numbers of gamekeepers were gradually reduced after about 1975. In 1986, there were between 500 and 800 individuals on Islay during the winter and about 200 to 300 resident pairs. Flocks of 40 or 50 gather at stubble fields and in Feburary 1979, between the Airport and Port Ellen, 36 gathered for three days following a peat fire. The winter visitors are from Scandinavia; they arrive in late August or September and depart between mid-February and mid-March. There is a record of large numbers flying west-southwest past the Rhinns of Islay in October 1884 and continuing until 18th November; probably this was a hard-weather movement.

'Hoodies' are distributed throughout the island over moorland, farmland, machair and shore, most thinly over the moorland, and there is still a marked difference in the densities over unkeepered and well-keepered parts. They obtain their food by pecking, probing and clod-turning; the males do more probing than the females and certain individuals develop special abilities to capture particular prey. Their main foods are grain, wild seeds, small live animals and carrion, including carcases of sheep, lambs, Rabbits and hares. The smaller rodents are caught live, and incapacitated lambs and ewes are sometimes attacked. A problem arises when ewes are in poor condition at lambing time or when they roll over and cannot regain their feet. These voracious birds also steal eggs and take young birds, and are frequently chased off by ground-nesting birds such as Lapwing, Curlew and Oystercatcher. They also search seaweed for crustaceans and shellfish, which they crack open by dropping them from a height on to rocks or pebbles. They may carry bone to a fence post, where they hold it with one foot, leaving their beak free to pick off the meat. Other foods include berries, beetles, spiders and craneflies.

In the Outer Hebrides flocks of hundreds fly to roost in trees, but this happens only where they are unmolested and on Islay roosting appears to be in small scattered groups. At dusk on 29th December 1985, a few were seen flying towards woods northeast of Callumkill; on 22nd February 1986, ten flew up the Kilchoman Gorge towards dense scrub at the upper end of that glen; on 14th March 1986, seven roosted in the wood south of Knockdon; and another group regularly gathers on dead trees or pasture near Avenvogie Cottage prior to roosting in the nearby conifer plantation. Hooded Crows keep themselves separate from other corvids roosting in the same wood.

Raven   *Corvus corax*

In the mid-1980s Islay held about 100 Ravens. Earlier records have shown that this resident population is linked with others across the North Channel. A pair leaving Texa on 6th January 1910 was lost to sight heading for the Mull of Kintyre. Birds ringed in Kintyre have been found in Northern Ireland, and one ringed there in 1980 was found at Daill on 3rd November 1980.

Nesting takes place from February on traditional ledges on the higher coastal cliffs, such as those at Maol an Fhithich and Dun an Fhithich on the Oa. More rarely an inland cliff is used and one east of Loch Gruinart, called Beinn nam Fitheach, is also named after this species. A site at Laggan Point, which was used in the 1970s, had eggs in 1886. Ravens sometimes ward off the mock attacks of Peregrines, which may be nesting nearby, by half-rolls to present claws and beak in flight.

Ravens hunt over all parts of the island but spend most time in moorland and coastal areas, especially searching around the moorland-farmland boundaries and in extensive dune areas. Pairs appear to require a home range of 15–20 sq. km (6–8 sq. miles) These birds feed largely on sheep, Rabbit and hare carrion, and may worry incapacitated lambs. They also take live voles, mice and

Raven (Brett Westwood)

rats, steal eggs and nestlings and sometimes search for shoreline carrion. Young are fed for their first few days on insects, especially maggots and beetles from carcases. Adults are capable of holding food under one or both feet when tearing off pieces, and may hide a surplus from competitors. In contests with the similar-sized Great Black-backed Gull, either may dominate.

Breeding Ravens roost in territory, but from late August they form communal roosts in trees together with non-breeders. A roost in the Islay Estate woods has a long history and is probably the only one on Islay (Figure 12). Normally located near Daill, it contained 95 birds in December 1973, over 100 early in 1975, and 72 in December 1977. In the 1985/6 season it was in the wood south of Knockdon and 105 birds were present in November. Prior to entering the latter site, the birds assembled at a nearby slope-soaring site and performed aerobatic rolls and spectacular dives with partially closed wings.

Starling   *Sturnus vulgaris*

On Islay the Starling is now a resident, passage migrant and winter visitor, but in the early 19th century it retreated from northwest Britain, leaving outposts in the

Outer Hebrides and Shetlands (*S.v.zetlandicus*). From about 1830 the Continental form (*S.v.vulgaris*) spread from England into Scotland and Ireland, reaching Islay in 1843 when it was recorded at Torrabus on 27th February; this race then became common by the turn of the century. Independently, immigration of birds from the mainland begins annually in mid-August and birds mainly from Scandinavia, entering Scotland in September, quickly reach Islay. The flocking of juveniles begins in mid-June; 200 were at Sunderland on 18th June 1973, and 800 were on the Gruinart Reserve in July 1985. After the arrival of immigrants, these flocks may be swollen to form thousands; maximum numbers of over 2,000 were at Foreland on 31st August 1979 and 6,000 at Sunderland on 11th November 1975. Normally, residents and immigrants form flocks fewer than 500 and often fewer than 250 strong. A migrant ringed at Banff on 6th July 1972 was found dead at Port Ellen in December, and a first-year female ringed at Gdańsk, Poland, on 26th July 1972 was at Carnmore on 2nd December. Many birds in this autumn movement are thought to continue on to Ireland, and large numbers were recorded at the Rhinns Lighthouse on 15th and 21st August 1885 and on 19th October 1977. There is no evidence of a return passage.

The residents nest in holes in mature trees in the estate woodlands, in many farm buildings, some abandoned houses and caves; in June 1973 some were seen taking over holes in the banks of the River Laggan, and a pair was nesting in a high old cliff near Smaull on 19th June 1987. Most parents collect food from nearby farmlands; a white juvenile was being fed at Port Ellen on 25th May 1971. Starlings forage on the short grass of grazed permanent pastures and leys, in fields with freshly cut silage, in stubble, root crops and ploughings, but unlike gulls do not follow the plough. They visit livestock feeding stations, the Gartbreck refuse dump and birdtables, rummage among rotting seaweed, fallen leaves and cowpats, and hawk insects; in the breeding season they collect caterpillars.

Starlings walk-pick or walk-probe and have a special open-beak probe: the beak is opened after entering the soil, pushing it apart, and at the same time the eyes are drawn forward, eliminating any need to turn the head to one side. They sometimes search close to the feet of livestock, enhancing the likelihood of prey movement and consequent detection. They may also perch on a sheep's back, using this as a viewpoint, sheltering from strong wind or collecting ectoparasites. On pasture, a flock often forages upwind in parabolic close formation, with individuals constantly leapfrogging to the front. In all of these activities a wide range of small invertebrates is taken, as well as weed seeds, cereals, berries, fruits, potatoes and roots.

On Islay, Starlings frequently associate with flocks of Lapwings, which probably provide a warning of the approach of a Peregrine or other potential predator. Less often, they accompany other species such as gulls, Curlews, Golden Plovers, Fieldfares, Redwings, Choughs and Jackdaws. Any disturbance is likely to be followed by the Starlings engaging in close-formation flying. A Peregrine is sometimes about as Starlings gather prior to entering a roost. Roost sites are to be found in certain coastal caves, in abandoned buildings such as

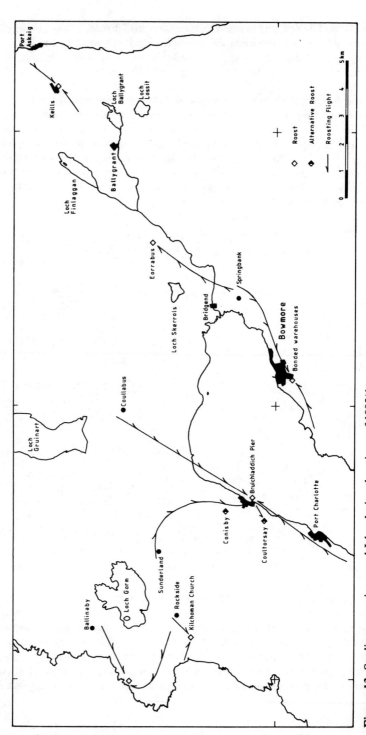

Figure 13: Starling roosts in central Islay during the winter of 1985/6

Kilchoman Church, and at many farms and some distilleries. The largest are at Bowmore Distillery and under Bruichladdich Pier (Figure 13).

Rose-coloured Starling *Sturnus roseus*

A vagrant that normally breeds in the Balkans and across Turkey and southern Russia into Iran; it winters in the Indian subcontinent. Following irruptions a few, mainly adults, reach Scotland. This happens in most years and they usually arrive in June, July or August. One arrived at Esknish on 22nd July and stayed on Islay until 10th September 1977; another was at Portnahaven from 10th August to 10th September 1987.

House Sparrow *Passer domesticus*

A resident that probably colonised Islay in the first half of the 19th century and was first reported abundant in 1913 (Ross). It is closely associated with villages, farms and distilleries throughout the island; some of the more isolated houses, however, are rarely visited by this opportunistic species. There are now probably between 800 and 1,200 pairs on the island. Six pairs bred at the RSPB farm, Aoradh, in 1984 and 1985, and a maximum of 28 was on the reserve on 4th June 1984. Flocking begins in July and continues until spring; 200 were at Bruichladdich on 18th March 1978, and some were with a finch flock near Port Mias-sgeire, Portnahaven, on 18th March 1979. A pale bird with 'oatmeal' plumage was at Machrie on 27th November 1907; another was on Oronsay during the summer of 1974.

House Sparrows feed on the shore and in fields near farms and villages, and at birdtables. They have broad, thick bills, enabling them to peck a wide variety of seeds from weeds, grasses, cereals, and birch or elm trees; they also take insects whenever they are readily available. Both seeds and insects are obtained from plant and ground by hovering, pouncing and pecking; insects may be picked off a sunny wall or even off a motor car. Pairs roost in their nest holes, but birds of the year and non-breeders form communal roosts in the dense cover of evergreens such as ivy, or in farm steadings.

Tree Sparrow *Passer montanus*

A resident near the changing northern limit of its range that is occasionally replenished by a few immigrants. Movement is suggested by seven out of 13 sightings having occurred in April and September. It was probably on Islay in the early part of the 20th century, when it was reported to be on Hebridean islands; it was then absent for a few decades, and was next recorded in June 1969 at Port Ellen. Typically, most subsequent records were in or near deciduous woods at Carnmore, Craigens, Kildalton and Bridgend, but the last record was of three or four at the young conifer plantation just northeast of Sunderland on 29th October 1985. It now appears to be very scarce again, and at its peak in the early 1970s is not likely to have exceeded ten breeding pairs.

The Tree Sparrow may join seed-seeking finch flocks, and usually takes small seeds from grasses and annual weeds such as goosefoot and chickweed; it also takes spilled grain and insects.

Chaffinch   *Fringilla coelebs*

A resident, winter visitor and passage migrant that has been common since at least the late 19th century. Probably about 800 to 1,000 pairs of the British race (*F.c.gengleri*) nest on Islay in virtually all woodlands, dense scrub and even birch scrub patches in small glens. A pair was feeding young in a few birch trees west of Gearach on 4th June 1986. Slightly larger and paler birds (*F.c.coelebs*), predominantly males, arrive in Scotland from Fennoscandia in mid-August and continue passing through during September to at least mid-October; the return migrants have left by mid-April. Outside the breeding season, Chaffinches on Islay form flocks of up to 200 or 300 birds. Exceptionally, thousands were reported on passage on 22nd October 1880, about 550 were near Cluanach on 16th February 1980, and 1,800 were on the Gruinart Reserve in January 1985.

Throughout the island the large flocks forage on open farmland, while small groups of the native race search in or near woodlands and other areas having good cover such as gorse scrub, and also around farm steadings and anywhere grain is spilled. All feed on a wide range of weed seeds and cereal grain pecked from the ground, or in the few good beech years take beech mast. Insects, especially caterpillars, are collected for dependent juveniles, and birdtables are visited. Roosts are in evergreens, conifer plantations or other thick cover, the local birds usually staying in small groups in or near their territories.

Brambling   *Fringilla montifringilla*

A winter visitor to Scotland from Scandinavia, penetrating west in small numbers to the Hebrides. Very rarely, a flock of a few tens is seen; 25 were at Kintour on 1st January 1970. Passage visitors may cross to Ireland, but Bramblings migrate at night and evidence is lacking. The first few migrants arrive in mid-October and the last ones are seen in March, although a pair in breeding plumage was at Loch Gorm on 18th May 1976.

These birds have been found in most parts of the island, usually fewer than ten feeding on the ground with Chaffinches, Greenfinches or Linnets. A beak that is slightly larger and sharper than that of the Chaffinch enables the Brambling to select beechnuts as its primary food. Where this source fails, it joins other finches on rough pastures and open fields to take weed and cereal seeds; it is in such cirumstances that it is normally found on Islay. Bramblings roost with other finches, usually in rhododendrons or young conifers.

Greenfinch   *Carduelis chloris*

A resident and passage migrant that was reported as scarce in 1876 but became common in the 20th century. Some tens of pairs breed, perhaps 50 or so. Both numbers and sightings peak in November and to a lesser degree from mid-February to early April, suggesting passages to and from Ireland of birds breeding to the north and northeast. Flocks of up to 40 individuals and exceptionally more are recorded in autumn and winter: from 16th to 20th November 1981 about 100 were at Ballygrant, 80 at Nerabus, and 70 at Gartachossan. Other sightings were well distributed over much of the island.

The Greenfinch often joins flocks of Chaffinches or Linnets and is found on both pastures and arable land, in stubble fields, around steadings, at birdtables and along woodland margins, or in young conifer plantations. With a short but broad bill it takes cereal seeds and the larger weed seeds, including those of charlock, persicaria or redshank; insects are added to the diet of nestlings. Rhododendron clumps or other evergreens accommodate communal roosting.

Goldfinch   *Carduelis carduelis*

A resident that may have bred in the 19th century, but in the last quarter was a prized cagebird and became scarce. Pairs were seen at Laggan Bridge in 1957 and at Loch Skerrols in 1959, and the species was heard singing at Kildalton in 1971. Nesting was proved in the Bridgend district in 1971 and it has probably bred on the island ever since 1973. The maximum flock size also increased year by year to 20 on 21st March 1977 at Laggan Bridge. Since then, numbers have remained similar; 22 were seen on the Gruinart Reserve in July 1985. Some birds from the west of Scotland may winter in Ireland, and the species is considered to be a partial migrant in mainland Britain, but no evidence of movement was collected on Islay until 120 were seen at Gruinart in September 1986.

Records now come from all parts of the island and additional evidence of breeding has been noted in small woods at Carnmore, Blackrock and Gruinart Farm. Flocks are formed in late August and disbanded in mid-April; they rarely unite with other finches. The Goldfinch forages on farmland, especially on the rougher pastures and in weedy patches; it is occasionally seen on the machair. It takes seeds from Compositae—dandelions, thistles, teasels, groundsel and ragwort—and also a few insects. The females have relatively short bills and seldom feed from teasels, which require the longer bills of males. Dense scrub or trees, including conifer plantations, provide roosting for this species.

Siskin *Carduelis spinus*

The Siskin is present in small numbers in most years, but is rare in January, February and March. Some are probably passage migrants, while others are longer-staying visitors, some of which breed. This is an irruptive species, generally migrating southwest from breeding haunts in Scandinavia and the Scottish mainland. The birds migrate when the food crop is poor, apparently staying where it is good. Large numbers enter Britain in autumn; up to 25 were on the Gruinart Reserve from 15th to 31st October 1985. Three left Islay from Frenchman's Rocks on 14th April 1974, perhaps bound for Ireland. A pair bred near Port Askaig in 1972; pairs or singing birds were recorded at Ballygrant, Bridgend and Carnmore Wood from May to June 1986, and others were noted at Ardtalla, Bruichladdich, Cluanach and Loch Allan in that summer.

The Siskin has been found in many woodlands on Islay, especially mixed ones; 14 were seen in Bridgend Woods in early July 1978. It benefits from afforestation and is likely to increase on Islay as the large numbers of conifers currently being planted reach cone-bearing age. Like other finches, it takes seeds from a succession of species through the year. The main sources in autumn and winter are birch, alder and larch, then in spring and summer spruce and pine follow; lesser supplies come from elm, dandelion and thistle species. Siskins also visit the gardens of houses, and since the mid-1960s they have taken peanuts offered by householders.

On trees, this species usually starts to forage at the top and then works downwards. It is an agile feeder and takes up various perching positions, including hanging upside down; it can also use its feet to pull in or firmly hold food items. It can prise apart the scales of cones to gain access to seeds, by inserting and then opening its bill. Siskins roost in small groups in clumps of tall conifers or in scrub.

Linnet *Carduelis cannabina*

A resident that was said to be common by Gray (1871) and Baxter and Rintoul (1953). It has apparently decreased to the present few hundred pairs as agriculture has intensified. Most Linnets breeding north of Islay in western Scotland probably winter to the south, as do a proportion of those elsewhere in the British Isles. Some are likely to be passage visitors that help form the exceptional flocks of western Islay, such as 350 at Easter Ellister on 4th October 1975, 200 at Ardnave on 19th October 1975, and 325 at Craigens on 15th September 1977. On return migration, there were 150 at Kilchiaran in mid-March 1977 and 150 in a mixed flock near Port Charlotte on 21st March 1981.

Flocks of Linnets first form in mid-July and break up in April; throughout the island they normally contain fewer than 100 birds, sometimes associated with other finches and buntings. Linnets are widespread at all seasons on the lower ground, on arable and pasture fields, in scrubby areas and on machair. They nest among gorse or dense scrub and in young conifer plantations.

This species seldom feeds in trees, but spends most time on successive crops of seeds from weeds of cultivation and meadow grass, and on grain in stubble fields. It roosts communally in gorse and other scrub or in reedbeds. On 25th March 1978, sleet driven by a gale-force wind caused 90 feeding Linnets to retire to crevices in a stone wall near Craigens.

Twite   *Carduelis flavirostris*

There are probably fewer than 100 resident pairs on Islay, but this species is also present as a passage migrant and winter visitor in small numbers. Some move regularly between Scottish islands, and ringed birds from Scotland have been found in Donegal. Twites passed over Carnmore on 18th October 1974 and 40 flew by Frenchman's Rocks on 10th December 1974.

Flocks are formed in mid-August; most contain up to 100 birds and disband in April. Since 1975, however, 200 to 300 Twites have been counted fairly regularly in February; in addition, 200 were at Ardnave on 2nd January 1983 and 264 on the Gruinart Reserve on 28th September 1984. These larger winter flocks probably contain immigrants and have not been found in March or April.

Most records are within 1 km (0.6 miles) of the coast on well-grazed pastures, including that of machair and old dunes. A quarter of the records are from the Ardnave Peninsula, but similar open areas such as that northeast of Loch Gruinart are probably of equal importance to this species. The Twite usually feeds on short turf or other equally low vegetation, taking the grain in stubble fields and small seeds from farmland weeds and maritime flowers, using its feet to steady the food plant. It roosts in dense scrub, gorse, heather or bracken, often with Linnets; typically 50 to 100 birds gather together.

Mealy Redpoll   *Carduelis flammea flammea*

An eruptive subspecies of the Redpoll that breeds in northern Eurasia and normally migrates southeast out of Fennoscandia. Varying numbers, however, erupt annually and are seen on the east coast of Britain between September and December. In some years a few penetrate to the west, and one was at Bridgend on 9th October 1976.

Lesser Redpoll   *Carduelis flammea cabaret*

The Lesser Redpoll was first reported in 1913 (Ross). It bred before 1953 (Baxter and Rintoul) and still does in small numbers, probably fewer than 40

197

pairs. Flocks of up to 150 birds seen in the Kildalton area in the latter half of March and June of the years 1970, 1972, 1979 and 1983 were probably irruptive birds from northern Scotland.

Sixty per cent of all records are from the Bridgend or southeastern woods, especially Kildalton; others are from widely scattered localities with small plantations or well-developed birch scrub. None has been reported from the Rhinns. There are likely to be local increases in the resident population as conifer plantations grow, followed by reductions as the canopies close. These Redpolls feed on successive crops of seeds from sallow, birch, alder and some herbs and grasses, and also on a few insects. They roost in thorn, birch or sallow scrub, and in young conifer plantations.

Crossbill *Loxia curvirostra*

An irruptive visitor and very rare temporary resident that normally breeds on mainland Britain and across Eurasia in the temperate conifer forests. Two were in Bridgend Woods in July 1963, another two were near the Wool Mill in September 1976, and four males were at Skerrols in October 1979. Nesting was suspected in 1980 when a male and a probable juvenile were found at Cluanach on 5th June, and again when a pair was carrying nesting material at Cluanach on 14th April 1982. An invasion produced 15 at Kildalton Woods on 21st June 1986.

It is not known if the Scottish Crossbill (*L. scotica*) is among these records; it prefers Scots pine to the plantation spruces and both occur in the vicinity of Cluanach and Bridgend. The spruce plantations between Cluanach and Avenvogie Cottage may encourage nesting if they are thinned out and mature so that well-spaced tall trees yield good cone crops. A decade or so later, the recent afforestation may continue to encourage this species in various parts of the island. The Crossbill's main food is conifer seeds prised out of cones. It roosts in the dense cover of tall conifers.

Bullfinch *Pyrrhula pyrrhula*

Probably about twelve pairs are resident (*P.p.pileata*). Occasionally there are also irruptive visitors, such as the 30 at Portnahaven on 7th December 1985. These may have been of the larger and more brightly coloured race *P.p.phyrrhula* from Scandinavia, which is seen in most years in the Northern Isles in October, November and December.

There are many records in the breeding season from May to August; a pair had five young in Bridgend Woods on 28th June 1986. Two-thirds of all records come from the three larger mixed woodlands; others are from smaller woods with oak or hazel. This species has increased markedly in recently afforested areas on the mainland and may do so on Islay while new conifer plantations retain open canopies.

The Bullfinch forages in bushes and trees, taking kernels from seeds, buds, berries and other fruits; the young are fed on caterpillars, spiders and small snails. It roosts at temporary sites in evergreen shrubs.

Hawfinch *Coccothraustes coccothraustes*

A very rare visitor that is resident on mainland Britain south of the Highlands, but not in Ireland. Two pairs were in the Gruinart district on 23rd February 1986, the first Islay record.

American Redstart *Setophaga ruticilla*

A very rare vagrant that breeds across North America from British Columbia to much of the eastern seaboard, and winters in the tropical Americas. The first Scottish record was from Portnahaven, where a female or immature bird was found on 1st November 1982; others have since been found in the British Isles in October.

Lapland Bunting *Calcarius lapponicus*

A rare passage visitor that breeds around the world near arctic coasts. Those arriving in Britain in autumn are probably from southern Greenland; two were at Ardnave on 15th October 1974 and one was on the Oa on 23rd February 1975. Up to 14 were seen at Kilchoman, Coul Point and Sanaigmore from 19th October to 7th November 1987. The spring migration yields fewer records and no birds have been noted during this period on Islay.

Snow Bunting *Plectrophenax nivalis*

A winter visitor in small numbers, normally arriving near the end of September and leaving in mid-April. Seventy were at Kilchiaran and Portnahaven on 6th October 1985, and flocks of 55 and 40 have been recorded in November and January respectively. There is one summer record, of a pair on 22nd June 1964, and a few breed on the mountains of the Scottish mainland. These birds usually migrate at night, but parties of up to eleven have appeared at Frenchman's Rocks during daytime seawatches; they probably come from Iceland (*P.n.insulae*) or Greenland (*P.n.nivalis*). The males of these subspecies are recognised by the amount of white on the rump; the Icelandic rumps are relatively dark.

199

Snow Buntings are found on expanses of grass near the coast, the seashore itself, and upland pastures. These grasslands may be well grazed or rough, and dry or damp with rushes. The pastures of Laggan Bay from the golf course to the northern dunes, and the Ardnave and Killallan areas, are good places to search for this species. In autumn and winter they feed mainly on seeds, and buds and insects are added to their diet in summer. The seeds of rushes and grasses are especially important in the autumn. They feed in tight flocks, and like Starlings progress across poor pastures by a 'leapfrog' or 'roller-coaster' motion, if in sufficient numbers and concentration for competition between individuals to be restrictive.

Yellowhammer   *Emberiza citrinella*

A resident that was reported in 1871 (Gray) and 1892, and was described as local in 1938 and 1953 (Baxter and Rintoul); only 14 pairs were found in 1954, but it was 'singing everywhere' in 1971. Numbers appear to change markedly from year to year, perhaps as a result of variable immigration. A spread of some 35 localities and rare visits to the Gruinart Reserve suggest that there are usually well below 100 pairs.

In the breeding season from May to August, this species is thinly distributed over farming areas, on pasture, arable and stubble fields, in scrubby areas and open woodland, and occasionally on machair. It is also found at livestock feeding stations, on farm tracks and in the vicinity of steadings. It flocks with finches and Reed Buntings during the autumn and winter, normally up to 50 birds being involved, but exceptional numbers were noted in mid-November 1981: 70 at Gartachossan near Bridgend, 80 at Nerabus on the Rhinns, and 100 at Ballygrant.

The Yellowhammer eats spilled grain and other seeds from a variety of plants, and in the breeding season, insects, spiders, millipedes, slugs and earthworms are added to its diet. It roosts in dense vegetation, sometimes in woods.

Rustic Bunting   *Emberiza rustica*

A rare vagrant that breeds in the coniferous forests from northern Scandinavia to easternmost Siberia, and winters in east and southeast Asia. In some years it reaches Scotland, mainly in May; in others the majority are found between mid-September and mid-October. One was at Easter Ellister on 23rd May 1980.

Reed Bunting   *Emberiza schoeniclus*

The Reed Bunting was first recorded in 1892; it is now a resident and a probable passage migrant. Birds on the move were noted at Carnmore on 13th September 1974, and one followed the ferry from Islay to Gigha on 14th April 1979. These passages appear to involve only small numbers, but it is possible that some birds may come from Scandinavia and winter south of Islay.

In the breeding season from May to August, this species is thinly but widely distributed; ten pairs bred on the Gruinart Reserve in 1985. In 1947 and 1954 it was described as common in all low-lying damp places, but, as on the mainland, it has now spread to drier farmlands and scrub patches on the moors. In recent years it has been seen in about 70 possible breeding sites, strongly biased towards road access; probably over 100 pairs are present in summer. In autumn and winter, flocks of up to 50 birds have been found in several areas; 65 were at Gruinart in January 1986. Smaller numbers feed with finches and other buntings, often on stubble, at livestock feeding stations and in the vicinity of farms or on tracks where grain has been spilled. This species is primarily a vegetarian, taking seeds from a variety of plants, but in the breeding season it also takes insects and their larvae, especially caterpillars. In autumn and winter it roosts communally in reedbeds and other tall vegetation.

Red-headed Bunting *Emberiza bruniceps*

A probable escape that is commonly kept in captivity. In the wild, it breeds east of the Caspian Sea into China and south to the borders of India. It migrates southeast into much of India and Pakistan, where it stays for the northern winter. One was at Easter Ellister on 31st July 1976.

Black-headed Bunting *Emberiza melanocephala*

A rare vagrant or escape which in the wild breeds from eastern Italy, through the Balkans and Turkey to the Caspian Sea, and winters in much of India. A male was at Ardnave on 11th June 1968.

Corn Bunting *Miliaria calandra*

An occasional visitor, very rarely recorded in summer and winter. It was regarded as very abundant in 1892 and common in 1913 (Ross), remaining resident until perhaps the 1940s. Prior to 1913, some reports came from the Port Ellen district: in winter, 20 were in trees at Cragabus and 25 at Leorin. In 25 years to 1986 all 14 records were of ones and twos confined to the Rhinns, and the last record is of one at Clachantachree on 21st October 1987. Thus, during this century, the species has declined on Islay, just as it has throughout Ireland.

Seventy per cent or eleven of the records are dated mid-February to late July, with the three others in November. Most have been noted in the 'singing' season and it is probably under-recorded at other times. Short-distance movement south from the breeding areas in the Outer Hebrides, Tiree and Coll may account for most records collected since it was resident on Islay.

This species prefers open, well-cultivated arable land. It feeds by walking and picking weed seeds, grain and some insects, including grasshoppers, caterpillars, butterflies and beetles. In winter it joins flocks of other buntings and finches, especially in severe weather. It roosts communally in stubble or long grass.

Sources of Information

Baxter, E. V., and Rintoul, L. J. 1953. *The Birds of Scotland*. Oliver and Boyd, Edinburgh.

Bibby, J. S., and Heslop, R. E. F. 1986. *Land capability classification for forestry of the island of Islay, Argyll*. Macaulay Institute for Soil Research, Aberdeen.

Booth, C. G. 1969–82. Records in the care of the Islay Natural History Trust, Port Charlotte, Islay.

Booth, C. G. 1981. *Birds in Islay*, 2nd edition. Argyll Reproductions Ltd, Port Charlotte, Islay.

Boyd, J. M., and Bowes, D. R. 1983. *Natural environment of the Inner Hebrides*. Proc. Royal Soc. Edinburgh, 83B.

BTO, RSPB and Wildfowl Trust. Data from organised birds counts, including the Birds of Estuaries Enquiry.

Bullock, I. D., Drewett, D. R., and Mickleburgh, S. P. 1983. The Chough in Britain and Ireland. *Brit. Birds* 76, 377–401.

Clyde River Purification Board. 1974. *Survey of the River Sorn*. Technical report for Islay Estates.

Cramp, S. 1977, 1980, 1983 and 1985. *Handbook of the Birds of Europe, the Middle East and North Africa*, vols. I, II, III and IV. Oxford Univ. Press, Oxford.

Cunningham, P. 1983. *The Birds of the Outer Hebrides*. Melven Press, Perth.

Darling, F. F. 1947. *Natural History in the Highlands and Islands*. Collins, London.

Department of Agriculture and Fisheries for Scotland and Nature Conservancy Council. 1977. *A guide to good muirburn practice*. HMSO, Edinburgh.

Elkins, N. 1983. *Weather and Bird Behaviour*. Poyser, Calton.

Elliott, R. E. Unpublished Islay bird records 1976 to 1987.

Elliott, R. E. 1981. Orbital ring colours of Herring Gulls in Britain. *Bird Study* 28, 66–8.

Elliott, R. E. 1982. Movements and inland foraging of *Larus* gulls on Islay outside the breeding season. Unpublished manuscript.

Evans, P. R., Goss-Custard, J. D., and Hale, W. G. 1984. *Coastal Waders and Wildfowl in Winter*. Cambridge Univ. Press, Cambridge.

Feare, C. 1984. *The Starling*. Oxford Univ. Press, Oxford.

Francis, I. M. 1986. *Greenland White-fronted Goose in Britain: 1985–1986*. Greenland White-fronted Goose Study, Univ. College of Wales, Aberystwyth.

203

Fuller, R. J. 1982. *Bird Habitats in Britain.* Poyser, Calton.

Galbraith, C. A. 1984, 1985 and 1986. Argyll bird reports for 1983, 1984 and 1985. Argyll Bird Club.

Goodwin, D. 1976. *Crows of the World.* Cornell Univ. Press, New York.

Gray, R. 1871. *The Birds of the West of Scotland.* Murray, Glasgow.

Hale, W. G. 1980. *Waders.* Collins, London.

Islay Estate Papers, Islay Estate Office, Bridgend, Islay.

Islay Natural History Trust. Confirmed data for 1985 to 1987 received from visitors and other sources.

Jardine, D. C., Clarke, J., and Clarke, P. M. 1986. *The Birds of Colonsay and Oransay.* Stornaway Gazette Limited.

Lack, P. 1986. *The Atlas of Wintering Birds in Britain and Ireland.* Poyser, Calton.

McKay, M. M. 1980. *The Rev. Dr John Walker's Report of the Hebrides of 1764 and 1771.* John Donald, Edinburgh.

McVean, D. N. 1959. Muir burning and conservation. *Scottish Agriculture* Autumn 1959, 79–83.

Meiklejohn, M. F. M., and Stanford, J. K. 1954. June notes on the birds of Islay. *Scot. Naturalist* 1954, 129–45.

Monaghan, P., and Thompson, P. M. 1984. The breeding ecology of the Chough on Islay, Inner Hebrides. Report held at Univ. of Glasgow, Glasgow.

Monaghan, P., Shedden, C. B., Ensor, K., Fricker, L. R., and Girdwood, R. W. A. 1985. *Salmonella* carriage by Herring Gulls in the Clyde area of Scotland in relation to their feeding ecology. *J. Appl. Ecol.* 22, 669–79.

Moore, P. 1985, 1986 and 1987. Barnacle Geese at Loch Gruinart RSPB reserve, winters 1984/85, 1985/86 and 1986/87. RSPB internal reports.

Moore, P. 1987. A survey of Corncrakes on Islay 1986. *Argyle Bird Report* 4, 50–3.

Morrison, A. 1980. *Early Man in Britain and Ireland.* Croom Helm, London.

Nature Conservancy Council. 1986. *Nature conservation and afforestation in Britain.* NCC, Interpretive Services Branch, Peterborough.

Nature Conservancy Council. 1963–87. Citations of Sites of Special Scientific Interest on Islay.

Nelson, J. B. 1978. *The Gannet.* Poyser, Berkhamsted.

Newton, I. 1972. *Finches.* Collins, London.

Newton, S. F. 1984. *Observations of birds and mammals: Isle of Islay 1981–83.* Field studies report no. 40, Brathay Exploration Group, Ambleside.

Ogilvie, M. A. 1975. *Ducks of Britain and Europe.* Poyser, Berkhamsted.

Ogilvie, M. A. 1978. *Wild Geese.* Poyser, Berkhamsted.

Ogilvie, M. A. 1987 and 1988. Islay bird and natural history reports for 1986 and 1987 Islay Natural History Trust, Port Charlotte, Islay.

Ogilvie, M. A., and Booth, C. G. 1970. An oil spillage on Islay in October 1969. *Scot Birds* 6, 149–53.

Ogilvie, M. A., and Ogilvie, C. G. 1984. Jackdaws roosting on the shore with Oystercatchers. *Brit. Birds* 77, 368.

Owen, M. 1980. *Wild Geese of the World.* Batsford, London.

Owen, M., Atkinson-Willes, G. L., and Salmon, D. G. 1986. *Wildfowl in Great Britain* Cambridge Univ. Press, Cambridge.

204

Parslow, J. 1973. *Breeding Birds of Britain and Ireland.* Poyser, Berkhamsted.

Pennant, T. 1774. *A Tour in Scotland and a Voyage to the Hebrides, 1772.* Chester.

Perrins, C. M. 1979. *British Tits.* Collins, London.

Petty, S. J., and Anderson, D. 1986. Breeding by Hen Harriers (*Circus cyaneus*) on restocked sites in upland forests. *Bird Study* 33, 177–8.

Prater, A. J. 1981. *Estuary Birds of Britain and Ireland.* Poyser, Calton.

Ratcliffe, P. R., and Petty, S. J. 1986. The management of commercial forests for wildlife. In: *Trees and Wildlife in the Scottish Uplands.* Edited by Jenkins, D., Institute of Terrestrial Ecology, Cambridge.

Riddiford, N., and Findley, P. 1981. *Seasonal movements of summer migrants.* BTO, Guide no. 18, Tring.

Ross, A. 1913. Birds of Islay. *Glasgow Naturalist* 1913, 7–32.

Royal Society for the Protection of Birds. Poison—what is at risk? Pamphlet issued by the RSPB, Sandy, Bedfordshire.

Royal Society for the Protection of Birds. Systematic lists of birds on the Loch Gruinart Reserve, 1983–7.

Royal Society for the Protection of Birds. 1986. *Wild birds and the law.* RSPB, Sandy, Bedfordshire.

Ruttledge, R. F., and Ogilvie, M. A. 1979. The past and current status of the Greenland White-fronted Goose in Ireland and Britain. *Irish Birds* 1, 293–364.

Scottish Ornithologists' Club. Scottish bird reports for 1970 to 1985.

Sharrock, J. T. R. 1976. *The Atlas of Breeding Birds in Britain and Ireland.* BTO, Tring.

Simmons, I. G., and Tooley, M. J. 1981. *The Environment of British Prehistory.* Duckworth, London.

Simms, E. 1985. *British Thrushes.* Collins, London.

Storrie, M. C. 1981. *Islay: biography of an island.* The Oa Press, Islay.

Thaxton, R. W. 1984. Observations of Barnacle Geese (*Branta leucopsis*) wintering at Loch Gruinart, Islay. Internal report for RSPB.

Thom, V. M. 1986. *Birds in Scotland.* Poyser, Calton.

Verrall, K., and Bourne, W. R. P. 1982. Seabird movements around western Islay. *Scot. Birds* 12, 3–11.

Voous, K. H. 1977. *List of Recent Holarctic Bird Species.* British Ornithologists' Union, London (reprinted from *Ibis*, 115, 126–38; and 119, 223–50 and 276–406).

Warnes, J. M. 1982. A study of the ecology of the Chough (*Pyrrhocorax pyrrhocorax* L.) on the Isle of Islay, Argyll 1980–1981. Report held at the Univ. of Stirling.

Watson, A. 1971. Key factor analysis, density dependence and population limitation in Red Grouse. In: *Dynamics of Populations.* Edited by P. J. Den Boor and G. R. Gradwell, Pudoc, Wageningen.

Williamson, K. 1972. Breeding birds of Ariundle Oakwood Forest nature reserve. *Quart. J. Forestry* 66, 243–55.

Appendix 1: The legal status of Islay's regular birds

Species	LS	Species	LS
Red-throated Diver	Ps	Hen Harrier	Ps
Black-throated Diver	Ps	Sparrowhawk	P
Great Northern Diver	Ps	Buzzard	P
Little Grebe	P	Golden Eagle	Ps
Fulmar	P	Kestrel	P
Manx Shearwater	P	Merlin	Ps
Gannet	P	Peregrine	Ps
Cormorant	P	Red Grouse	Q3
Shag	P	Black Grouse	Q2
Grey Heron	P	Partridge	Q1
Mute Swan	P	Pheasant	Q4
Whooper Swan	Ps	Water Rail	P
White-fronted Goose	Px	Corncrake	Ps
Greylag Goose	Q1	Moorhen	Q1
Barnacle Goose	Px	Coot	Q1
Brent Goose	P	Oystercatcher	P
Shelduck	P	Ringed Plover	P
Wigeon	Q1	Golden Plover	Q1
Teal	Q1	Grey Plover	P
Mallard	Q1	Lapwing	P
Pintail	Q1s	Knot	P
Shoveler	Q1	Sanderling	P
Pochard	Q1	Purple Sandpiper	Ps
Tufted Duck	Q1	Dunlin	P
Scaup	Ps	Snipe	Q5
Eider	P	Woodcock	Q1
Long-tailed Duck	Ps	Bar-tailed Godwit	P
Common Scoter	Ps	Whimbrel	Ps
Goldeneye	Q1s	Curlew	P
Red-breasted Merganser	P	Redshank	P

206

Species	LS	Species	LS
Greenshank	Ps	Blackbird	P
Common Sandpiper	P	Fieldfare	Ps
Turnstone	P	Song Thrush	P
Arctic Skua	P	Redwing	Ps
Black-headed Gull	P	Mistle Thrush	P
Common Gull	P	Grasshopper Warbler	P
Lesser Black-backed Gull	K	Sedge Warbler	P
Herring Gull	K	Whitethroat	P
Great Black-backed Gull	K	Garden Warbler	P
Kittiwake	P	Wood Warbler	P
Common Tern	P	Chiffchaff	P
Arctic Tern	P	Willow Warbler	P
Little Tern	Ps	Goldcrest	P
Guillemot	P	Spotted Flycatcher	P
Razorbill	P	Long-tailed Tit	P
Black Guillemot	P	Coal Tit	P
Rock Dove	P	Blue Tit	P
Woodpigeon	K	Great Tit	P
Collared Dove	K	Treecreeper	P
Cuckoo	P	Chough	Ps
Barn Owl	Ps	Jackdaw	K
Tawny Owl	P	Rook	K
Short-eared Owl	P	Hooded Crow	K
Skylark	P	Raven	P
Sand Martin	P	Starling	K
Swallow	P	House Sparrow	K
House Martin	P	Chaffinch	P
Tree Pipit	P	Brambling	Ps
Meadow Pipit	P	Greenfinch	P
Rock Pipit	P	Goldfinch	P
Grey Wagtail	P	Siskin	P
Pied Wagtail	P	Linnet	P
Dipper	P	Twite	P
Wren	P	Redpoll	P
Dunnock	P	Bullfinch	P
Robin	P	Snow Bunting	Ps
Whinchat	P	Yellowhammer	P
Stonechat	P	Reed Bunting	P
Wheatear	P		

Birds not listed are protected at all times, some with special penalties.

Key
LS: legal status.
P: protected at all times.

Q: quarry species protected during a closed season: 1 = 1st February to 31st August and 21st February to 31st August for waterfowl in areas below high-water mark; 2 = 11th December to 19th August; 3 = 11th December to 11th August; 4 = 2nd February to 30th September; 5 = 1st February to 11th August.
K: may be taken or killed by authorised persons at all times.
s: special penalties apply.
x: licensed shooting on Islay is reviewed annually.

The above table is based on the Game Acts and Wildlife and Countryside Act 1981. Further details and information relating to restrictions on the sale of birds and their eggs, the exhibition of birds, prohibited methods of killing and taking wild birds, birds in captivity and the release of birds into the wild is given in a booklet entitled 'Wild birds and the law', obtainable from the RSPB, The Lodge, Sandy, Bedfordshire, SG19 2DL.

Appendix 2: Code of conduct for birdwatchers

Those members of the public interested in birds include birdwatchers, photographers, artists, sound-recordists, ringers, scientists, wildfowlers and natural-history lovers in general. This is a continually growing section of the population and it is vital that a responsibility for the heritage of bird life be taken seriously.

Ten points from the RSPB's 'Code of conduct for birdwatchers' are given below.

1: The welfare of the birds must come first.
2: Habitat must be protected.
3: Keep disturbance of birds and their habitat to a minimum.
4: When you find a rare bird think carefully about whom you should tell.
5: Do not harass rare migrants.
6: Abide by the bird protection laws at all times.
7: Respect the rights of landowners.
8: Respect the rights of other people in the countryside.
9: Make your records available to the local bird recorder.*
10: Behave abroad as you would when birdwatching at home.

*On Islay, report to the director of the Islay Natural History Field Centre, Port Charlotte.

Glossary

Arthropods: Animals with an external skeleton, including crabs, insects, spiders and centipedes.

Beaufort Scale: An international scale of wind strengths varying from force 0 to 12, representing calm air and a hurricane respectively. Intervening strengths may be measured in terms of wind speed at a standard height of 10 m (30 ft), or judged by observing smoke, the motion of trees and waves, and structural damage, etc.

Bronze Age: A cultural period ranging from 2100 to 600 BC in Britain and characterised by the first metal objects produced by man.

Club: A gathering of seabirds at the edge of a colony, comprising failed breeders and non-breeders.

Comfort station: A convenient location, used for bathing, feather maintenance, cleaning of bare parts, and various shaking and stretching movements. Lapwings, Curlews, gulls and other birds often assemble for these purposes by shallow water at the mouth of a stream entering a loch or the sea.

Control: The recovery and release of a bird previously ringed or marked in some way.

Distraction display: A parental display having the effect of diverting the attention of a potential predator away from eggs or young; for example, the 'broken wing' displays of some waders such as Ringed Plovers.

Drumming: A sound produced when a Snipe's beating wings cause air to be deflected past its outer tail feathers during aerial evolutions in the breeding season. Vibration of these specially strengthened feathers creates a characteristic buzzing at varying speeds.

Erupt: see Irruption.

Fennoscandia: Finland and Scandinavia.

Feral: Gone wild; applied to domestic animals that have reverted to a free existence.

Geo (Gaelic *Geodha*):   A long, narrow opening in a cliff eroded by the sea along a line of weakness caused by a fault, joints or a weathered igneous dyke.

Gley soil: A bluish, compact, sticky soil.

Holarctic Region: A zoogeographical region, the Palearctic and Nearctic Regions combined; that is the entire Northern Hemisphere north of the tropics.

Invertebrate: Any animal lacking a backbone, including sponges, jelly-fish, worms, snails, shellfish, arthropods (q.v.), starfish and sea-squirts.

Irruption: A form of migration that involves greatly varying numbers of birds and distances travelled. Variation is from year to year and is related to fluctuations in food availability. Birds are said to erupt out of the region losing them and to irrupt into the region gaining them.

Loafing: A term applied to flocks or individuals which are quiescent but not roosting, often at a habitual site, and sometimes indulging in comfort behaviour (see Comfort station), or simply digesting after a period of feeding.

Machair: A florally rich turfed habitat in flat sandy areas on the leeward side of dunes in the Hebrides. The coastal grassland on Islay, referred to as machair in this book, is not so rich in species as the archetypal machair of the Outer Hebrides.

Mesolithic: A cultural period ranging from about 10,000 to 3500 BC in Britain and characterised by the appearance of small man-made flint tools known as 'microliths'.

Mineral soil: That part of a soil lying below superficial litter or other organic accumulation such as peat.

Muir: Moorland.

Neolithic: A cultural period ranging from about 3500 to 2100 BC in Britain and characterised by primitive agriculture and polished flint tools.

Peaty lochan: A small loch bounded by peat or by land largely covered by peat so that the water draining into it is weakly acidic.

pH value: A scale of the acidity or alkalinity of a solution, with seven representing neutral, lower numbers acidity and higher numbers alkalinity; measured in terms of the hydrogen-ion concentration.

Plunge-diving: A feeding method entailing entry into water head first from the air, followed by the capture of prey underwater.

Productivity: The productivity of any habitat in terms of the abundance or otherwise of vegetable and animal life.

Pursuit-diving: A feeding method in which the bird starts from a surface swimming position, glides gently into the water and pursues prey underwater.

Pursuit-plunging: A form of plunge-diving in which the bird sights prey while airborne, dives head first into water and chases the prey underwater.

Quarry species: Any species of quadruped animal, bird or fish that is hunted, especially by man.

Raptor: A bird of prey, a species that hunts and kills other animals for food; applied to hawks, buzzards, eagles, falcons and sometimes owls.

Rhizome: A rootstock or underground stem bearing buds from which new plants grow.

Roding: The twilight display of the Woodcock, performed by the male when searching for females with which to mate.

Roosting: Applied to birds at, or travelling to and from, a habitual site specifically allocated to sleeping, often punctuated by resting. A roost is a safe place at which birds rest and sleep.

Ryegrass: Any grass of the genus *Lolium*, especially *L. perenne*, widely cultivated as a forage crop. Has a flattened flower spike and hairless leaves.

Salmonella (plural: *Salmonellae*):   A group of non-sporing rod-shaped aerobic bacteria associated with food poisoning.

Salmonellosis: The disease of animals, including humans, due to an infection of *Salmonellae*; food poisoning.

Silage: Any crop harvested for fodder when green, and kept succulent by partial fermentation in a silo.

Stitching: The feeding action of a wader in which it makes a rapid series of closely spaced trial probes into the ground.

Stolon: A runner; a slender horizontal stem that grows along the surface of the soil and propagates by producing roots and shoots at intervals.

Strand line: A line along which many items, carried up a beach by wave action, are left behind by the receding tide. Pieces of seaweed, seeds, dead crabs, and other marine animals and flotsam may be distributed along such lines.

Surface-diving: The action of a bird propelling itself head first under water from a floating position, using feet and in some species wings.

Surface-seizing: Feeding by pecking at food floating on the surface of water.

Swash area: The area of a beach being washed by to-and-fro wave action.

Thermal: A pocket of low-density air rising from locally heating or drying ground, earth or rock. On Islay, thermals commonly arise at the edge of an area just ploughed, while ploughing continues further across the field. Buzzards, gulls and Choughs may enter such rising air in order to gain height while using the minimum amount of energy.

Trochoidal flight path: The flight path generated by a bird flying in circles and at the same time drifting in a moderate breeze of force 4 or 5.

Vagrant: A bird wandering outside the normal migration range of its species or subspecies.

Whiffling: Rapid descent from high flight involving fast side-slipping first one way and then the other.

Windthrow: The uprooting of trees by strong winds; usually requires storm force 10 or stronger, but also dependent on degree of exposure and the ability of the soil type to provide good anchorage.

Index

This index contains all localities and English names referred to in the text. Six-figure British National Grid references are given for each locality (or four figures where appropriate) rather than page numbers. The conventional two-letter references identifying 100,000-m squares are given for places lying outside Islay.